A COUNTRY
HERBAL

A COUNTRY HERBAL

LESLEY GORDON

Webb&Bower
EXETER, ENGLAND

Also by Lesley Gordon:

PEEPSHOW INTO PARADISE:
A HISTORY OF TOYS

POORMAN'S NOSEGAY

GREEN MAGIC

(*half-title page*) AN ILLUSTRATION FROM *Tacuinum Sanitatum, c.* 1385.

(*title page*) A TRAVELLING grocer appears in this engraving by M. Engelbrecht, dated about 1735. His accoutrement includes 1, a coil of tobacco; 2, a pipe; 3, boxes of preserves; 4, feathers; 5, small cornets; 6, sugarloaf; 7, barrel of oil; 8, paper; 9, Dutch cheese; 10, oranges; 11, lemons; 12, cheese knife; 13, scales; 14, a measure for oil; and 15, a round box; The drawers contain 16, cloves of garlic; 17, nutmeg; 18, cinnamon; 19, tea; 20, coffee; 21, almonds; and 22, raisins.

First published in Great Britain 1980 by
Webb & Bower (Publishers) Limited,
33 Southernhay East, Exeter, Devon, EX1 1NS

Distributed by WHS Distributors
(a division of W.H. Smith and Son Limited)
St John's House, East Street, Leicester, LE1 6NE

Designed by Vic Giolitto

Picture research by Anne-Marie Ehrlich

Copyright © Webb & Bower (Publishers) Limited 1980

British Library Cataloguing in Publication Data

Gordon, Lesley
    A country herbal.
    1. Plants, Useful
    I. Title
    581.6'1   QK98.4
    ISBN 0-906671-09-4

Phototypeset in Great Britain by Filmtype Services Limited, Scarborough, Yorkshire

Printed and bound in Hong Kong by Mandarin Publishers Limited

CONTENTS

FOREWORD

Our grandmothers' recipes usually contained 'a little of this and a little of that', and it is on this somewhat haphazard principle that this book has been compiled. A little history, a little folklore, some facts about cosmetics, the making of perfumes, the art of dyeing, a few hints about herb-growing: all this adds up to an attempt to tell in brief the story of herbs and spices.

It is impossible to write of herbs without writing of the men and women who discovered the plants and dared to taste them for the first time. Among them were the simplers who searched the hedgerows and waste ground for a possible rare herb, but who found only nettles and dandelions; nevertheless these were healing and useful plants to be taken to market or to the apothecary's shop. There were the housewives who cooked the plants for the family meals, or pounded and mixed them for curing the sick; the pioneers who must have suffered many a catastrophe in gaining knowledge; and the gardeners who transplanted the wild herbs to their own backyards, discovering by trial and error how best to propagate and coax them to flourish.

Some of the same plants that provided food, drink and medicine could also be employed in spinning and weaving, making women into more than willing spinsters. Women were also interested in seeking out dye plants, finding that woad gave them blue, madder produced red, and agrimony a splendid yellow; they then combined one with another to dye their garments. Artists also experimented with these same plants to find colours and fixatives to reinforce their palettes.

The pleasure of beautifying themselves and each other gave women the satisfaction of gathering the plants from their own gardens, or from the surrounding countryside, to make the little luxuries of hair-dyes and freckle-removers, skin-lotions and washing-balls, starch for laces and perfume for gloves, and all the charming nonsenses of sweet-bags and pot-pourri bowls.

Even small houses and farms had their still-rooms, with dried plants hanging from the rafters and aromatic herbs contained in pots, 'which pots you may let down at your pleasure in apt frames with a pulley from your Chamber window into your garden, or you may place them upon shelves without the Room, there to receive the warm Sun, or Temperate rain at your pleasure . . .' Sir Hugh Platt described this splendid idea in 1594 and further suggested how 'You may also hang in the Roof, and about the sides of this Room, Small Pompions or Cowcumbers, pricked full of Barley, first making holes for the Barley, and these will be overgrown with green spires . . .'

A GERMAN engraving by M. Engelbrecht, dated about 1735, of a female grocer and her divers trappings. Among these are 4, St John's bread, the fruit of the carob tree; 7, a container of coarse, dried tobacco; 8, brazil-wood, which provides a red dye; and 15, a jar of oil of jasmine. The drawers in the cabinet beside her contain the following: 17, rice; 18, prunes; 19, barley; 20, anise; 21, alum; 22, tartar; 23, soap; 24, vegetables; 25, powders; 26, vermicides; 27, beeswax; 28, pepper; 29, ginger; 30, galingale (the roots of certain East Indian plants, once put to culinary and medical use); 31, nutmeg; 32, incense; 33, glue; 34, sugar candy; and 35, antimony.

But these pretty things were only the shining surface of life. Beneath the gloss lingered magic and witchcraft, darkness and superstition, the terror of the plague, and human spite and human fear. There were plants in plenty for those who knew where to look: mandrake and henbane, belladonna and vervain — some poisonous in root and berry, others harmless in themselves, but with rank scent, sad colour or strange form and texture to excite the imagination.

Most remarkable of all is how men like Gerard, Parkinson and Culpeper, growing distrustful of magic, learnt by experience and carefully controlled dosage that even the most poisonous of plants could be used as cures. The old-fashioned word 'wort' has a comfortable if antique sound, but for many people today the word 'herb' implies cleanliness and instils confidence.

There are, of course, many herbs and spices that are still in use that have not been included, for lack of pages to accommodate them all, but let Parkinson sum up, for as he says, it is not only for food and medicine that we owe them so much. 'And thus I have shewed you all the varieties of nature . . . pointing unto them and describing them one after another. And now . . . I bring you to rest on the Grasse, which yet shall not be without some delight, and that not the least of all the rest.'

A COUNTRY HERBAL

AGRIMONY
Agrimonia eupatoria

UNDER JUPITER AND THE SIGN OF CANCER

One of the fifty-seven herbs in the Anglo-Saxon *Holy Salve* believed to protect man from goblins, evil and poison, agrimony has been in continuous use until today. Its name comes from *argemone,* a Greek word given to plants employed in the relief of eye troubles, and was used by the Greeks in the treatment of cataract. It owes its Latin name *eupatoria* to the King of Pontus, Mithridates Eupator, who discovered its use, and so 'the plant hath a roiall and princelie authoritie'.

With its roughly cut leaves, fragrant yellow flowers and the clinging hairy burrs that follow, it may be found in hedgerows and on waste land. It still maintains its past reputation as a popular English 'simple', that is, a herb that may be used alone, as distinct from a 'compound', when it is combined with others.

Wounded deer were said to cure themselves by browsing on the plant. Monks grew agrimony in their medicine gardens as a cure for stomach-aches and as a compress for open wounds. It appears as Egremoyne in the list of remedies supplied in 'The Canon's Yeoman's Tale' of Chaucer, and Gerard recommended its use for 'those with naughty livers'. Culpeper advised that 'Outwardly applied and being stamped with old swine's grease, it helpeth old sores, cancers and inveterate ulcers, and draweth forth thorns and splinters of wood, nails, and other such things gotten into the flesh'. He also gave:

A drink most excellent

Take a pottle of white wine, steep these hearbs overnight, finely shred wood betony, mugworth, branch-leaved planton, avis, sanich, ribworth, dandalion, whitebottles, as grown in wheat, dazy roots and leaves, crowfery [comfrey?], buglos, woodruff, the male strawberry leaves, revenue[?] root, wild valerian, poly-podium of ye oak, sink-foil, sage, mouse-ear, aggrimoney, speedwell, self-heal; boyle these in ye white wine — then straine them and boyle ye same again with a quantity of honey. A draught evening and morning, you must guess the quantity.

Its country name of church-steeples refers to its rising spires of yellow flowers; and the names cockleburr and sticklewort refer to the burr which attaches itself to the clothing of the unwary passerby. Because of its use in the treatment of liver complaints, it is known also as liverwort. Agrimony wine, taken for colds, gave it yet another name, the lemonade flower.

There is a larger and more fragrant form, *Agrimonia odorata,* which Philip Miller, in his *Gardener's Dictionary,* says should not be wanting in the garden. It blooms between June and August. Because the whole plant, including the root, retains its scent after it is dried, it makes an

AGRIMONY, as depicted in an English manuscript from about 1100, now in the possession of the Bodleian Library, Oxford.

[8]

excellent filling for sweet-bags and herbal pillows.

It contains tannin, and has in the past been used for dressing leather. The whole plant yields a yellow dye.

Our grandmothers valued it as a substitute for the still expensive tea, or as an addition to make the tea go further and add a delicate aroma. It was even more popular in France, where it is still drunk as a 'tisane' — a handful of flowers, stems and leaves infused in boiling water. For medicinal purposes this drink should be taken first thing in the morning, but because of its fragrance French country people drink it cold with meals as a refreshing beverage.

The following recipe for an agrimony tea was used in 1817:

Sanative English tea

Agrimony and ground ivy, equal quantities. Half as much of sweet marjoram, pennyroyal, lavender, rose and cowslip flower leaves. Chop and mix together and use them as Indian tea.

Agrimony wine also makes a pleasant drink.

Agrimony wine

A good bunch of agrimony, leaves and flowers
2gal (9l) water
7lb (3.1kg) sugar, demerara or white
3 lemons
6 oranges
4oz (113g) lump ginger

Crush ginger, and put with agrimony and water in a large saucepan. Boil until a good colour. Pour onto sugar, add lemons and oranges (sliced) and allow to stand for 2–3 days. Strain, put into a large jar and leave to work. The wine can be used after 6 months.

ALFALFA
Medicago sativa

A perennial of the Pea family, the plant originated in Medea where it was discovered by King Darius, who ruled Persia from 521 to 486BC. The name medick or medicle is derived from the Latin *Herba medica,* the Median herb. Alfalfa is the old Spanish name. It is also called lucerne.

It is a deep-rooting trifoliate plant, now grown widely for commerce. The blue and violet clover-like flowers are borne on upright spikes 12–18in (30–45cm) long, from June to August. Its succu-

ALFALFA, from the second volume of *La Botanique mise à la portée de tout le monde,* 1774, by F. and C. Regnault.

lent herbage and the fact that it yields two crops annually makes it perhaps the most valuable of the world's fodder plants, much esteemed for increasing the milk of cows. The plant also has the virtue of lasting longer in the ground than most cattle plants.

The Romans cultivated it as a fodder plant at the beginning of the first and second centuries AD and it was grown for the same purpose in Italy and Spain. It is an important healing herb to the Chinese, who make it into tea and drink it as a daily beverage. They regard it as a cure for stomach ulcers. In recent years its value as a health food has been discovered, and alfalfa sprouts have reached a high degree of popularity as a salad vegetable. It is rich in vitamins and protein, and the seeds can be sprouted in the home to be ready and fresh when needed. It has the flavour of fresh garden peas.

To sprout alfalfa seeds

Pick over seeds, discarding damaged ones. Wash

¼ cup seeds and place in a bowl of lukewarm water. Leave overnight. Drain and retain liquid for use in soup or stew. Rinse seeds thoroughly and drain. Put two or three tablespoonfuls of the soaked seeds in a quart (1l) jar, cover top with cheesecloth and tie. Place jar on its side so that seeds form a thin layer, and leave in a dark warm cupboard. Rinse sprouts three times a day by pouring lukewarm water into jar, swirling around and emptying the excess. After 3–5 days, when the first young leaves appear, place jar in direct light until ready for use. Seeds may be stored in a refrigerator 3–5 days.

Although usually used for salads, they may be used in egg dishes, and are excellent and nourishing in sandwiches. They also make appetizing omelettes.

Alfalfa omelette for two

4 lightly beaten eggs
2tbsp water
1½tbsp butter
1 cup alfalfa sprouts
1tbsp parsley
salt and pepper

Mix eggs, water and seasoning. Heat butter in omelette pan and pour in egg mixture, stirring gently with fork until it begins to set. Fold in sprouts and chopped parsley and serve with rolls or thin wholemeal bread and butter.

ALLSPICE
Pimento officinalis

A small, bushy evergreen tree, allspice has a pleasant combination of the flavours and scents of cinnamon, clove and nutmeg. It is native in the West Indies and South America, but is extensively cultivated in Jamaica: in all these areas it is called Jamaica pepper or pimento, owing to the likeness the berry bears to a peppercorn.

The tree begins to fruit when it is three years old, and its small white flowers appear from June to August. The berries, the size of currants, are purplish-black when ripe but, since they lose their aroma on ripening owing to loss of volatile oil, are harvested while still unripe and green. The oil is obtained by distillation, and is comparable to oil of cloves. In Jamaica the berries are used as a substitute for pipe tobacco.

An infusion called pimento water is made for flatulence, and this is also used as a vehicle to disguise the flavours of other less acceptable medi-

ALLSPICE, here shown in an illustration from *Flora Medica*, 1829.

cines. Pimento oil is taken as a digestive, and in cases of hysteria. The crushed berries when boiled until thick are used as a poultice for rheumatism and neuralgia.

Powdered allspice is used to flavour cakes, milk puddings, soups, preserves, pickles and chutneys. It is a valuable addition to pot-pourri. Sliced oranges dipped in a mixture of allspice and brown sugar and fried make a delicious accompaniment to roast duck and pork. It is a useful spice in curry powder.

The following recipe is appetizing and economical, and may be served with pasta or rice.

Spiced giblets

giblets	1 dssp mushroom
1 onion	ketchup
2 cloves	2 peppercorns
1 blade mace	2 allspice berries
butter	pinch of salt
	flour, lemon

ANGELICA, from Joseph Roques' *Phytographie Medicale*.

Clean giblets and put into a saucepan with 1qt (1l) of cold water. Boil and remove scum. Add onion, cloves, mace, peppercorns, allspice berries and a pinch of salt. Simmer gently until giblets are tender. Take out when cooked, and thicken sauce with flour and butter. Boil for ½ hour. Remove giblets and cut into small pieces, return to sauce with juice of half a lemon and a dessertspoonful mushroom ketchup. Serve with snippets of toast.

ANGELICA

Angelica archangelica, or *Angelica officinalis*

UNDER THE DOMINION OF THE SUN AND THE SIGN OF LEO

The virtues of this herb were believed to have been revealed by an angel to a monk during a time of plague; the angel may have been Michael himself, for it is reputed to bloom on his day, 8 May. Regrettably, this holy herb is commonly known as bellyache root.

It is a native of northern Europe, but has been cultivated in Britain since the 16th century. With its huge lobed leaves and vast umbels of green-white flowers it can rise to between 4 and 10ft (between 1 and 3m), and every part of the plant is aromatic. The wild archangel, *Angelica sylvestris,* is smaller and less aromatic than the garden species. It has purplish stems and white flowers tinged with purple which appear in July. The plant gives a good yellow dye.

Our ancestors prized angelica highly, and its leaf-stalks were commonly blanched and eaten with bread and butter just as celery is today. A piece of the root would have been held in the mouth as an antiseptic when plague was feared.

As a home remedy it was rated by Parkinson, apothecary to James I, ahead of all the medicinal plants. 'Having showed you all the herbs that are most usually planted in kitchen gardens for ordinarie uses, let me now adde a few others that are also noursed up by many in their gardens to preserve health, to cure such small diseases as are often within the compasse of the gentlewoman's skill, who help their own family and their poore neighbours that are farre remote from Physicians and Chirurgeons, to take much pains both to doe goode unto them, and plant those herbes that are conducing to their desires.' He advised the gentlewoman that the 'dryed roote made into pouder, and taken in wine or other drinke, will abate the rage of lust in young persons'.

The plant is usually raised from seed in April and is treated as a biennial, although it often does not bloom until its third year, after which it dies. A splendid plant for the semi-wild garden, particularly near water and in shade, it is also a good bee-plant. The seed loses its germinating properties so it should not be kept longer than the spring after flowering.

The ribbed fruits are raised as a commercial crop for the distillation of an essential oil employed in herbal medicine and in perfumery. Angelica is also used in certain Rhenish wines, to which it gives a flavour of muscatel. In France it is cultivated on a large scale near Clermont Ferrand and sold for making liqueurs — Chartreuse, anisette and some vermouths. Sometimes it is added to gin.

In medicine, herbalists use it as a tonic and for coughs and colds. The stems, if chewed, reduce flatulence. A tisane with lemons and honey is a

ANGELICA, from an illustration by F. Regnault, now in the possession of the Bibliothèque Nationale, Paris. The oil from this plant is used in the making of perfumes and to flavour liqueurs.

good and pleasant cold cure. Seeds and roots are used in medicine, and roots and stems are sold for confectionery; it was for this latter purpose that angelica used to be cultivated in moist fields around London. The confectionery, known simply as 'angelica', is perhaps the herb's best known product. The candied leaves and stalks are used as a decoration on cakes, trifles and chocolates, as well as on ice puddings and cassatas.

Pears baked in syrup and garnished with a candied angelica leaf and stalk make a simple but attractive sweet. An infusion of the leaves is a good aromatic tea, and a little of this added with a slice of lemon to stewed apples or rhubarb improves the flavour. Angelica may be used to flavour green tomato and ginger jam, and it makes a good sauce for white fish.

To candy angelica

Cut stems and leaf stalks into 4–5in (10–12cm) pieces, and place them in a crockery vessel. Pour over a boiling solution of 1pt (550ml) water and ¼lb (113g) salt. Cover and leave for 24 hours. On the following day, drain, peel and wash the stems in cold water. Make a syrup of 1½pt (825ml) water and 1½lb (680g) sugar, and boil for 10 minutes. Immerse the angelica carefully in the boiling syrup for 20 minutes, then lift out and leave to drain. Dry in a cool oven. Sprinkle with sugar and store in airtight jars. The operation takes time, but when done it will keep for a considerable number of parties.

ANISE
Pimpinella anisum

Grandmother's gentle cure-all, anise is a herb with no vice in it. It is equally accommodating in culinary matters, cosmetics and cures, and has the added distinction of supplying us in our youth with those round, brown sugary aniseed balls.

Its history is long: it was known as a wild plant in ancient Egypt, Greece, Crete and Asia Minor, and was mentioned by Dioscorides and Pliny; and in cultivation it was known to the ancient Egyptians and to the Romans. At Roman weddings a cake flavoured with aniseed was part of the marriage feast — powdered and mixed with honey, anise was considered to have aphrodisiac qualities, which possibly was the reason for its use.

An aromatic umbelliferous plant, which may be wild or cultivated, it is an annual, whose small white flowers appear in July and August, followed by downy brown seeds. These seeds are dried and used in a tisane, made of a half-teaspoonful of seeds to a cup of hot water, for flatulence and constipation.

It is regarded as carminative, expectorant and tonic, and is an old and tried soothing syrup for babies. Its pleasant flavour is used in combination with other medicines, and the dried seed may be chewed as a digestive. Taking a few seeds in a cup of hot milk at bedtime is helpful against insomnia.

Oil of anise relieves cramp and stomach pains, and is used also as a flavouring for Pernod and other drinks and in the preparation of soap.

The leaves may be used as pot-herbs. The seeds help to flavour curries, and are cooked with red cabbage, but the most usual use is in cakes and bread.

Aniseed cookies

2 cups flour
½ cup mixed butter and lard
4tsp baking powder
¾ cup cold milk or milk and water
lump sugar
orange juice
aniseeds

Sift together dry ingredients, rub in butter and lard, and mix with liquid to make a soft dough. Roll lightly to about ¾in (2cm) thick. Cut out with a floured biscuit cutter. Dip small lumps of sugar into orange juice and press one on each biscuit, sprinkling a few aniseeds on top. Bake (Gas Mark 4, (350°F, 180°C) for 10–15 minutes.

ARROWROOT
Maranta arundinacea

An herbaceous perennial, arrowroot is native to the West Indies; it is cultivated there and in tropical America, South and West Africa, and India. It was introduced into England, but only as a stove plant, and was taken by John Williams, a missionary, to the South Sea Islands. Its common name is said to be derived from the custom of the American Indians of applying the roots to wounds received from poisoned arrows. The generic name *Maranta* was given in memory of Bartomeo Maranto, a 16th-century physician.

It grows to a height of 2–3ft (60–90cm), has broad pointed leaves and bears a spike of creamy flowers which grow in pairs. The farinaceous

Plumbe's arrowroot sponge cake

Take 4oz (113g) arrowroot, 4oz (113g) butter, 2tsp baking powder and mix well together. Beat 3 eggs, yolks and whites separately, and add to them 4oz (113g) castor sugar. Beat together, flavour with a few drops of vanilla or almond essence and beat again. Put mixture into a buttered tin, papered all around 2in (5cm) deeper than the tin, and bake in a hot oven for an hour.

BALM
Melissa officinalis

UNDER THE DOMINION OF JUPITER AND THE SIGN OF CANCER

A modest herb with little beauty, balm is nonetheless one of the best loved plants of the cottage garden, for it is the sweetest of all herbs. Beekeepers in particular esteem it, hence the name *Melissa*: honey, mead and wax were an important part of rural economy in the days when sugar was scarce and expensive. Pliny wrote that 'Bees are delighted with this herbe above all others ...

BALM, shown here from William Woodville's *Medical Botany*, 1832.

ARROWROOT, as illustrated in P. J. Redoute's *Liliaceae*, 1802. From the rhizome of this plant an edible starch is derived.

substance which we call arrowroot is obtained from its fleshy rhizome when not more than a year old, by maceration, washing and drying. The resulting powder is finally spread on clean white cloths and dried in the sun. It is principally used in blancmange, or in a thin and easily digested gruel for invalids and babies, although the roots can also be candied. To add a little interest, it can be flavoured with lemon and sugar, with wine, or with nutmeg and other spices.

For culinary and medicinal purposes, it seems to have been put on the British market by H. M. Plumbe, who advertised it at 1s 6d per pound as suitable for breakfast, luncheon, dinner and supper, for the making of biscuits, blancmanges, breakfast cakes, custards and creams, gruel, baked pudding, jelly, omelettes and as a thickening for soups.

His recipe for sponge cake is certainly well worth trying. The version that follows has been modernized for the benefit of today's cook.

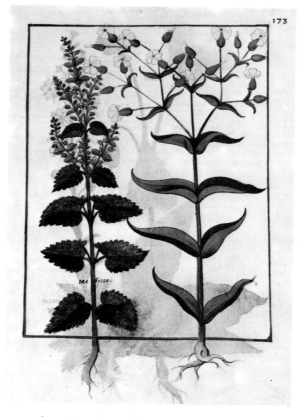

BALM, from Jean Bourdichon's 16th-century *Hours of Anne of Burgundy*, now in the possession of the Bibliothèque Nationale, Paris.

Close by Gerard's garden was the shop of a nurseryman, William Lucas, where balm could be purchased. John Harvey, the garden historian, has found out the precise date and situation — at the sign of The Naked Boy, also known as The Three Naked Boys, near Strand Bridge, London, in 1677. Alas, the Naked Boys, whatever their number, have disappeared, but three hundred years later balm may still be found in the catalogues of herb specialists.

Thomas Coghan, a 16th-century Oxford don, said, 'It is an hearbe greatly to be esteemed of students, for by a special property it driveth away heaviness of mind, sharpeneth the understanding and encreaseth memory'. Evelyn wrote of it too. He recommended it as a cordial for its calming effect on the heart. He pictured the London of the future as a great garden city, planted with flowering trees and shrubs. In *Fumifugium: or the Inconvenience of the Aer and Smoke of London dissipated,* he suggested that the 'beds and bordures should be planted with scented flowers and herbs, including balm'.

It was grown in large quantities in the neighbourhood of London to supply the markets, where bunches were sold at from 6d to 1s a dozen. For gardeners, balm was one of the 'sweet smelling hearbes whether they be such as beare no flowers, or, if they beare any, yet they are not put in Nosegaies alone, but the whole hearbe with them' that Lawson instructed the *Countrie Housewife* to plant. It was not only for a remedy for a cold on the chest that the country housewife valued her plants of lemon balm, but also for polishing her few chairs:

The several chairs of order look you scour
With juice of balm, and every precious flower.

So Mistress Anne Page, in *The Merry Wives of Windsor,* bids her elves polish the chairs with a handful of balm leaves, to scent them and give them a gloss.

Balm was also used as a strewing herb, and picked for the kitchen, where its juice was made into a tansy with eggs, rosemary and sugar.

In the 17th century the Carmelite monks in Paris made a perfume, a forerunner of eau de cologne, a distillation of balm leaves called Carmelite water. It is still used in perfumes, and in the home in pot-pourri, sweetbags and sachets. A herbal pillow, filled with the dried flowers of hops, cowslips, mignonette and balm is a recognized aid to peaceful sleep, and makes a very welcome present. One of the properties of balm is

when they are straied away they do find their way home againe by it', which is why bee-keepers still rub their hives with balm, knowing that their bees will never leave and hoping that other bees will come. It is said also to improve the flow of milk in cows, and a tea of balm and marjoram given to cows after calving strengthens them.

This valuable perennial was introduced into Britain by the Romans, and has been naturalized in the south of England. Its virtues have been known from earliest times — for nervous troubles, menstrual irregularity, and 'good against a surfeit of mushrooms'.

Gerard says that 'The juice of Balm glueth together greene wounds', and it is now recognized that balsamic oils of aromatic plants make excellent surgical dressings. It was cried in the London streets, and presumably in other towns:

Here's balm and hissop and cinquefoil,
All fine herbs, it is well known.

that the dried leaves retain their scent for a long time. As a bath additive, 2oz (56g) of the leaves, steeped in boiling water for fifteen minutes, is relaxing and sedative.

Balm was one of the ingredients of Henrietta Maria's nourishing morning broth. The following recipe was given by Sir Kenelm Digby in his *Closet Of Cookery,* 1669:

The Queen's morning broth

A hen, a handful of parsley, a sprig of thyme, three of spearmint, a little balm, half a great onion, a little pepper and salt, and a clove, as much water as will cover them; and this boiled to less than a pint, for one good porrengerful.

In cooking its uses are numerous. It flavours marrow jam and apple jelly; it is useful in chicken stuffing; and it improves stewed fruit and jellies. Thin slices of orange marinated in a French dressing to which balm has been added are delicious. To enhance tea's refreshing and invigorating qualities, add a few dried leaves of balm to the pot.

Balm is used commercially in the making of liqueurs, and is useful in the home in a refreshing summer drink made with lemon peel, sugar and an infusion of the leaves. In fact, all fruit cups are improved by a sprig or two of balm, and the crushed fresh leaves can be added to cider.

Claret Cup

Mix one bottle of claret, 1pt (550ml) bottle soda water, balm, borage, 1 sliced orange, ½ sliced cucumber, a liqueur-glass of brandy and a little sugar. Place in a covered jug in a refrigerator for an hour and then strain.

BASIL

Ocimum basilicum

UNDER THE DOMINION OF MARS AND THE SIGN OF SCORPIO

Basil has been growing in Britain since the 16th century, although it will not survive a British winter and therefore must be treated as an annual. It flowers in July and August.

Its name, *basilicum,* comes from the Greek *basilikon,* 'royal', which may have signified that it was the king of herbs, or perhaps that it was used in some royal unguent or medicine.

Common basil has always been popular with Greek, Italian and French cooks, but *Ocimum sanctum,* holy basil, is a sacred herb to the Hindus. It is grown in pots near temples and outside nearly

BASIL, from *Tacuinum Sanitatum, c.* 1385, now in the possession of the Bibliothèque Nationale, Paris. The leaves of this herb are an essential ingredient for the production of Chartreuse.

every house, watered daily and worshipped by all the members of the household. The root is made into beads and worn around the neck and arms, and the seeds are made into rosaries. A leaf is placed on the breast of the dead, so that it may open for them the gates of heaven. It is sacred to Krishna and to Vishnu; and Lakshmi, the wife of Vishnu, was transformed into the *tulasi,* the holy basil. The plant is a native of India. In spite of its holiness, Brahmins eat a few leaves after lunch for digestive purposes.

In Egypt, basil is scattered over graves. A strange superstition, common to the ancient Greeks and Romans and persisting until today, is that basil seeds must be planted with cursing and abuse, otherwise they will not flourish. It must be sown late in the year, and this is no superstition, for the plant is tender.

Faire Basil desireth it may be hir lot
To growe as the gilly flower trim in a pot
That Ladies and Gentils whom she doth serve
May help hir as needeth life to preserve.

[16]

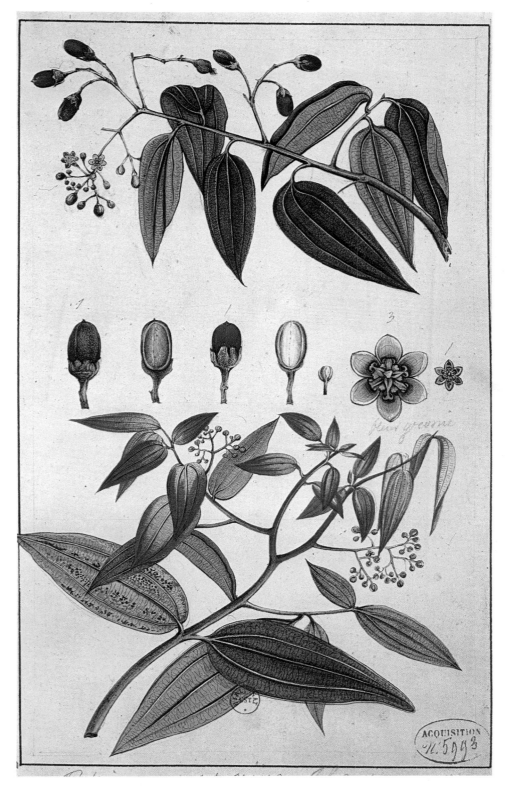

BAY, from a 19th-century French watercolour, showing the blossom in various stages of development.

'To make that a woman shall eat of Nothing that is set upon the Table:- Take a little green Basil, and when Men bring the Dishes to the Table put it underneath them that the Woman perceive it not; so Men say that she will eat of none of that which is in the Dish whereunder the Basil lieth.' Crafty instructions for checking obesity from an old herbal.

Basil, especially bush basil, *Ocimum minimum,* is excellent grown as a pot plant, since on a sunny kitchen windowsill it will provide its aromatic leaves for much longer. The flowers are best pinched out — no great loss, since they are undistinguished.

Culpeper comments: 'This is the herb which all authors are together by the ears about, and rail at one another like lawyers. Galen and Dioscorides hold it not fit to be taken inwardly; and Chrysippus rails at it with downright Billingsgate rhetoric' — which tells us rather more about Billingsgate in the 17th century than it does about basil. He continues: 'Something is the matter this herb and rue will not grow together, no, nor near one another', a fact known to the ancient Greeks, and endorsed by scientists today. He ends on a mysterious note: 'It helps the deficiency of Venus in one kind, so it spoils all her actions in another. I dare write no more of it —'. And Culpeper was no timid man.

Basil may dislike rue but it has an affinity with tomatoes. Any tomato dish, hot or cold, may be improved with chopped basil. Egg, potatoes and cold rice respond equally well. Brought in fresh from the garden, chopped finely and put in a salad bowl, with French dressing added and the salad finally tossed in, it gives, as the name implies, a salad fit for a king.

The standard infusion — ½tsp in a cup of water — should be taken slowly for all stomach troubles, vomiting, constipation and enteritis. Sweetened with honey, it is soothing for coughs.

Bush basil, which we have mentioned, grows to only 6in (15cm), and it is rather less tender. It is an attractive pot plant; and there was a charming custom in Tudor times for a miniature basil plant in a pot to be presented to visitors on leaving. In Crete it was grown in pots as a love-plant, signifying 'love washed with tears', and in Italy it was called 'Kiss-me, Nicholas' and worn by provocative young women in their hair. In contrast to all this, the Greeks portrayed the figure of Poverty as a ragged woman with a pot of basil at her side.

In today's kitchen it is used in soups and sauces. The leafy tops of both bush basil and sweet basil are used in seasoning and salads, casseroles and sausages; the nipping out of the tops helps to keep the plants well shaped and bushy. It is used also in vinegars and as a flavouring for fish.

Cheese, carrot and basil flan

6oz (170g) frozen pastry
4oz (113g) finely grated raw carrot
3oz (85g) coarsely grated cheese
½tsp fresh or dried basil
2 eggs
½pt (275ml) milk
salt and pepper

Line a flan ring or a sandwich tin with the pastry. Beat eggs lightly into the milk, and add carrot, cheese, basil and seasoning. Pour mixture into the pastry case and bake for about ½ hour (Gas Mark 5, 375°F, 190°C).

BAY
Laurus nobilis

A TREE OF THE SUN, UNDER THE SIGN LEO

A tree of the Laurel family, bay is native to southern Europe, where it reaches heights of 40–50ft (12–15m). It is a bushy shrub in England which needs protection from searing winds and hard frosts.

The bark is smooth, reddish or olive green. The leaves are alternate, smooth and thick, of a rich shining green with wavy margins. The small flowers grow in clusters and are yellowish-green in colour. Both the oval berry and the leaves yield an essential oil. William Turner described the bay in his great Herbal: 'The leaves of the Bay tre are always grene and in figure and fashion they are lyke unto periwincle. They are long and brodest in the middest of the leaf. They are blackishe grene namely when they are olde. They are curled about the edges, they smell well. And when they are casten into the fyre they crake wonderfully. The tre in England is no great tre, but it thryveth there many partes better and is lustier than in Germany.'

Laurus nobilis, the sweet bay or bay laurel, was dedicated to Apollo. It was the classical garland tree, and great men in Greece and Rome were crowned with its leaves. When a battle was won every Roman soldier carried a sprig of bay to denote victory. To be awarded a wreath of bay leaves was a sign of academic distinction — hence the term 'poet laureate'. University students who graduate are called Bachelors, from the French *bachelier,* which is derived from the Latin *bacca-laureus,* 'laurel and berries'. At one time these scholars were not allowed to marry lest the duties of husband and father should distract them from an academic career; thus all unmarried men came to be called bachelors.

In Roman times the aromatic quality of the leaves gave the bay the reputation of resisting contagion, and during a time of plague the Emperor Claudius and his court moved to Laurentium, celebrated for its bay trees. Pliny the younger built his favourite villa nearby. Theophrastus wrote that many people kept a bay leaf in their mouths as an antiseptic, and the leaves were also eaten to prevent intoxication. In 1629, foreshadowing the great plague, all the bay trees around the University of Padua withered and died. In this same year Parkinson's *Paradisus Terrestris* was published, in which he said, 'Bay leaves are necessary both for civil use and for physic, yea, both for the living and the dead. It serveth to adorn the House of God, as well as man, to crown or encircle, as with a garland, the heads of the living, and to stick and deck forth the bodies of the dead, so that from the cradle to the grave we have still use of it'.

The bay was one of the 400 simples used by Hippocrates, and through the centuries it was in constant demand for hysteria, ague and many human ills. Culpeper wrote that 'it resisteth witchcraft very potently, as also all the evils old Satan can do to the body of man, and they are not a few'. He prescribed a decoction of 'equal parts of Bay berries, cummin seed, hyssop, origanum, and euphorbia, with some honey' which, he said, 'settleth the palate of the mouth into its place', a restoration greatly to be desired.

During the reign of Elizabeth I it was customary to strew the floors of the homes of distinguished persons with bay leaves.

A 17th-century stillroom book includes a recipe for the treatment of 'All Manner of Fits', including 'baye' among thirty-two other herbs, but since they must be combined with '12 swallows alive' and 'a quart of piggons dung' the recipe is little used.

Every part of the tree has healing properties when used externally for such things as sprains and ear-ache. Although rarely used internally, both berries and leaves are excellent for restorative baths.

The oil expressed from the berries is green and strongly aromatic. It has been used in perfumery and in the making of bay rum, which combines an extract of the leaves blended with cloves, cinna-mon and pimento, to make up a well known hair tonic and a refreshing after-shave lotion.

Sweet bay has been cultivated in Britain since the 16th century. The trees may be grown from cuttings taken in April, or by layering in March or August; good plants may then be expected by the second spring. By growing a small bay tree in a pot you can not only use its leaves to add a pleasant flavour in cooking but, if you are super-stitious, it will protect your house from being struck by lightning. A bay tree adds distinction to a house if stationed at the front door, but it is handier outside the kitchen. Wherever it stands, take it inside on a frosty night or in a freezing wind. When the tree needs trimming dry the leaves for culinary purposes, but they will lose their flavour if kept too long.

One of the earliest culinary uses of bay leaves was in the decoration of the boar's head for festive occasions: all the company rose in honour of the boar's head and, to the sound of music, it was carried in by the chief cook on a silver dish, wreathed with bay, having in its mouth a lemon or a roasted pippin, and in its ears sprigs of rosemary.

French cookery may be said to be based on the bay leaf, since a French cook uses half a bay leaf in every *bouquet garni.* The leaves give a distinctive flavour in a marinade and to many soups, in fish and meat dishes, and in milk puddings. Bay leaves are best when used in slow cooking; they should be removed before serving. They also lend an appetizing aroma to kebabs.

Chicken liver and bay leaf kebabs

8 chicken livers
2 medium-sized onions
4 tomatoes
8 button mushrooms
rice
bay leaves
oil, salt and pepper

Wash livers and dry them thoroughly. Cut into handy-sized cubes. Peel and quarter onions. Halve tomatoes. Wash button mushrooms and the bay leaves. Thread each skewer with a bay leaf, liver, mushroom, tomato and onion, and repeat in the same order until skewer is full, ending with a bay leaf. Thread each skewer in the same order, place on a large dish and brush with oil, pepper and salt. Leave to marinate for ½ hour. Grill, turning so that they cook evenly. Serve on a bed of rice, with herb-butter sauce, or parsley and lemon juice, and a green salad. (Serves four people.)

BAY and garlic are the herbs being sold by the man depicted in this print by Delpech after an original by Vernet.

BELLADONNA (DEADLY NIGHTSHADE)

Atropa belladonna

The beautiful lady of this plant's name owed her loveliness to a solution of its juices which she dropped in her eyes to cause dilation or enlargement of the pupils: this used to be a traditional cosmetic practice among the young and, by nature, black-eyed beauties of Spain. Today the drug atropine is still indispensable in dilating the eye for examination and surgery. Taken internally, belladonna can accelerate the heartbeat, but its main use is in preventing spasms of the stomach and

BELLADONNA, as illustrated in Joseph Roques' *Phytographie Medicale* (*left, above*) and by F. Regnault (*left, below*), the latter illustration now in the possession of the Bibliothèque Nationale, Paris. Belladonna, or deadly nightshade, should not be confused with the woody nightshade or bittersweet, *Solanum dulcamara*: the leaves and berries of this shrub are less poisonous and are used in herbal treatments for rheumatism and skin complaints. Amateur medical use of either plant is of course dangerous.

inhibiting the production of mucus in the lungs and of saliva — these properties also make it useful in the operating theatre. A cosmetic lotion called dwal water, from the early English name for belladonna, dwal or dwale, was used by young women for removing freckles; dwale, it is thought, connects with the Scots word *dule*, and the French *deuil*, both signifying sorrow. The juice of the ripe berries gives to paper a beautiful and durable purple colour.

The generic name, *Atropa,* is derived from Atropos, the daughter of Erebus and Night. She was one of the three Parcae, the Fates who govern the lives of men, and her duty was to cut the thread of life without regard to sex, age or quality. She was represented by the ancients in a black veil, with a pair of scissors in her hand.

Belladonna is a perennial of the Potato family, native to England and throughout Europe; it is an introduced plant in the USA. Its appearance does not belie its reputation, for it is of lurid colour and unpleasant smell, with solitary flowers described variously as yellowish-brown or brownish-purple. Gerard, with his genius for description, notes that it is 'an overworn purple'. The flowers are succeeded by large and shining black berries, which, although by no means common, every child should be warned against. The whole plant is poisonous although, as we have seen, it contains a useful and powerful medicine when properly used. 'The naughtie and deadlie nightshade' had many warning names among our forefathers: for example, the furious, the raging or the sleeping nightshade; and the death-herb, the devil-berry and the devil's cherries.

Belladonna plants are seldom seen today, yet they once grew so luxuriously around Furness Abbey that the district was known as the Vale of Nightshade. As one might half-expect from its sinister reputation, it thrives on old ruins. It prefers a lime-rich soil — but is not suitable for the garden!

It has been cultivated as a commercial crop in the UK in Hertfordshire and Suffolk. Its leafy tops are mown in its second year, and the harvest repeated for three or four years. The leaves, roots and berries which contain two alkaloids, atropine and hyoscyamine, are used medicinally.

Small domestic animals seem to be immune to belladonna's poison, although people have been poisoned by eating rabbits which had fed on it. For mass murder in the past it had no rival. A legend tells that the Scots under Macbeth, during a truce with the Danes, treacherously mixed nightshade with the ale; they then basely fell upon the Danish troops and destroyed them in their sleep.

A few grains of the dried leaf or an infusion causes delirium, madness or a strange somnambulism, followed by complete loss of memory. Plutarch, in his account of the Parthian war, says the troops of Marcus Antonius sought herbs but found few that they were accustomed to eat, and those who had eaten belladonna lost all memory and sanity, and would busy themselves moving every stone they met with as if engaged in some very important pursuit.

Under medical direction this dangerous plant has been used for scarlet fever, but no part of it should be taken except with a doctor's advice.

BERGAMOT

Monarda didyma

One of the handsomest of the perennial herbs, bergamot or monarda is a native of eastern and central USA.

It received its botanical name from Nicholas Monardes, a Spanish physician who discovered it in the 16th century, but it was not until 1745 that it was first grown in the UK, by Peter Collinson. It is now a welcome cultivated plant in British gardens, with its splendid scarlet flowers — and the crimson, purple, pale blue, pink and white varieties — which bloom from June to August and attract the bees so vital for pollination, from which it has earned the name of bee balm. Unfortunately, it is hard to grow. Since it is a swamp plant, it requires a good damp soil and partial shade, and unless supplied with these is likely to die down. It should in any case be split annually and the dead centre removed.

Bergamot is a member of the Mint family. It has little medicinal value except carminative and digestive, but in the past it was important in the USA both as a substitute for tea and as a fragrant and invigorating tea in its own right, known as oswego tea: so popular was this beverage at one time that the plant itself was known as oswego tea. The dried leaves can be used in combination with ordinary tea.

The oil of bergamot that is so widely used in perfumery comes not from monarda but from a citrus tree, *Citrus bergamia*, which has a similar perfume, although monarda itself is used extensively in its dried form for pot-pourri and in sachets. In Edwardian England small silk bags containing, mixed with bergamot, any or all of dried lemon verbena, scented geranium leaves, thyme, mint, lavender, rosemary and southernwood, were hung on the backs of chairs to scent winter drawing-rooms.

Bouquet de victoria

Mix well and distil 1oz (28g) essence of bergamot; ½ drachm (2g) oil of cloves; 3 drachms (10g) oil of lavender; 6 grains musk; ½ drachm (2g) aromatic vinegar; 1½pt (825ml) spirits of wine.

Today we use the chopped leaves of bergamot to flavour our sauces and salads, and the pungent scarlet tubular flowers, each with a drop of honey in its base, as a last minute decoration to cold dishes — and we may still enjoy a cup of oswego tea.

BETONY

Betonica officinalis or *Stachys betonica*

UNDER THE DOMINION OF JUPITER AND THE SIGN OF ARIES

In the Middle Ages betony was cultivated in monastery gardens where it was used against almost every evil that flesh is heir to. It seemed that a man with a bottle or two of betony syrup and oil, a pot of ointment and a plaster or two could face the world with confidence, and could deal with such disasters as jaundice, palsy, convulsions, gout, dropsy, headaches, shortness of breath, stitches and pains in sides and back, and, of course, the bites of serpents and mad dogs. More than this, small pieces could be worn round the neck as a charm and protection against evil spirits, and for this purpose betony was often planted in churchyards.

The plant is somewhat similar to but brighter and so a little prettier than the nettle, and has no sting. Through the ages, it could be found in most cottage gardens, ready when needed for coughs, colds and just 'feeling low'. Anne Pratt wrote some time in the 1870s: 'We have often seen in cottages in Kent, and doubtless there might be seen also in other counties, large bundles of the "medicinal Betony", as Clare calls it, hung up for winter use.'

The dried leaves could be taken as tea, mixed with tobacco and smoked, or mixed with marjoram, orris root and a little eyebright and reduced to powder to be taken as a snuff for headaches. A British herbal snuff and tobacco were both made of equal quantities of betony and eyebright.

Cosmetic baths of betony were enjoyed by the fortunate, not only to cleanse and strengthen the body but also to beautify the skin. Vapour baths of this same versatile herb were found efficacious 'for them that be ferfull'. It was found to be best picked for these purposes as it began to flower.

The story of betony is sad. Not pretty enough for the front row of the herb garden, and over-praised and over-valued for her slender skills, life passed her by, and she is now almost forgotten. In her day, a whole treatise was written on her virtues by Antonius Musa, chief physician to the Emperor Augustus. Even verses were composed in her honour.

A rare recipe for 'Conserve of Betony After the Italian Way' remains, from *The Queen's Chest Opened,* by W. M., Cook to Queen Henrietta Maria, 1655: 'Betony new and tender, one pound, the best sugar, three pound, beat them very small in a stone mortar, let the sugar be boyled with two quarts of betony water to the consistency of a syrup, then mix them together by little and little over a small Fire, and so make it into a Conserve, and keep it in Glasses.'

But the time came when no place was found for betony in the perfume garden, and she was elbowed out of the kitchen. Coughs and colds are still with us, and painful backs as well, but betony is redundant. She has not lost all her skills by any means, but anything she can do other herbs can do better. We must remember, however, Antonius Musa's prayer: 'Betony, you who were discovered first by Aesculapius or by Chiron the centaur, hear my prayer. I implore you, herb of strength, by Him who ordered your creation and ordered that you should be useful for a multitude of remedies. Kindly help in making these seven and forty remedies.' We may remember also that Gerard 'found a rare white betony in a wood by a village called Hampstead', and transferred it, with great pleasure and care, into his garden.

Betony may yet return to favour.

BIRTHWORT
Aristolochia species

UNDER THE DOMINION OF VENUS

A perennial plant native to southern Europe and introduced to England, where it is now rare. The Aristolochiaceae comprise a group of 6 genera and about 220 species, many of which, but not *A. clematitis*, common birthworts, are native to America.

Birthwort was introduced from central or southern Europe to the physic gardens of the English medieval monasteries, and it is among the ruins of such establishments as Carrow Abbey that it may still be found. It was recorded at Carrow in 1793, and was then believed to have been grown by the nuns in the same place probably since the 12th century.

The young shoots resemble a vine, hence *clematitis*. The stalks, square and dusky green, grow to 1½ft (45cm), and the leaves are large, smooth and heart-shaped, with a rank odour attracting the flies that play an important part in their continuing existence. As with the wild arum, small insects are trapped on entering the trumpet-shaped flowers which have down-pointing hairs to prevent their escaping before they are plentifully dusted with pollen. As each flower opens the stigmas reach maturity before the stamens, so that flies carrying pollen from the older flowers effect fertilization on arrival. The flowering season lasts from May to September, when spherical striped capsules develop, packed with flat triangular seeds. The fruit hangs down on curved stems, allowing the seed to drop on the ground beneath. So these colonies survive, renewing their tenancy but seldom widening their horizons.

The name *Aristolochia*, meaning 'best birth', probably arose from the strange formation of the flower. The greenish-yellow tube-like perianth, swollen at the base, symbolized the womb and the birth-passage, and was thus accepted by the *Doctrine of Signatures* as being visible proof that the plant must be of aid to women in childbirth. Parkinson says that 'it is good to help women that are ready to be delivered, and that are delivered, but not those that are with child, not ready to be delivered, for in such it may cause abortment'.

The root only was used in medicine to promote evacuations after birth. Brook says that the roots of two other varieties, long birthwort and climbing birthwort were also kept in apothecaries' shops, and these possessed the same virtues to a lesser degree.

According to Pliny, if an expectant mother desired to have a son, she employed birthwort with the flesh of an ox, but we are not told whether the results were satisfactory.

Although the plant is poisonous, it has been used in ointments and poultices, and an ancient prescription for a plaster made of opopanax, bedellium and *Aristolochia* root still remains; but this strange-looking frequenter of monastery gardens is now of historic rather than obstetric interest.

BISTORT
Polygonum bistorta

A PLANT OF SATURN

A handsome perennial plant, native to many parts of Europe and the USA, and common in the moist grassy areas of northern England and southern Scotland, bistort is cultivated not only for its valuable medicinal properties but, in gardens, for

BISTORT, as shown in an illustration by W. Clark from *Medical Botany*, 1834, by John Stephenson and J. M. Churchill.

[23]

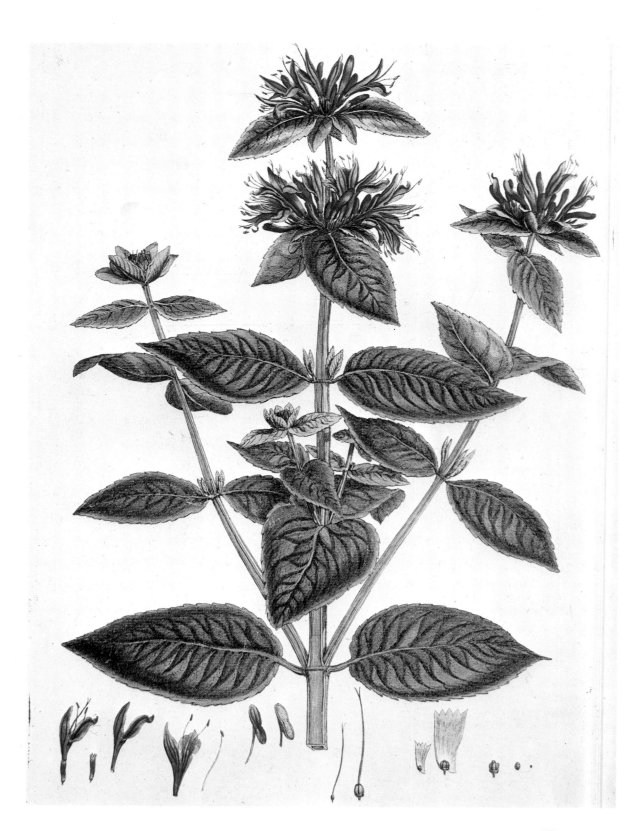

The underground stem is black outside and red within, and powerfully astringent. It contains tannin and gallic acid, and the tannin has been employed in the making of leather. When the tannin has been removed from the root, there remains a starch-like substance which can be used for food; in Russia this substance has been made into bread.

The leaves and tender shoots may be cooked as greens, and in the North of England, where the plant is prolific, it is traditional at Easter to eat bistort pudding, a herb pudding whose local variations have given rise to other country names. In Manchester it was called patience or passion dock, because the pudding was eaten during the last two weeks of Lent. It was also called Easter mangient, a corruption of *mangient,* to be eaten, to which the nursery pudding blancmange is also related. Easter mangient, eaten in the Lake District, was yet further corrupted into Easter giant and Easter ledges, and all have given their name, at some time, to what we call here dock pudding.

BIRTHWORT, from William Woodville's *Medical Botany,* 1832.

BETONY, illustrated in an English manuscript herbal dated about 1100, now in the possession of the Bodleian Library, Oxford.

its bluish-green leaves, backed with ashen-grey and purple, and the tall spikes of rose-pink flowers which it bears from June to September.

The name 'bistort' means twice-twisted, and refers to the underground stem which is twice bent, like the letter S — old herbalists called it English serpentary, dragon wort and snakeweed; some discovered in its image the virtue of curing snake-bites.

It possesses 'a powerful faculty to resist all poison, and may be used in the treatment of cholera, dysentry, smallpox, measles, diarrhoea, jaundice and gonorrhea. It is excellent for gargles and as a mouthwash for sore gums, and for the clearing of pimples and stings'. It is claimed to heal internal ulcers. The powdered root will stop the bleeding of small wounds, and a bistort poultice is used for sores and haemorrhages. It is a good tonic, and was in the past used against the plague. It was also an old country cure for toothache. It is used in decoctions and lotions, and was recommended by the ancients against miscarriages and as a birth-plant.

(*left*) BERGAMOT, an English 18th-century engraving by J. F. Miller from the Victoria and Albert Museum, London.

Aristolochia   Serpentaria

No one knows how or when dock pudding originated, but it has become part of the traditional cookery of Yorkshire, celebrated in modern times at the Calder Valley Arts Festival as the Dock Pudding Championship. Claims to this essential herb are staked out in the local countryside, numbered, and outsiders warned off, and that area allowed two years to recover before the next onslaught.

During the Second World War, so great was the fame of *Polygonum bistorta* that Lord Haw Haw announced over the air that the food situation was so critical in Yorkshire that people were reduced to eating grass.

Dock pudding

Gather bistort, nettles, dandelion leaves, a few blackcurrant leaves, an onion or leek, or any greens available. Wash and dry, chop finely and place in a pie dish with a handful of oatmeal and one of barley. Add salt and pepper to taste. Cover with water and leave overnight for oatmeal and barley to swell. Put in a freshly greased pie dish and bake slowly for 1½ hours. Just before serving add a beaten egg and return to the oven for a few more minutes. An alternative method is to fry the mixture in bacon fat, and serve with bacon and chips.

BONESET

Eupatorium perfoliatum

A native of North America, boneset is found in swamps and water-margins. The pairs of opposite leaves, the lower of which are joined by their bases around the stems, so that the stem seems to grow through the leaves, have given it the common names of thoroughwort, thoroughgrow and thoroughstem. The flat leaden-white flowers spread in broad panicles from July to September.

To the children of colonial days the word boneset sounded the knell of doom. If only the bitter draught had been kept for administering to those with broken or misplaced bones it might have been bearable; but to 'writhing children into whom copious draughts of bitter, nauseous teas were poured every time they took cold, while a paternal hand, as relentless as that of Fate, held their little noses until the last drop was gulped down', boneset was the most bitter and the most nauseous of herbs.

However, as an indication that the herb was efficacious as a mender or setter of broken bones,

BONESET, from R. Bentley and H. Trimmen's *Medicinal Plants*, 1880.

the name was entirely misleading: it came from the name of a form of influenza which was once rife in the USA, so painful that it was given the name of break-bone fever, for which the plant was found to provide a successful cure. Small comfort this to young America: like the early Christian martyrs before them, they suffered for the faith of their fathers, their terrors of the disease increased a hundredfold by the anticipation of copious doses of boneset tea, administered by old women outside the 'regular practice'. Only those who were allowed instead to munch boneset taffy ever regained their faith in humanity.

The sufferings of the Pilgrim offspring leave us in little doubt as to the value of the herb as an emetic. It is described also as a mild tonic. It is used by the southern US negroes for fevers, and by the American Indians for malaria and ague, therefore earning the name of ague weed.

The Chinese use boneset in combination with peppermint leaves and dried elder flowers for influenza and its accompaniment of headache, aching muscles and general feverish conditions. The medicine is called tse-lan, and is made by first simmering the elder flowers for ½ hour. 1pt (550ml) boiling water is then poured on to ½oz (14g) boneset and ½oz (14g) peppermint leaves, but the infusion must not be allowed to continue to boil; after standing for 30 minutes, it is strained and added to the strained elder-flower tea, and then a cupful of the hot tea is given to the patient every 15 minutes until relief is obtained.

BORAGE
Borago officinalis

A HERB OF JUPITER AND UNDER THE DOMINION OF LEO

The borage flowers' five-pointed azure stars, with their purple-black anthers and clean white eyes,

BORAGE, from the first volume of *La Botanique mise à la portée de tout le monde*, 1774, by F. and C. Regnault.

La Bourrache.
Borago Officinalis. Lann.
Ital. Borragine. Esp. Borraia. Angl. Borage. Allem. Borragen.

are among the loveliest flowers of the herb garden. Borage was once known as one of the four 'cordial flowers most esteemed for cheering the spirits' — the other three being rose, violet and alkanet. Borage was also considered good for the heart. It was cultivated in gardens in the 15th century, having been introduced from southern Europe, and these charming blue flowers, so useful and so decorative, may be recognized in the embroideries of the 16th and 17th centuries.

It is an annual which may be sown in September for May flowering, or in March for flowers in July. The stalks are tinged with red and the flowers have the odd characteristic of turning red if hot vinegar is applied. It is valuable as a companion plant in the vegetable patch, where it is much visited by the bees, who will fertilize the surrounding plants. Grown near tomatoes, it deters the tomato worm. Strawberries and borage seem to have formed a mutual pact, and each prospers in the other's company.

The old saying, 'Borage for courage', seems to be not merely a glib rhyme but to have some foundation in fact, for chemicals present in the herb act upon the adrenal gland, the 'organ of courage'. Borage contains potassium and calcium and is useful in medicine for its emollient properties, and is still one of the finest remedies for all bronchial, lung and chest disorders. Borage tea is an excellent lotion for sore eyes, and taken internally cleanses the blood and reduces fever. It is used also as a gargle for sore throats and ulcerated mouths.

The flowers are added to pot-pourri, but the dried herb has no virtue. For whatever purpose, the leaves should be used young, as old leaves are covered with prickly hairs. Indeed, the dried up leaves and stalks of the dead plant, encountered among the grass, are very unfriendly to bare legs and feet.

Borage leaves may be added to pickles, but their most popular use is as a cool flavouring to claret cup and fruit drinks. An old drink known as cool tankard was made with wine, water, lemon, sugar, and the flowers and young leaves in summer. The young leaves are delicious and, because of their slight cucumber flavour, make a good filling for sandwiches, particularly with cream cheese. They are useful in a cosmetic bath to cleanse and strengthen the body.

Borage flowers are decorative in salads and, like primroses and violets, are especially suitable for crystallizing. To do this a cooking thermometer is a help. Take two heaped tablespoonfuls of the flowers, 1lb (450g) castor sugar and one cup of water. Bring the sugar and water to the boil over a steady heat, and stand the thermometer in a jug of hot water. Test the syrup with the thermometer and when it reaches 240°F (115°C), drop the dry flowers a few at a time into the syrup. Boil gently for one minute, then lift them out with a perforated spoon and lay them on a sheet of foil. Drop in each batch until they are all coated, then place them on the foil in a slightly warmed oven to dry, turning once during the process. The remaining syrup may be used for crystallizing grapes, oranges, or simply for sweetening stewed fruit.

In a little book of 1713, *The Art of Gardening,* Leonard Meager in 'Sundry Sorts of Useful Herbs', says that 'Borrage and Bugloss are wholesome Pot-Herbs, and very Cordial Herbs otherwise used'. At that time borage seed was comparatively expensive, being sold for 1s an ounce.

To make a tart of borage flowers

Take Borage flowers and parboil them tender, then strayne them with the yolkes of three or foure egges with sweet curdes, or els take three or foure apples, and parboil withall, and strain them with sweet butter and a little Mace, and so bake it.
A Proper New Boke of Cookery, etc. (Anon, 1575)

CAPER

Capparis spinosa

Capparis spinosa, the common caper, gives its name to the whole family of Capparidaceae, which is widely scattered in many parts of the world, including Portugal, Sicily, southern USA and Canada. It is extensively cultivated in France and Italy.

A stiff, prickly shrubby plant, it grows to a height of 3–4ft (approx. 1m); it is deciduous and its shiny blue-green leaves have two curved and spiny stipules at the base, giving the whole its thorny character. The large handsome flowers have four sepals and four white petals, which grow in a cross, and long decorative purple stamens. Left unharvested, the buds grow quickly and burst. This always occurs towards evening and moths attracted to its glimmering beauty feed ecstatically on the brief honey feast offered to them. Next morning, its mission over, the flower withers. The time of honey and sweetness continues throughout the summer, as more and more new flowers open.

After fertilization the long stalk of the ovary curves like a hair pin, bent double with the burden

CAPERS being measured out by a herbalist, as illustrated in *Tacuinum Sanitatum, c.* 1385.

of its small cucumber-like fruit. This time the party is for the birds who, in extracting the sweet and sticky pulp, carry away the seeds in their beaks and so help to propagate the plant.

The medicinal qualities are antiscorbutic and aperient, and the roots were once used as a preservative for teeth.

Pickled capers have been known since about 1480, and a scented tea was made of them in the middle of the 19th century. When harvested commercially, the caper buds are pickled for use in sauces and salads. They are more popular on the Continent than in Britain, where the Sunday ritual of boiled mutton, caper sauce and turnips is now almost forgotten. However, a more modest dish of lamb stew or white fish is still made appetizing by the addition of caper sauce. Keep your caper bottle closely corked and the capers well covered with the liquor to prevent them from spoiling.

CAPERS, shown in this charming 19th-century plate from *Flora of India* with a jungle wren warbler.

D. 172-99.

The cook's oracle's recipe for caper sauce, 1817

A tablespoonful of capers, and two teaspoonful of vinegar; mince one third of the capers very fine, and divide the others in half; put them in a quarter of a pint of melted butter. Remember to stir them into butter which has been cut up small and melted with a teaspoonful of flour and a tablespoonful of milk. When these are well mixed, add three tablespoonsful of water and stir until it looks like cream.

Observation Some boil and chop a few leaves of parsley, and add these to the sauce; others squeeze in a quarter of a Seville orange, or half a lemon; take care that nothing but the clear juice goes in.

CAPSICUM

Capsicum species

A member of the Nightshade family, the capsicum is native to all of tropical South America. Its original home was probably Brazil. It is cultivated in the East and West Indies, Africa, and in many other parts of the world, in temperate as well as in tropical zones. It is too tender for outdoor cultivation in Britain, but fruits well under glass, and even on a sunny windowsill, where it makes an attractive pot-plant. Sown in the greenhouse from January to mid-March, the pods may be harvested in their green state in late July to August, and in late August onwards when red. They may be hung to dry in the kitchen, where they continue to look ornamental, but for indefinite keeping hang them only when they are red.

There are many varieties of these highly ornamental plants which are equally desirable in their bright green, yellow or brilliantly glossy red states. The flowers are white and drooping, and in their native tropical America perennial, although elsewhere they must be treated as annuals. Whether long- or short-podded varieties, all are known as pod pepper.

For medicinal purposes capsicums are a fine natural body purifier and internal disinfectant, and a protection against infectious diseases. They may be taken in powder and tablet form to build up resistance at the beginning of a cold. Plasters are made for arthritic and rheumatic pains, but excessive use can cause blisters and possibly dermatitis. Too frequent internal doses can cause gastroenteritis. A little ground capsicum may be put in shoes to warm the feet, and an infusion can be used for chilblains.

CAPSICUMS, from an illustration in *Flora Medica*, 1829. The fruits of the capsicum are used as a vegetable in their own right and in the making of condiments such as cayenne pepper and paprika. The fruits of several *Capsicum* species provide us with chilies.

In the West Indies the capsicum is considered a certain cure for all ills, including the dreaded yellow fever. There they drink a tea of it, and chew the pods, a habit inadvisable to those with unseasoned palates. They also make a drink for fevers by soaking the pods in water and adding the juice of oranges and sugar.

The small fruits known as chilies are mostly from *Capsicum annuum* or *C. fastigiatum*. Other spices, such as cumin and coriander, are usually added to chili powder.

Cayenne pepper comes from the dried pod of *C. frutescens var. longum,* and is used in curries. It was introduced into the UK from India in 1548.

Hungarian paprika veal

Beat 4 fillets of veal and dip into seasoned flour. Fry the meat lightly in oil, turn once, and then remove and keep hot. Mix 1tsp paprika (the ground fruit of *C. frutescens*) with a small carton of soured cream, add to the fat, stir and replace meat. Simmer for a few minutes before serving with new potatoes and broccoli.

CARAWAY
Carum carvi

A HERB OF MERCURY

A biennial plant found wild in Europe, Asia and northern USA, caraway has been cultivated for so long in the UK that it is now frequently found growing wild there. In gardens, it is best sown in autumn, although it may be sown in March or April: like parsley, it is difficult to start. The commercial crop is raised by sowing one year and harvesting the next.

It belongs to the Carrot family, and has a white carrot-shaped root which may be cooked and eaten as a vegetable. The small white or yellow flowers appear in May and June, followed by the dark brown double fruit containing the curved ridged seed, the source of the aromatic oil in which lies its chief value. The root, however, has its place in history, since it provided the bread for the soldiers of Julius Caesar's army. It has been cultivated in Norfolk, Essex and Kent, but mainly comes from Holland.

Parkinson grew it in his garden in Long Acre in 1629, and recorded: 'The seed is much used to be put among baked fruit, or into bread, cakes etc., to give them a rellish. It is also made into comfits and put into Trageas or Dredges, that are taken for cold or wind in the body, as also are served to the table with fruit.' The seeds, or a tincture of them, are used for flatulence, coughs, headaches and indigestion, and a poultice was made of the crushed seeds to relieve ear-ache.

Its chief medicinal virtue, however, is as a nursery nostrum for hiccupping babies. The matter of the hiccup was dealt with by Parson Mather, in a medical treatise entitled *The Angel of Bethesda,* in no light manner. 'The Hiccough or the Hicox rather, for it's a Teutonic word that signifies to sob, appears a Lively Emblem of the battle between the Flesh and the Spirit in the Life of Piety. The Conflict in the Pious Mind gives all the Trouble and same uneasiness as Hickox. Death puts an end to the Conflict.' To combat this affliction in church the three 'meetin' seeds', dill, fennel and caraway, were given to children in America to eat during the prayers and sermons.

The essential oil of caraway is used in perfumery and the making of soap. In Germany and Austria it is particularly popular — in bread and cakes, in sauerkraut and in Kümmel, a liqueur of the same name as the herb. The famous caraway comfits were made in a hot copper pan by putting the seeds into a syrup, which was kept constantly turning over a hot fire until the seeds were saturated and coated.

It must have been in Shakespeare's day that caraway as a flavouring and digestive reached the height of its popularity, and a dish of caraway seeds appeared on the table at most meals. In *Henry IV, Part 2,* Justice Shallow, welcoming Sir John Falstaff into his garden, says, 'Nay, you shall see mine orchard, where, in an arbour, we will eat a last year's pippin of my own graffing, with a dish of caraways . . .'

Roasted apples were served with caraway sauce, and Canon Ellacombe noted that little saucers of the seeds were traditionally served at some of the London Livery dinners; a similar custom is still maintained in some colleges in Oxford and Cambridge. The seeds are used in puddings and cakes, soups, bread and cheese; in Norway and Sweden they are used to flavour black bread. Caraway seed cake was traditional in English farmhouses after wheat-sowing.

Caraway seedie-cake

5oz (140g) flour
4oz (113g) castor sugar
2oz (56g) butter
1 gill (275ml) milk
the whites of 2 eggs
1tsp baking powder
2oz (56g) candied peel
1 large tsp caraway seeds
salt

Beat butter and sugar to a soft cream, stir in milk gradually and when it is quite smooth add stiffly whipped whites of eggs. Mix baking powder with a pinch of salt and stir in lightly, followed by candied peel chopped small and caraway seeds. Pour into a well greased tin and bake in a moderate oven for 1¼ hours.

CARDAMOM
Elettaria cardamomum

Hecate, the Grecian goddess of the infernal regions and patroness of witches and sorcerers, was acquainted with the properties of every herb, and imparted this knowledge to her daughters, Medea and Circe. The herbs dedicated to this malevolent trio were necessary to witches in their spells and so were persistently sought by them. The fact that cardamom, a powerful love potion, was one of

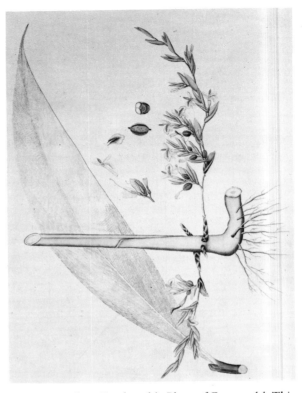

CARAWAY, shown here as illustrated in *Flora Medica*, 1829, is related to the carrot and is a plant with many uses. Its oil is used for carminative and stimulatory purposes and to flavour liqueurs, while its fruits, misleadingly known as caraway seeds, can be infused to give a refreshing tea or used to flavour or garnish foodstuffs such as cheese and bread.

CARDAMOM, from Roxburgh's *Plants of Coromandel*. This spice plant is often cultivated on tea and rubber plantations as a crop additional to the principal one.

these vital ingredients must have presented many witches with a problem, since the plant is native to southern India.

The flowering stems of this perennial herb spread horizontally near the ground and are a few inches to 2ft (60cm) long. It is a handsome plant of the Ginger family, producing yellow flowers with a purple lip in April and May. The fruit is smooth and yellowish-grey and contains dark reddish-brown seeds. The seeds are aromatic and stimulant, and are used as an appetizer and carminative and as a condiment. They are also used to disguise the flavour of disagreeable medicines. They are picked when ripe, and washed in special water to which soap nuts (a kind of acacia) are added. The old-fashioned patent medicine called Solomon's Balm of Gilead was prepared principally from cardamom seeds.

A somewhat exotic aphrodisiac combining cinnamon, cloves, nutmeg, pepper, pyrether, car-damom, gilliflowers and other ingredients, to be taken night and morning, was advised by the Arabian Shaykh Nafzawi. Another, slightly less extravagant, recipe contained green peas boiled with onions, with the addition of cinnamon, ginger and cardamoms. A lady botanist, writing in 1859, recollects 'in our young days, seeing old ladies carry Cardamoms in their pockets, and eat them as if they were sweetmeats'. No doubt this was for digestive or tonic purposes.

Powdered cardamom is used in curry, cakes and liqueurs, and a whole seed-pod may be added to hot punches, spiced wines, marinades, pickling liquids and coffee. For home cookery purchase whole cardamom seed when possible and grind or powder it as desired.

Spiced semolina

few cloves
pinch of cardamom
pinch of cinnamon
1oz (28g) raisins
1oz (28g) chopped almonds
4oz (113g) butter

1 cup semolina
2 cups sugar
1½ cups water
whole almonds and cream

Fry spices, raisins and chopped almonds gently in butter, add semolina and fry until brown, stirring always. Add sugar and water, mix, cover and lower heat, then simmer gently, stirring frequently, for 10–15 minutes, until quite dry. Serve hot, decorated with almonds and cream.

CARRAGHEEN MOSS

Gigartina mamillosa
Chondrus crispus

One of the most useful of algae, carragheen moss has a nomadic nature: where it is abundant one year, the next year it may not be found. Roughly speaking, however, most is found around the shores of North America; it grows on submerged rocks off the coast of France, and is most faithful

CARRAGHEEN MOSS, from the fourth volume of R. Bentley and H. Trimmen's *Medicinal Plants*, 1880.

to Ireland, a habit which has earned it the name Irish moss.

A sea plant of the Dulse family, it may be found all year round. Its shape is the best guide for identification, for its colour varies from red and purple to green, and it sometimes reflects prismatic colours. It turns yellow when dried. It hangs in branched tufts from rocks and stones, with many fronds growing from one root, and has roundish cells hollowed like small spoons. There are two types, *Gigartina mamillosa* and *C. crispus,* and both are important sources of carragheenan, a vegetable gelatine for thickening sauces, making jellies and blancmanges for invalids, and emulsifying ice-creams.

When the moss is boiled it forms a cloudy, somewhat spongy jelly, with a very faint mossy flavour which requires some sort of addition to make it palatable. It is considered in some places as a remedy for coughs, bronchitis and intestinal ailments. After being washed, dried in the sun and bleached, it may be stored in its dried state until it is required for use. When boiled and dissolved into a thick colourless jelly, it may be taken by invalids in tea.

This jelly is strongly adhesive and useful in book-binding as a size for making water-marbled papers. The moss is boiled and diluted, and left in the marbling-tank for 24 hours to form a skin, on which the colours, mixed with ox-gall, lie until combed into patterns, when the paper is carefully lowered on to the surface to receive them. Carragheen size is also used by painters, and in dressing silk and glazing calico.

It is a good fattening food for calves when boiled in milk; pigs also thrive on it when it is mixed with potatoes or meal. It can be grown successfully in an aquarium.

Dried carragheen moss can be obtained from stores, but with increasing difficulty, and so whenever possible it is useful to collect one's own supply. If this is done, wash the moss several times, and allow it to soak overnight in fresh water. It can then be dried and stored.

Carragheen blancmange

Soak ½ cupful in water for 10 minutes; drain and simmer in milk with a flavouring of dried elder-flowers (2tsp) or a bay leaf, or vanilla or spices for 15 minutes. Strain and sweeten with honey or sugar, and allow it to set. Serve with cream.

A fruit jelly can be made with it by using orange or lemon juice, or the strained juice of any summer fruit. Refrigerate for several hours.

CASTOR OIL PLANT
Ricinus communis

The castor oil plant, or bush or tree, according to the climate in which it grows, is one of the most ancient sources of medicine known. Castor oil seeds have been found in Egyptian tombs, where they have lain for some 4,000 years. The plant was mentioned by Hippocrates 400 years BC. Herodotus wrote that it furnished an oil used by the Egyptians in their lamps and in their unguents. In the first century AD Dioscorides described the plant and the process of extracting its oil. Pliny speaks of it as a laxative, and for that purpose it has been used throughout the centuries. It was employed in the Middle Ages for the cure of skin diseases, and as a healing medium after the removal of foreign bodies from an injured eye.

It is a member of the Spurge family, originally a native of India, but is now found not only in tropical countries, where it may grow to a height of 30–40ft (9–12m), but in temperate climates also. In the South of France it may attain 15ft (4.5m); in Britain, where it is usually treated as an annual or a greenhouse plant, it seldom reaches more than 5ft (1.5m).

The leaves are deeply lobed and glossy. In Germany they have been used to feed silkworms, and trees were grown specially for this purpose.

There are male and female flowers on the same plant. The male flowers, which appear on the lower spike, have a green calyx and yellow stamens, but no corolla. The female flowers grow on the upper part of the spike and likewise have no corolla, but the calyx is reddish and the ovary in its centre is crowned by deeply divided red threads. The whole of the plant, except for the oil, contains an irritant poison. The flowers appear in July and August, followed by the three-celled nut, covered with tough spikes, which contains the seed.

The oil is used for leather-dressing, and in the manufacture of artificial leather for furniture. It is also employed commercially in the making of transparent soaps.

CASTOR OIL PLANT, from Sibthorp's early 19th-century *Flora Graeca*. Once widely used as a notoriously effective laxative, the extract from this plant is now used mainly in the making of oils and varnishes and as a lubricant.

CAYENNE is prepared from capsicums, many forms of which cluster together in this lushly coloured plate from Hibberd's *The Floral World*, 1872.

CATMINT
Nepeta cataria

A HERB OF VENUS

The catmint, catnip, catnep or nep is an aromatic plant of the Mint family, common in North America and many parts of Europe; in the UK the wild flower is a perennial of the hedgerows, and is usually known as calamint. It was an old simpler's herb, catmint tea being a drink enjoyed by country people long before China and Indian teas were imported. It was believed that the root when chewed made the quietest person fierce and quarrelsome, and a tale was told of a hangman who could not face his job until he had eaten it. It prefers chalky or gravelly conditions and, unlike other mints, does not require a moist soil in which to flourish.

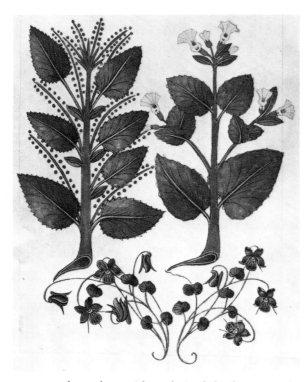

CATMINT, shown here with nettle (on left), from an early 16th-century manuscript.

The wild flowers are almost white, with corollas dotted with crimson. Introduced into cultivation, it has become a valued rockery- and border-plant, where from June to September it produces grey leaves and cool bluish flowers, which have become an almost necessary part of an English country garden.

It is a well known fact that cats love it. Gerard records: 'The later Herbarists doe call Nep *Herba Cattaria*, and *Herba Catti*, because cats are very much delighted herewith; for the smell of it is so pleasant unto them, that they may rub themselves upon it, and wallow and tumble in it, and also feed on the branches and leaves very greedily.' Modern herbalists claim that cats are aware of its medicinal value. Whether or not that is the case, a small bag stuffed with dried catmint makes an acceptable present for any cat. Catmint is also attractive to bees, and bee-keepers would do well to rub some on the inside of a hive to welcome a new swarm.

Culpeper claimed that catmint 'taketh away barrenness . . . and the pains of the mother', and it was used in baths for women 'to make them fruitfull'. With wine, it was 'good for those who have fallen and are much bruised'. Catmint ointment was used also to relieve piles.

In modern medicine catmint is regarded as a digestive herb, and is prescribed for stomach pains and flatulence. It is good for feverish colds and coughs, and if drunk at night it encourages peaceful sleep. It is mild enough to be given to children. Catmint tea may be made from the fresh or the dried herb. An infusion of 1 tablespoonful of fresh or ½ tablespoonful of the dried herb is good for nerves and headaches, or it can be used for the same purpose in combination with skullcap and peppermint, or sage, peppermint and marjoram.

The plant has little culinary value, although the French use the young shoots in salads.

CAYENNE
Capsicum species

Cayenne is the ground product of the various dried capsicums. There are many distinct varieties, such as cherry pepper, *Capsicum cerasiforme*; bird pepper, *C. baccatum*; bell pepper, *C. grossum*, and spur pepper, *C. frutescens*, which are grown in different countries, in temperate as well as tropical zones.

C. annuum belongs to the Nightshade family, and is believed to be native to South America, but is now cultivated in all tropical countries. It is an annual, growing to a height of 12–18in (30–45cm), and is grown in greenhouses in England, or as a decorative pot-plant for sunny windowsills. Sown under glass from January to mid-March, the pods may be harvested in their green state in late July to August, and in late August onwards when red. They may be hung to dry in the kitchen, where they continue to look ornamental, but for indefinite keeping, they should be hung only when red.

Taller and more woody than *C. annuum*, *C. frutescens*, cultivated in the warm regions of both hemispheres, produces the largest and mildest of the capsicum fruits. These are ground for paprika.

Hungarian goulash
1lb (450g) cubed beef
1 large onion
2oz (56g) dripping or lard
1 clove garlic
1tsp paprika
1lb (450g) tomatoes
½lb (225g) small potatoes
salt
chopped parsley

Fry chopped onion gently, add cubed beef and stir until meat is evenly browned. Add seasoning and sliced tomatoes, cover and simmer for an hour. Add potatoes and continue to cook for 20 minutes. Garnish with chopped parsley.

The capsicums are all highly pungent, and derive their genetic name from the Greek, *kapto*, 'I bite'. Cayenne pepper was introduced into Britain in 1548. Here are two recipes for use with fish.

Essence of cayenne

1qt (1l) vinegar to 1oz (28g) cayenne pepper. Put the pepper in a jar, pour the vinegar over it. Cover it closely and let it stand for a month. Strain and bottle.

Chili vinegar for fish

40–50 scarlet chilies to 1pt (550ml) vinegar. Pound chilies, put them in a jar, pour over them 1pt (550ml) vinegar, cover closely for a fortnight. Strain and bottle for use.

Stuffed sweet peppers

4oz (113g) rice
8oz (226g) minced pork or beef
1 onion
tomato sauce
5 green peppers
1 clove garlic
1 egg
salt and pepper

Boil the rice. Cut the peppers near the stalk end, removing seeds and ribs, but leaving 'lids'. Mix minced meat with chopped garlic and onion, cooked rice and seasoning. Stir in beaten egg and fill the peppers with the mixture. Replace the pepper 'lids', leaving partially open, and pour over a little tomato sauce. Bake in a moderate oven until tender.

CELANDINE

Chelidonium majus

A HERB OF THE SUN UNDER THE DOMINION OF LEO

This plant of the Poppy family is a perennial native to many parts of Europe and the USA. It may be found on waste land, in hedges along the highway, in shady lanes, in churchyards and, uninvited, in gardens, where it is seldom turned away since it is an attractive and well behaved visitor.

CELANDINE, as illustrated in a 13th-century English herbal.

The leaves, which are deceptively frail, are of a yellowish-green, and the delicate four-petalled flowers blossom throughout the summer. The rootstock is brown outside and orange-yellow within, and contains an acrid juice which turns red on exposure to the air. The long curved and pointed pods split into two when the seeds are ripe. Both the rootstock and the herb are used in medicine. They are gathered in the spring before flowering, for the dried plant is less efficacious than the fresh.

It is a herb much used in homoeopathic medicine, but skin poisoning can result from handling the crushed plant and, taken internally, celandine may have a narcotic effect on the nervous system, so it should be used only under medical direction. With knowledge and care it may be prescribed for diseases of the digestive system, stomach, gall-bladder and liver. An ointment is used for skin troubles.

[37]

CELANDINE, from *Ortus Sanitatus*, 1485. The greater celandine, illustrated here, is a member of the Poppy family and should not be confused with the unrelated lesser celandine, or pilewort, which is a member of the Buttercup family.

It owes its generic name *Chelidonium*, or swallow-wort, to the ancient belief that the juice brought sight to young swallows which had not yet opened their eyes, or which had been blinded. All the old herbalists repeat this story; some even state that doves made use of vervain, swallows of celandine, linnets of eyebright and hawks of hawkweed to restore lost eyesight to their fledglings. It is refreshing to read a vigorous denial from Gerard: 'It is called Celandine not because it first springeth at the coming in of Swallows, or dieth when they go away, (for as we have said, it may be found all the yere) but because some hold opinion, that with this herb the dams restore sight to their yong ones when they cannot see. Which things are vain and false.' He did hold, however, that 'the juice of the herbe is good to sharpen the sight, for it clenseth and consumeth away slimie things that cleave about the ball of the eye, and hinder the sight, and especially being boiled with honey in a brasen vessell'. Francis Bacon also believed in the efficacy of celandine in eye diseases:

'Saladyne hath a yellow milk which hathe also much acrimonie for it cleanseth the eyes and is good for cataract.' Modern practitioners are still using celandine as an eye lotion.

The other names wart flower, wartweed and wart plant, point to its use in the removal of warts. The juice is still employed for this purpose, but should be mixed with vinegar and used sparingly on the skin. Modern medicine does not confirm the ancient belief that celandine leaves worn in the shoe cure jaundice.

In the 19th century the distilled water of the leaves and roots of celandine was used as a depilatory. A hair bleach was made by mixing the roots with 1qt (1l) lye (made of ashes of vine-twigs), ½oz (14g) each of briony and turmeric; saffron and lily roots, flowers of mullein, yellow stechas, broom and St John's wort.

It has the dubious fame of being incised on a memorial stone not to its own glory but to that of the poet Wordsworth. Unfortunately, Wordsworth's much quoted celandine was the lesser celandine, *Ranunculus ficaria*, which is related to the buttercup.

CENTAURY
Erythraea centaureum

UNDER THE DOMINION OF THE SUN

This small and pretty annual is a native of the UK, flourishing on dry chalk downs, in sandy pasturage or barren fields. It is common throughout Europe.

It has fibrous woody roots, paired oval leaves, and numerous clusters of tubular flowers that explode into stars like bright pink earthbound fireworks. Unfortunately, like fireworks, they are evanescent: they open early but are closed again by noon; a single cloud in the sky is enough to cause them to remain tightly furled. It is possible to outwit them by bringing a small cluster indoors where, in a glass of water and the right amount of warmth, they may expand fully. The name *Erythraea* comes from the Greek *erythros*, red, referring to these flowers, although white ones are not unknown.

(*right*) CENTAURY, from a superb detail adorning a page of Jean Bourdichon's *Hours of Anne of Burgundy* from the 16th century.

(*far right*) CENTAURY appears in the margin of an English manuscript from the early 13th century — complete with a centaur to bear it.

Menu lyc .

larata facies. quasi malagma. y impo
nes. perfectissime sanat. Hom̄ ihus
herbe Centauria maior. h Angl'
huius genera sunt duo. Cente
· has autem centaurias
duas chirocentauros̄ di
citur inuenisse. Inde ex
nomine ipsius centau
ri nomen eis iposure.
Ipse uero. de his herbis
herbis medicina instru
it. primisqz egrotā
tibus tradidit.

Quidam uocant eam. charonion.

[39]

For medicinal purposes, the tender leaves, shoots and flowers should be collected in July. The herb, which is extremely bitter, is used by herbalists for jaundice and general biliousness. A tisane is made as a tonic, to stimulate appetite and digestion. It is strongly antiseptic and good for cuts and scratches, and is also used as a mouthwash.

It was much used by country folk, and such was their belief in its medicinal properties that they called it febrifuga (from *febrifuge*, meaning 'anti-febrile'). Culpeper advises to 'give it inwardly for inward diseases, and use it outwardly for outward diseases . . .' ''Tis very wholesome, but,' he admits, 'not very toothsome.'

CHAMOMILE (CAMOMILE)

Matricaria chamomilla
Anthemis nobilis

UNDER THE DOMINION OF THE SUN

The wild chamomile has an obvious desire for the companionship of man for it inhabits the fields and lanes and waste patches around our houses, on gravelly and stony soils. This aromatic daisy plant, with feathered leaves, is inclined to loll about on dusty verges, showing no great desire to stand upright. It was early recognized as a good friend in both house and garden. Parkinson wrote in 1629: 'It is a common hearbe, well knowne, and is planted of the rootes in alleyes and walkes, and on bankes to sit on, for that the more it is trodden on and pressed downe, in dry weather, the closer it groweth, and the better it will thrive: the use thereof is very much both to warm and to comfort and to ease paines, being applied outwardly after many fashions.'

For the past 200 years the seats in the arbours — or the herbares, as they were called — and those hollowed out of the banks that enclosed the herb garden were frequently covered with chamomile; and lawns of it were planted before grass lawns were introduced into our gardens. It was also used for paths, seeming to thrive underfoot, and repaying such treatment by its sweet scent. It is no doubt for this reason that the meaning of 'Chamomile' in the language of flowers is 'patience in adversity'. It was also an old strewing herb. It was dedicated to St Anne, mother of the Virgin Mary.

Evelyn mentioned that 'October it will now be good to Beat, Roll and Mow carpet walks and camomile for now the ground is supple and it will even out all inequalities'. Shakespeare grew it in his garden, and it is said that Sir Francis Drake

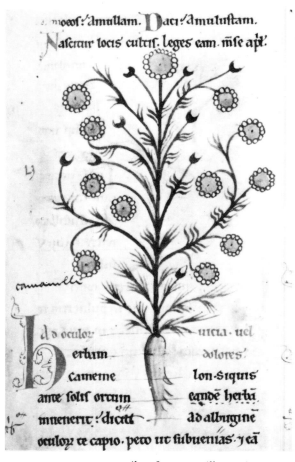

CHAMOMILE, or camomile, from an illustration in a 13th-century English herbal.

played his historic game of bowls on a lawn of clipped chamomile.

For a chamomile lawn the seedlings should be planted 6in (15cm) apart. They must be kept free from weed until they are established, and then cut and rolled about three times a year; the lawn will be found to be both fragrant and hard-wearing. There is a famous chamomile lawn in the gardens of Buckingham Palace.

Anthemis nobilis, or the Roman chamomile, is a double variety, and is the best known for lawns as it is more compact in growth. The name *nobilis* is an indication of how well thought of the plant was by the old herbalists.

It is an excellent companion plant, a fact acknowledged by generations of gardeners, and which has earned it the name of 'the plants' physician'. A plant or two grown in the greenhouse helps against the damping-off of seedlings. Bee-keepers should remember, however, that the sweet scent of chamomile is unaccountably offensive to bees.

Chamomile was loved and respected by our ancestors as a grave plant. Chamomile tobacco used to be smoked for asthma. As a medicinal plant it was recommended in 900 BC by Asclepiades, a physician so skilled in the use of herbs that he pledged himself to cease to act as a physician if he ever became ill: he died at a ripe old age as the result of an accident.

Only the flowers of the herb are used, and the oil from these, with crushed poppy heads, was made into a poultice for toothache and neuralgia, as well as for boils and inflamed swellings. It has been claimed that chamomile tea is the only certain preventative of nightmares. Chamomile oil can be made by steeping ½oz (14g) fresh or dried flowers in olive oil for 24 hours; it can be used as a massage oil for painful joints or to soften callouses. A few drops on a lump of sugar are good for stomach pains.

The flower heads in a tisane relieve nausea and diarrhoea, and the generations of flushed and restless babies who have been soothed with chamomile tea and honey can never be counted. Chamomile and pennyroyal boiled and strained make a good tonic drink for menstrual periods; mixed with white wine the tonic was taken for jaundice. The tea is considered an effective sedative, and both the perennial *A. nobilis* and the German annual, *Matricaria chamomilla,* may be used. Chamomile tea has been found efficacious as a drink for sick cows.

There is a tincture prepared by homoeopathic chemists, and for this, *M. chamomilla* is considered most valuable. A salve is made for piles. The tea is an excellent wash for sore eyes.

The name is derived from the Greek *chamœmelon,* meaning 'Earth apple', because it was considered that the scent resembled that of apples. The name of manzanilla, a light Spanish wine flavoured with chamomile, also means 'little apples'. An old Saxon name was *maythen.*

For cosmetic purposes the flowers are commonly used as a shampoo for blonde hair, to which it adds highlights. The flowers are boiled for 10 minutes, then left to steep for 15 minutes, strained, and the water used for the final rinse.

An infusion of chamomile flowers, rose petals, leaves, hips and white willow bark is used as a bath additive for fatigue. As a wash for face and arms it is useful as a preventative of insect bites and stings.

Chamomile has been cultivated in immense quantities in the UK, Italy, Hungary and Poland.

Early in the 19th century in Mitcham and Tooting, English farmers employed many people to gather the flowers from the beginning of July until the end of August. Local schools were closed for this chamomiling season. There were often as many as 200 women and children gathering flowers in a 10-acre field. The villagers relied on the money they earned in the chamomile season to clothe their children and pay the rent for their houses for the year.

The essential oil of *A. nobilis* is a bright blue, which turns to yellow on exposure to the air; there is also a dyer's chamomile, *A. tinctoria,* used in dyeing, particularly in France.

Today both the dried flowers and chamomile teabags can be purchased, and there are several soaps, shampoos and other cosmetic products to be found in herbalists' shops and pharmacies.

CHERVIL, from a 13th-century English herbal, is a herb with many culinary uses. The loosely related *Chaerophyllum bulbosum,* also known as chervil, has carrot-like roots which can be eaten as vegetables.

CHERVIL
Anthriscus cerefolium

A HERB OF JUPITER

This annual herb of the Carrot family is a native of Europe. A graceful plant, it reaches a height of

about 2ft (60cm), is a welcome addition to the herb garden, and grows well in the company of dill, coriander and mallow. Since all the plants of this order resemble each other closely and some contain deadly poisons, it is of the utmost importance to grow chervil from seed rather than collect it from the wild. It prefers to be raised in the shade, and can be sown from February to August for a succession. August and September sowings will be ready the same winter, if under a little protection. The leaves should be harvested when young.

The first known references to it appear to have been by Columella, a Roman writer on agriculture, and Pliny, both of whom wrote at the beginning of the Christian era. It was quite probably brought to Britain by the Romans who planted it near their encampments, in the vicinities of which it is likely to be found growing still.

For over three centuries it has been cultivated in English gardens as an aromatic pot-herb. Parkinson grew it for that purpose in 1629, and described it as being 'of a pale yellowish greene colour, but when the stalke is growne up to seede, both stalkes and leaves become of a dark red colour: the flowers are white, standing upon scattered or thin spread tufts, which turne into small, long, round, and sharpe pointed seeds of a brownish blacke colour'. It was a necessary part of a witch's pharmacopoeia, for these long, black furrowed seeds had, so it was said, the effect of producing double vision.

It was far more commonly used in cookery in the 15th and 16th centuries than today. Gerard says: 'Chervill is used very much among the Dutch people in a kinde of Loblolly or hotchpotch which they do eat, called Warmus. ... The roots are likewise most excellent in a sallad, if they be boiled and afterwards dressed as the cunning Cooke knoweth how better than myselfe: notwithstanding I used to eat them with oile and vineger, being first boiled; which is very good for old people that are dull and without courage: it rejoiceth and comforteth the heart, and increaseth their lust and strength.'

Even today, chervil has not lost its reputation as a good restorative for the elderly and for those whose memory has begun to fail; it is because of

(*left*) CHAMOMILE appears as a marginal illumination in the 13th-century *Hours of Anne of Burgundy* of Jean Bourdichon.

(*right*) A FRENCH CARICATURE, dated 1721, showing in exaggerated fashion the many requirements of the travelling grocer.

its reputation as a powerful brain stimulant that it earned the name *cerefolium*. It is also digestive, diuretic and expectorant. The juice is used for dropsy, scrofula, abscesses, eczema and gout. A poultice may be made for stiff and rheumatic joints, and an infusion taken to lower blood pressure. Equal parts of chervil and olive oil relieves piles. The plant must be used fresh, except when the shredded leaf is smoked as a herbal tobacco, like coltsfoot.

Its slight anise flavour makes it a pleasant accompaniment to chicken, veal and fish. The flavour does not withstand long cooking, and so it is suitable in omelettes and soufflés, or sprinkled at the last minute over soup. French cooks use chervil more frequently than do the British or Americans, and it is an important ingredient in their *fines herbes*. There is a curled variety which makes an attractive garnish.

Chervil and other useful herbs of this kind should be gathered in the morning on a sunny day, and tied into small bunches, separately or in a suitable mixture. Leave a loop long enough to enable you to plunge the bunches into boiling water without scalding your fingers. Wash the bunches under a cold tap, and dry on absorbent paper. Keep a saucepan of water at the boil for blanching. Immerse herbs quickly, and keep them under for one minute. Next plunge them into a bowl of iced water, or hold them again under the cold tap. Drain. Put them into freezer bags, label, and they are ready to freeze.

Prawn and chervil mayonnaise

Shell the prawns (or use a packet of frozen prawns or shrimps) and stir them into a mixture of mayonnaise and cream. Serve, accompanied by thin rolled wholemeal bread and butter, in small glasses with a sprinkle of chopped chervil leaves on top.

The Cook's Oracle has done its best to recommend chervil:

Chervil and butter

'This is the first time this very delicious herb, which has so long been a favourite with the sagacious French cook, has been introduced into an English book. Its flavour is a strong concentration of the combined taste of parsley and fennel, but inimitably more aromatic and agreeable than either. I cannot account for its being so little known in the English kitchen. You may make a most exquisite sauce with it, etc., as we have directed for parsley and butter. [For method see Poached eggs and parsley sauce, page 129.] You may enrich it with the juice of half a lemon, and a tablespoonful of white wine.'

The anonymous author goes on to give a testimonial to Drs Lewis and Aitken who 'are most respectable and well-accredited writers on chemistry, etc. and I trust all men who feel "*l'esprit du corps,*" will forgive me for saying they have written also like men of taste on culinary subjects, as the following quotation from their *Materia Medica,* London, 1791, will testify. See *cherefolium or chervil.* "It is a salubrius culinary herb, sufficiently nutritive to the palate and stomach."'

CHICK-PEA
Cicer pinnatifidum
C. arietinum

UNDER THE DOMINION OF VENUS

The chick-pea has accompanied men into battle and travellers across desert tracts in long-forgotten times. It was known to the ancient Egyptians; and the 'roasted seeds' mentioned in Greek comedy are believed to have been chick-peas. Dioscorides called it *krios,* because of the resemblance of the pea to the head of a ram. It was the staple diet of the poor in Rome, and formed the parched pulse of the Hebrews when they went into battle. The custom of taking parched grains as provision still exists: in hot dry countries some travellers supply themselves with parched chick-peas, called 'leb-lebby', which require much chewing and thus stimulate the salivary glands. African fighting men carry these parched peas — sometimes having nothing else to eat for days at a time.

Cicer pinnatifidium is an annual of the Bean family, and is cultivated in India for its seed. When ground into meal it forms an important part of the diet and is called 'gram'. It has violet pea-shaped flowers.

The flowers of *C. arietinum* are bluish or white. This species is cultivated chiefly in Spain, and the peas are used for culinary purposes in the Spanish *olla,* a mixture of bacon, cabbage, pumpkin, and chick-peas, which they call *garvanzos* or *garbanzos*. Even prolonged boiling does not make the peas soft and pulpy, and so they are usually eaten raw or roasted as a garnish. In Spain *C. arietinum* is used as a dyeing ingredient as well as for food.

93
L. Cicer satiuum
G. Peis cices
A. Ciche peafe
Ge. Kichern

Chick-pea casserole

2tbsp oil
2 medium sized onions, finely chopped
1 can chick-peas
1 large can tomatoes
½ cup water
1 pinch each of coriander, cumin and turmeric
2tbsp chopped parsley

Heat oil in a saucepan and sauté onions, but do not brown. Add chick-peas, drained. Add tomatoes, water and spices, and simmer for 30 minutes. Sprinkle with parsley.

CHICORY

Cichorium intybus

UNDER THE DOMINION OF JUPITER

Chicory is a perennial both native to and cultivated in Europe and the USA. An attractive plant in the herb garden owing to its clear blue flowers with each rayed petal toothed like those of its relative, the dandelion, it grows to a height of 3–5ft (1–1.5m).

Chicory has certain disadvantages as a garden plant, for the beautiful blue flowers are strict clock-watchers — opening hours from 8am to noon — and not even the warmest sunshine can coax them to stay out any longer. Linnaeus actually used them in his 'horologe' or floral clock in Uppsala for their reliability as timekeepers. The flowers are short-lived, but the dead cling to their stems among the living in withered and prophetic gloom. The wild flowers bloom from July to September in cornfields and hedges, and occasionally a rare white one may be found. If the blue-flowered plants are placed on an ant-hill the petals change to brilliant red.

Parkinson says that 'the flowers pickled up as divers other flowers are used to be now a daies, make a delicate sallet'. 'Pickling up' the flowers appears to have meant coating them in sugar and making them into a kind of confection.

Pliny and Theophrastus both say that the plant was popular in Egypt as a vegetable. It is known to have been one of the bitter herbs which God commanded to be eaten by the Israelites with the lamb at the Passover: The whole plant contains a bitter milky juice which is digestive, diuretic and tonic. It is valuable in cases of gallstones and for jaundice, kidney troubles, gastritis and lack of appetite. The juice may be taken in milk or water. Poultices of the boiled leaves and flowers wrapped in a cloth are used for inflammations. Parkinson called it a 'fine cleansing jovial plant'.

Syrup of succory was a popular laxative for children, and it is by its old name of succory that the plant is known in folklore and legend. The German legend of the *Wegewarten,* the Watchers of the Roads, a name given to succory in Germany, tells how a young and beautiful princess was abandoned by her husband, a young prince of extraordinary beauty. 'Grief exhausted her strength, and finding herself on the point of death, she exclaimed: "Ah, how willingly would I die if I could only be sure of seeing my loved one, wherever I may be." Her ladies-in-waiting, hearing her desire, solemnly added: "And we also would willingly die if only we were assured that he would always see us on every roadside." The merciful God heard from heaven their heart-felt desires, and granted them. "Happily," said He, "your wishes can be fulfilled; I will change you

into flowers. You, Princess, you shall remain with your white mantle on every road traversed by your husband; you, young women, shall remain by the roadside, habited in blue, so that the Prince must see you everywhere''.' Unfortunately for the erring prince, the succory is a common wayside flower in most European countries, and so the story has a Germanic nightmare quality.

Special strains of chicory are grown in France, Belgium, Germany, and to a lesser extent in East Anglia, as a substitute for or adulterant of coffee. This is possibly the reason chicory has been made the emblem of frugality. The roots are sliced, roasted and ground for this purpose. In Belgium, chicory is drunk as a beverage in its own right, and the roots are also boiled as a vegetable and eaten with butter. The French grow it as a fresh food for horses, cows and sheep.

The young green leaves may be chopped and used in salads, but it is blanched chicory that is the favourite winter salad. A form with a much divided leaf is called *barbe de capucin*.

Chicory and tuna salad

1 lettuce
1 chicory leaf
1 hard-boiled egg per person
1 cup diced celery
1 tomato per person
1tbsp chopped chives
French dressing
½ clove garlic
1 tin of tuna

Rub salad bowl with cut clove of garlic. Chop chicory and mix with torn-up lettuce in the bowl. Add celery and tomatoes, and toss with the dressing. Arrange hard-boiled eggs and tuna and sprinkle with chives. Serve with warmed wholemeal rolls and butter.

[46]

AN 18TH-CENTURY
Indian
watercolour of a
travelling
apothecary, now
in the possession
of the
Bibliothèque
Nationale, Paris,
Étampes.

CHICORY,
illustrated left in
two varieties from
Mattioli's
Commentarii,
1554, that on the
far left being the
one commonly in
use today.

[47]

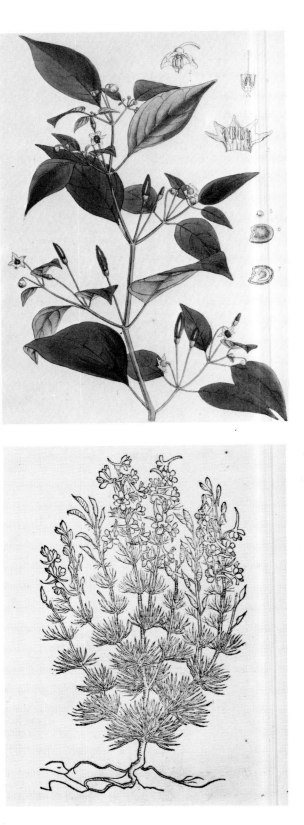

CHILI is the dried pod of this plant, *Capsicum fastigiatum*, illustrated here from the third volume of *Medicinal Plants*, 1880, by R. Bentley and H. Trimmen.

CHILI
Capsicum fastigiatum

Chili, or chilli, is the dried pod of a species of Capsicum or red pepper. The name is also given to the shrub which bears the chilies, known in Spain as *chile* and in Mexico as *chili*.

Parkinson, in his *Theatrum Botanicum*, treats the family of Capsicum, anciently called ginny or guiney pepper, with distrust: 'The Ginny Pepper, in mine opinion is fittest to follow next after the family of the Nightshades [Solanaceae], being in outward forme likest thereunto, as also being no lesse dangerous, although in a quite contrary nature. for it is as farre exceeding in heate, as other in cold: hereof there are found out, or at least brought to knowledge many sorts in these dayes, which were not knowne in former times, or neglected and not so heedfully regarded at least, as they have been of later time [1640], especially by Gregorius de Reggio, a Capuchine Fryer, who hath observed a dozen severall varieties at the least in the fruite or cods, although very little differing in anything else.' He later quotes this same *Gregorio de Reggio, his receipt*: 'for take, saith he, of the ripe cod of any sort of Ginny Pepper ... and dry them well, first of themselves, and then in an oven, after the bread is taken out, put into a pot or pipkin, with some flower [flour] that they may be thoroughly dried, clense them from the flower, and their stalkes if they have any, cut them and clip them very small, both huskes and seedes within them, and to every ounce of them, put a pound of fine wheaten flower ... make them up into cakes and small loaves with so much leaven as yee thinke may be convenient for the quantitie you make; and bake these as you doe bread of that size, and being baked cut it againe, that it may be as dry and hard as biskit, which beaten into fine pouder and sifted, may be kept ... to season meate or broth, or for sauce, ... (yea, and your wine and other drinke) ... Taken with Saxifrage water [it] expelleth the stone in the kidneyes, ... the pouder taken for three dayes together in the

CUMIN, shown here in an illustration from Mattioli's *Commentarii*, 1554, is a spice plant whose ground seeds are generally an ingredient of chili powder. The oil from the seeds of *Cuminum cyminum* is used in medicines and perfumes.

decoction of Pennyroyall, expelleth the dead birth, but if a peece of the cod or huske, either greene or dry to be put into the mother after delivery, it will make them barren for ever after.'

Gerard mentioned the Capsicum as being cultivated in his time, but after Parkinson there seems little interest in its medicinal properties, and Culpeper completely ignores the whole family. However, in the West Indies, the natives still regard a mixture of sliced cucumbers, shallots or onions cut very small, a little lime juice mixed with Madeira, and a few mashed pods of chili or bird pepper as an unfailing stimulant to the appetite. It is known as *man-dram,* and may be used as a sort of chutney.

The small pods are also the hottest, and have been used as remedies for cholera and for the dyspepsia and dilated blood vessels arising from drunkenness. A capsicum poultice, resembling a mustard plaster, has been used, with extreme caution, for the relief of aches and pains, but the plight of the unfortunate Mr Tasker Williams, who, with a musket-ball lodged in his thigh, fell into the hands of the enemy during the Ashanti war, should not be forgotten. The native treatment was to apply a poultice of pepper-pods, causing the patient agony and completely failing in its purpose of extraction.

Its modern usage by herbalists is in pill and powder form, or as a tincture or infusion used as liniments and gargles.

None of the family is indigenous to the old world, and the Greeks, Romans and Hebrews were not acquainted with them. In temperate climates Mexican chilies must be grown in a greenhouse and the resulting pods may be ground into chili powder for sauces, and for that well known dish chili con carne. They may also be used fresh in meat and rice dishes.

Ready-made chili sauce may be obtained, but in its powdered form should be kept in dark receptacles, as it is affected by light. The bought powder may be a mixture of chili peppers, aromatic seeds, spices and herbs, or the peppers alone, and the various brands may be mildly hot through several degrees to fiery. It is therefore advisable to proceed cautiously in this type of cookery, adding only a little at first, then tasting frequently and if necessary adding a little more.

Meat balls with chili sauce

You will need a tin of meat balls, or the required number of balls made of mince, pepper, salt, with egg to bind, dipped in flour and lightly fried in deep fat. The sauce is made from:

CHIVES, from an illustration from G. C. Oeder's *Flora Danica.*

2 onions
oil for frying
3tbsp chili sauce
2tbsp vinegar
½tsp paprika
1tbsp tomato puree

Fry sliced onions lightly; add rest of ingredients and simmer for 20 minutes. Pour sauce over meat balls and cook in preheated oven for 15 minutes (375°F, 190°C, Gas Mark 5). There are various accompaniments one can choose; a favourite is rice with green salad.

Chili con carne

1lb (450g) cubed lean steak
1 medium tin tomatoes
2tbsp cooking oil
1 chopped onion
¾lb (340g) dried kidney beans (or 1 large can)
1 chopped clove of garlic
1tsp chili powder
1tbsp plain flour
a little oregano and cumin seed
salt

Before proceeding, it may be well to note that the English translation is 'chilies with meat', and not 'meat with chilies'. This subtle difference should be considered carefully. A large can of red kidney beans may be thought to be an acceptable substitute for the ¾lb (340g) dried red kidney beans, which in preparation need to be soaked overnight and simmered until soft.

Heat oil in a heavy saucepan, add onion and garlic and cook gently until soft. Add chili powder and meat, turning meat until evenly browned. Blend in flour. Add tomatoes and liquid, oregano and cumin. Cover and simmer for 1 hour. Add prepared beans and salt, and cook a further 15 minutes. Serve piping hot with green salad and plenty of cold beer.

CHIVES
Allium schoenoprasum

UNDER THE DOMINION OF MARS

A hardy perennial of the Allium family, chives are allied to garlic, onions and shallots. Although native to northern Europe, they are rarely found wild in England other than on stream-sides in Cornwall and Northumberland. The Greeks and Romans must certainly have known of them since they grow wild in Greece and Italy, and no doubt made use of them for medicinal and culinary purposes.

The neatest, prettiest and most delicately flavoured of the onion tribe, chives make a useful border to the kitchen garden; they are even better, perhaps, grown in a sunny corner near the kitchen door, where they can be cut when needed. Seed sown in April will make little clumps by the autumn. Chives will remain good for gathering if the flowers are picked as soon as they appear, although it requires considerable determination to remove the attractive little globes of pinkish-mauve when they bloom in June and July.

Grown in rose-beds, chives combat black spot; set close to carrots, they discourage carrot fly. In other words, chives should be a welcome guest in any part of the garden. This virtuous little herb is a good companion plant to fruit trees also, as it is a good preventative of fruit scab. It scarcely ever succumbs to diseases itself, and it plays the part of an antiseptic and cheerful young nurse to other less fortunate plants. Chives tea sprayed on gooseberries, in strong solution, prevents mildew.

The 'grass', as it is called, appears like tiny rushes, and should be cut close to the ground when it is required.

In medicine chives are used as an appetizer and digestive, and are believed to be good for anaemia; they are not widely used for cures. In cookery, however, they play an important part in countless recipes: most popularly they are chopped and sprinkled in omelettes and scrambled eggs, on baked potatoes with butter and on salads. Chive sauce adds a delicate flavour to white fish or chicken.

Chicken with chives sauce

Prepare a boiling chicken and cook it in the usual way with onions, carrots and celery, pepper, salt and a bay leaf. Simmer gently for about an hour until tender. Lift and skin the chicken and put it on a large dish surrounded by the vegetables, and keep it warm in the oven with a little of the liquid poured over to prevent it from becoming dry. Put 4oz (113g) butter into a small saucepan and melt very slowly. Skim off any froth, being careful not to let the butter discolour. Add the grated rind of a lemon, a little freshly ground black pepper, a pinch of nutmeg and a heaped tablespoonful of chopped chives. Pour over the chicken and serve.

CINNAMON
Cinnamomum zeylanicum

An evergreen tree of the Laurel family, growing wild in the forests of India and Malaya, Cochin-China and Malabar, cinnamon was successfully cultivated in Ceylon between 1765 and 1770, but the species becomes easily naturalized as birds feed on the berries.

The cinnamon tree grows to a height of about 30ft (9m), and has willow-like branches with alternate oblong leaves. In early development the

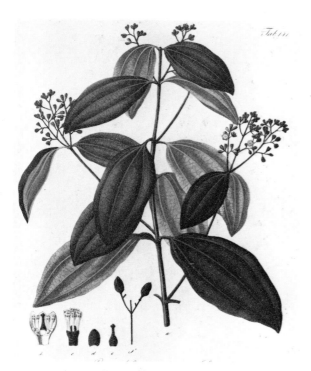

CINNAMON, as depicted in Daniel Wagner's *Pharmaceutisch Medicinisch Botanik*, 1828.

leaves are red and yellow, but later they become shiny green and leathery, with a lighter shade on their under-surface. The flowers grow in short white panicles, followed by a fruit that resembles a dark blue olive. After boiling, these yield an oil which, when it cools, becomes a solid wax and is used for fragrant candles. Oil of cinnamon is extracted from the bark and leaves for use in cold cures.

The spice is obtained from the inner bark of the young shoots and branches which are cut when about 1in (2.5cm) thick, and dried in the sun. The bark is then easily peeled, after which it is wrapped around a thin rod, and the outer skin scraped off. Quills of cinnamon are golden brown, have a pungent aromatic flavour and may be used whole or powdered.

Cinnamon has been continually used since ancient times, and was one of the oldest and most valuable items in the spice trade. For centuries the source of cinnamon had been kept a close secret by the Arabs, but it is said that when Alexander the Great was at sea, he perceived that he was near the coast of Arabia from the spicy scent wafting from the distant shore. It is mentioned in *Revelations*, predicting the fall of Babylon; and in *Exodus*, when the Lord said to Moses, 'Take thou unto

thee principal spices, of pure myrrh five hundred shekels, and of sweet cinnamon half so much — and thou shalt make it an oil of holy ointment'.

Cinnamon was brought to Western Europe by the Crusaders to enhance the flavour of bread, fish, salt meat and the unpalatable diet of the times. It was also valued for medicines, perfumes and love potions. Its use is now worldwide.

For medicinal purposes it is stimulant, tonic, stomachic, and carminative, and there are several preparations on the market. As a cordial it is used for cramps, and a tincture of cinnamon deadens the nerve in toothache. It also prevents vomiting. In the East it is used as a sedative in child-bearing. In the West, however, it is principally employed as an addition to other medicines.

In cookery it is useful in sweets and savouries. It is a traditional ingredient in Christmas puddings, Christmas cakes, mince pies and hot spiced drinks. Although the product of a warmer climate, it seems particularly comforting on a cold night, sprinkled on top of hot milk or on hot sweet black coffee. Cinnamon toast was an old-fashioned Sunday tea ritual on winter afternoons, timed with the drawing of the curtains and the lighting of the spluttering gas mantles.

Cinnamon was used by Eliza Acton in 1845 in a simple recipe given below.

Poor author's pudding

Flavour a quart of new milk by boiling in it for a few minutes half a stick of well-bruised cinnamon; add a few grains of salt, and three ounces of sugar, and turn the whole into a deep basin; when it is quite cold, stir to it three well-beaten eggs, and strain the mixture into a pie dish. Cover the top with slices of bread free from crust, and half an inch thick, cut so as to join neatly, and buttered on both sides; bake the pudding in a moderate oven for about half an hour.

New milk, one quart; cinnamon; sugar 3oz; salt; eggs 3; buttered bread; baked half an hour.

Cinnamon may be combined with other spices and in almost every curry dish. The following Indian recipe uses both herbs and spices. It is inexpensive, easy to make and delicious.

Chicken pilau

1 small chicken
2 onions
4oz (113g) butter

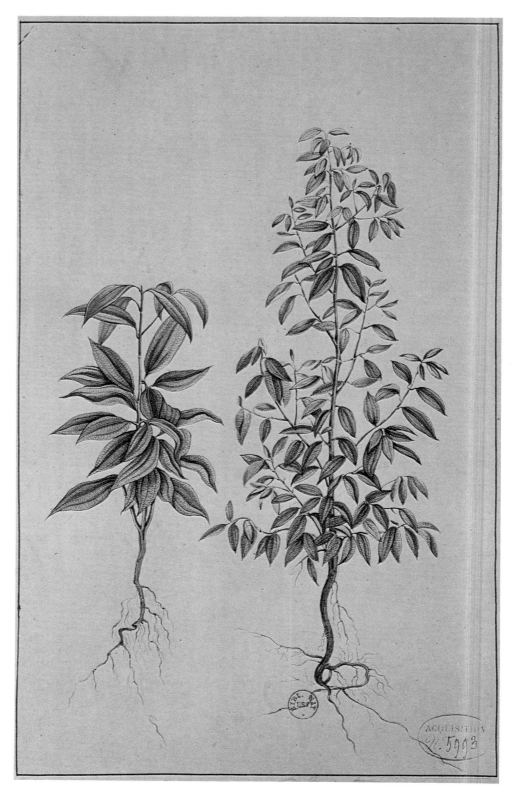

CINNAMON: young
plants of this
popular spice
shown in a French
19th-century
watercolour.

8oz (226g) rice
salt and pepper
pinch of ground cloves
pinch of ground cinnamon
pinch of thyme
pinch of sage

Boil chicken until tender and keep stock. Slice onions and fry in melted butter until brown. Remove from the saucepan and add rice. Fry until brown, then strain off remaining fat. Add about 1pt (550ml) chicken stock, spices, herbs, pepper and salt. When rice is tender, add chicken taken from bone and cut into small pieces, and browned onions. Heat slowly and serve.

CLARY

Salvia verbenaca

UNDER THE DOMINION OF THE MOON

The wild English clary or wild sage is a native of Europe, Asia, Africa and America. It is a biennial with square stems, paired hairy and wrinkled leaves, and spikes of purplish-blue sage-like flowers, which appear from June until August. It frequents dry chalky or gravelly pastures.

Gerard wrote in 1597 that 'it groweth wilde in divers barren places, almost in every country, especially in the fields of Holborne neere unto Grayes Inne, in the highe way by the end of a brickwall: at the end of Chelsey next to London, in the high way as you go from the Queenes pallace of Richmond to the waters side, and in divers other places.' Fifty years later, Culpeper reported it to be still growing in the same areas.

When put into water the seeds yield a mucilage which, if placed under the eyelid for a few minutes, envelopes any particle of dust which may be causing irritation or inflammation. It thus became clary or clear-eye, and eye-salves were consequently made of it. The old herbalists considered it the most efficacious herb in any eye complaint, including cataract, and respectfully named it *Officinalis Christi* or *Oculus Christi*, Christ's eye. Culpeper disapproved strongly. 'Wild clary is most blasphemously called Christ's Eye, because it cures diseases of the eyes. I could wish from my soul, blasphemy, ignorance and tyranny, were ceased among physicians, that they may be happy and I joyful.'

Another clary, *S. praetensis*, the meadow sage, is similar but less conspicuous. Both herbs are

CLARY derives its name from the earlier name 'clear-eye', which reflects the efficacy of its use in treating inflammation of the eyes. This engraving from 1937 by Kredel after Kock shows the meadow clary, *Salvia praetensis*.

smaller than the garden clary, but pleasantly aromatic, and both are thought to be more beneficial to the eyes.

Today clary is more popular with flower arrangers than with cooks, but our ancestors used it in many different ways for culinary purposes. Parkinson was probably the first to give a recipe: 'The leaves taken dry, and dipped into a batter made of the yolks of eggs, flour, and a little milk, then fryed with butter, until they be crisped, serve for a dish of meate, acceptable with manie, unpleasant to none.'

The young tops were used in soups, or simply as pot-herbs. There were clary omelettes and fritters and it was used in fruit jellies where it was said to taste like pineapple. Salads of the chopped leaves were sprinkled with its flowers. Most home-made wines and metheglins were flavoured with it. Clary wine was famous for its narcotic properties.

Clary was taken as a medicine for disordered stomachs, kidney diseases and as a digestive. It was also suggested that 'the seeds of it being beaten to powder, and drank with wine, is an admirable help to provoke lust'.

Today clary is cultivated on a small scale for ale and beer, and is one of the 'muscatel' flavours added to certain Rhenish wines. In France and Germany it is largely cultivated for its highly aromatic oil and used for its own perfume and as a fixative for other scents.

Clary fritters

Make a batter with ½pt (275ml) milk, 1 egg and enough flour to make a fairly thick mixture. Grate in a little lemon peel. Add a pinch of nutmeg, 2oz (56g) sugar and a dessertspoonful of brandy. Take several clary leaves, cut off the stalks, and dip them in the batter. Fry them quickly in a little butter and cooking oil. Take them out and let them drain on kitchen paper while you are frying the next batch. Sugar on both sides.

This is a modernized version of a recipe of 1788, which ends: 'Glaze them with a hot iron.' Try it at your own risk!

Clary wine

Time to boil, 1 hour; to make, 5 days; to stand, 1 year. 10 gallons water; 35lbs loaf sugar; 12 eggs; 2 pecks of clary blossoms; 1 pint good new yeast.

Mix sugar, water and well beaten whites of eggs. Let it boil gently ½ hour, simmering and skimming until it is quite clear. Leave until cold. Put it into a cask with 2 pecks clary blossoms stripped from stalk [flowers and floral leaves]. Add 1 pint yeast. Stir the wine three times a day for five days. Stop it up, and let stand for twelve months. It may be bottled at the end of six months if perfectly clear.

CLEAVERS

Galium aparine

UNDER THE DOMINION OF MARS

Cleavers, or clivers, is a native of Europe, Asia and North America. An annual herb, it frequents hedges and ditches where it scrambles horizontally, or climbs up banks and weaves its way among other plants and bushes. Less feeble than it appears, it has a grip that cannot be undone without breaking its jointed and bristly stems

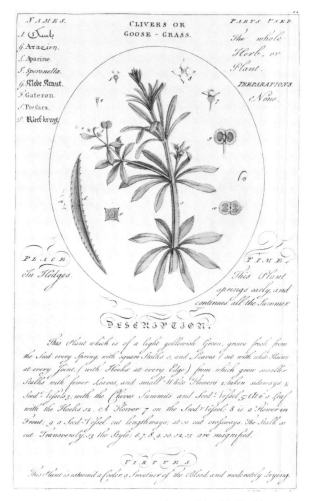

CLEAVERS, or goose-grass, as pictured by T. Sheldrake in *Botanicum Medicinale*, 1759.

which sometimes reach as much as 9ft (2.7m). The stem, the starry leaves and twin-globed seeds are covered with short hooked bristles that cling to clothing and animal fur.

The Greeks called it *philanthropon* because they considered that this clinging habit showed a love of mankind. English country people echoed the belief by calling it loveman. The minute four-petalled flowers, which appear in June and July, are white and develop rapidly into the seeds which fall in July and August, to establish next year's plants. The root contains a good red dye. Another name for this enterprising herb is goose-grass, since geese gobble it with enthusiasm, and farmers' wives chop it up to serve to their goslings. Horses, sheep, cows and poultry also enjoy it.

Most of its many names, including scratch-weed, catchweed, and in Scotland, grip-grass, allude to its rather trying habits. The name *aparine* means clinging and scrambling. An Anglo-Saxon name was *harriff*, meaning hedge-robber. Its scent is faint but pleasant. It belongs to the Bedstraw family, named for its strewing value for bedrooms in less hygienic ages. The Bedstraws are members of the Rubiaceae, which include the coffee shrub, the chinchona tree from which quinine is obtained, the ipecacuanha and the madder — so the humble cleavers has distinguished relatives.

In rural medicine it was used for jaundice, scarlet fever and measles. The crushed herb was folded in a cloth and applied hot in cases of ear-ache and toothache. A cooling drink was traditionally given every spring to 'clear the blood', and the whole plant gave a decoction equal, it was claimed, to tea.

Culpeper prescribed a course of it to the weight-watchers of his time: 'It is familiarly taken in broth, to keep them lean and lank, who are apt to grow fat.' It was eaten chopped and boiled to strengthen the liver, and the juice of the leaves applied to wounds to stop the bleeding. The dried herb was used in the same way.

Most usefully, the seeds were roasted and ground and used as a mildly stimulating substitute for coffee. A learned professor of that time wrote authoritatively, 'Our peasants would do well to set their idle children to collect the seeds, which are to be found in profusion in every hedge'.

Cleavers is used in homoeopathic medicine for skin diseases such as psoriasis and scurvy. The whole herb is considered one of the best remedies for kidney and bladder troubles. It is diuretic, tonic and aperient, and is also given in some cases of arthritis. Two handfuls of chopped herbs infused in 1pt (550ml) boiling water makes a hair lotion that clears dandruff; and a strong infusion of cleavers and lovage used directly on the skin, or in the bath, is a good deodorant.

CLEMATIS

Clematis vitalba

DEDICATED TO THE VIRGIN MARY

A perennial climber native to Europe, this is the only clematis that is found wild in Britain, where it grows on limestone and chalky soil mainly in the south. Its small petalless flowers have green and white sepals in May and June, but are far less noticeable than the smoky clouds of its seeds as they appear in August and September to drift

CLEMATIS, from J. Roques's *Phytographie Medicale*, 1821.

among the hedgerows. As autumn changes to winter, these soft white seed-clouds, torn by winds and soaked by rain, become grey and dirty, clinging to nearby twigs and stems like ragged cobwebs, and earning the name of old man's beard.

Gerard gave to this plant a pleasanter name, the traveller's joy, although until he described it it had been known as viorna, because it decorated the 'waies and hedges, where people travel'. It was also known as virgin's bower, as a compliment, some said, to Queen Elizabeth, but since in France it was called *le berceau de la vierge* it is more likely to have signified the bower of the Virgin Mary. Gipsies' bacca, Tom's bacca and smoking cane are yet other country names, because gipsies smoked the hollow stems.

The name clematis comes from the Greek *klema*, which signifies the young shoot of a vine and indicates its climbing nature. It clings without tendrils, making its way sometimes to a length of 20ft (6m) over a hedge, by means of its leaf-stalks. Both flowers and leaves are extremely acrid, and the whole plant is poisonous, like the buttercup to which it is related. In spite of this, the leaves when dried form good fodder for cattle. Birds and small animals make use of the downy seed-tails to line their nests. In France the long stems were woven into baskets and bee-hives.

Although *C. vitalba* is the only native British species, there are half-a-dozen in the USA, and more in New Zealand and Australia, mostly bearing similar names, such as Virginia virgin's bower, Western virgin's bower, purple virgin's bower and pipestem.

Clematis is used in homoeopathic medicine, but is too dangerous a plant to be handled except under medical direction, and for the same reason it should not be used in cookery or for cosmetics.

CLOVES are the dried, unopened flowers of the evergreen tree of the same name, shown here as depicted in Christoval Acosta's *Tractado de la Drogas*, 1578. Oil of cloves has a modern commercial use as a flavouring for toothpaste, and is believed to ease toothache.

CLOVE
Eugenia caryophyllata

An evergreen tree, the clove is native to the Spice Islands and the Philippines, but is cultivated in Sumatra, the West Indies, Ceylon, India, Brazil and many other tropical areas.

These handsome trees of the Myrtle family grow best near water and are so absorbent of water that nothing will flourish under their branches. They have soft grey bark and bright green leaves, resembling large bay leaves. At the beginning of the rainy season at the extreme ends of the branches appear long green buds from which the delicately peach-coloured flowers expand. When the corolla fades the calyx turns yellow and then red. The embryo seeds are then beaten from the trees and dried in the sun, for if the fruit is allowed to grow their marvellous spicy aroma is greatly dissipated. Each berry contains one seed, and the trees take eight or nine years to produce fruit.

It seems that their oldest medicinal use was in China, where it is reported that they were taken for various ailments as early as 240BC. Later, cloves were brought to the Mediterranean ports by Persians, Arabians and Egyptians, and here the trade flourished, until in 1511, the Portuguese discovered for themselves the growing areas. The Dutch soon gained monopoly of the trade. In 1797 Sir Joseph Banks introduced the clove into Britain.

The finest cloves are from Molucca, where girls wear its flowers, and children are given necklaces of clove seeds as amulets to preserve them from illness and the 'evil eye'. The strongly aromatic seeds are also regarded as aphrodisiac.

Medicinally, cloves are used for flatulence and diarrhoea, for most liver, stomach and bowel ailments, and as a stimulant for the nerves. Clove oil is a tried and trusted friend to sufferers from toothache: a few drops on a small pellet of cotton-wool gently pressed into a cavity give relief. It is also a breath sweetener. Clove tea, with the addition of a blade of mace, is good for nausea, and is soothing to the nerves. An inhalant of cloves, camphor, eucalyptus and pine is used for whooping-cough, and a liniment of cloves mixed with camphor, wintergreen and origanum is used as a massage for aching muscles.

For culinary purposes cloves are used in both seed and powder form. No apple-pie or ham is complete without these highly scented little brown 'nails', from which its name clove from the Latin *clavus,* is derived. Marinades, curries, and

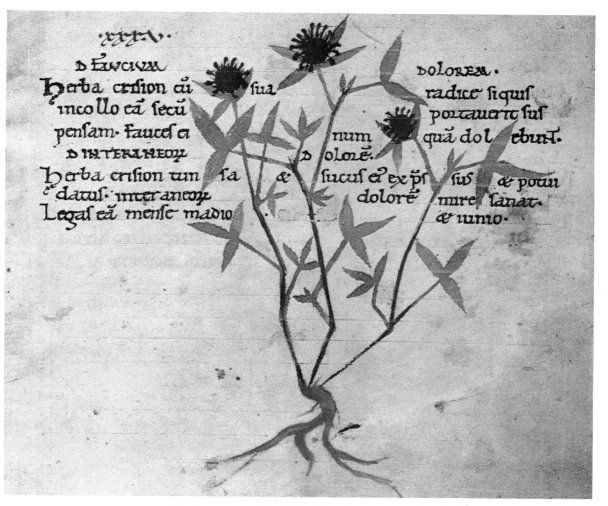

CLOVER has leaves normally divided into three parts, and to find a four-leaved clover has long been thought to signify good luck; however, four-, five and even six-leaved clovers are not uncommon. This illustration from an English manuscript of about 1100 shows red clover.

pickles may be spiced with cloves, and mulled claret and clove-scented punch are part of traditional Christmas fare. In *The Pickwick Papers*, at their very first meeting Mr Weller and the lacrimose Mr Trotter were 'occupied in discussing an exhilarating compound, formed by mixing together in a pewter vessel, certain quantities of British Hollands and the fragrant essence of the clove'.

The following recipe also might well have been enjoyed by Dickens himself.

Wine and clove soup

3 cups water
1 cup dry white wine
3 whole cloves
1 tin chicken soup or stock from a boiling fowl
2 chopped tomatoes
½ cup peas or diced celery
plain yoghurt
salt and pepper

Mix ingredients together and simmer for 15 minutes. Remove cloves. Cool and put in blender for 3 minutes. Return to saucepan and add a little milk if necessary. Heat and serve with a little yoghurt or cream and a dust of paprika.

CLOVER, RED

Trifolium pratense

UNDER THE DOMINION OF VENUS

A short-lived perennial, common throughout Europe, particularly in Italy, red clover was introduced into North America, where it grew so abundantly in Vermont that it became the official state flower.

It was introduced into English farming in 1645 by Sir Richard Weston of Sutton Manor, Surrey. He wrote a treatise on the cultivation of flax, clover and the turnip, which he also introduced. He valued clover at £12 an acre. 'Monie is the Queen that commands all', he declared in this document, which he left to his son as a legacy. 'You should then learn these things I have set down by example, which I am enforced to leave to you as a father's precepts, and with a father's blessing to you all, desiring God Almighty to guide you and direct you in all your actions. I will leave you to His divine protection and providence. Note that the Clover-grass seed will be ripe about a month after it appeareth in the husk.'

The true clovers belong to the genus *Trifolium*, of which there are over twenty wild species. The name *Trifolium* suggests that it possesses only three leaves, but the number of its leaves varies, and deep meaning was read into this fact. Three stood for the Trinity; four for luck; five for fame; six for money and seven for prosperity. Because it symbolizes the Trinity, it was considered to be a charm against witches.

The same plant is called both red clover and purple clover, but in fact the colour varies between the two, probably with the conditions under which it grows. It reaches 1–2ft (30–60cm) in height and the dark green leaves are lighter in the centre. The flowers, which bloom from May to September, grow in dense globular or egg-shaped heads, composed of bean-flower shaped florets. They are honey-scented, and a clover-field may be as sweet as a bean-field. They have the endearing habit of closing their leaflets at sunset, as if in prayer, and drooping in the evening dew or in the rain. Gerard quoted Pliny who 'writeth and setteth it down for certain, that the leaves hereof do tremble and stand right up against the comming of a storm or tempest'.

The flowers stand erect until fertilized by a passing bee, and then suddenly turn down as a signal that such attentions are no longer required. Red clover sets no seed in the absence of bees, a fact discovered when the plant was introduced into Australia and New Zealand, and bees had to be brought there for the continuance of the crop.

It is the white clover, *T. pennsylvanicum*, that is native to the USA, and large quantities of its seed are imported into Britain for cultivation. Although liking both varieties, bees show a distinct preference for white clover.

The common name clover, which comes from the Latin *clava*, a club, signifies a leaf composed of three leaflets. *Pratense* means 'growing in meadows'. Other country names are honeystalks, sweet kitty clover, marl grass, cow grass and bee-bread, a name special to Kent. Shakespeare called it triffoly.

Not only is clover a bee-plant — indeed, some beekeepers believe it to be the best of all — but butterflies love it as well. It will not, however, flourish in a field with buttercups.

The Druids venerated the Trefoil as a symbol of the earth, the sea and the heavens. The leaf is often used in ecclesiastical architecture and for decorating churches on Trinity Sunday.

Red clover is used in short-term leys, is harvested for hay and silage, or may be ploughed back in the earth as green manure.

In medicine, red-clover tea, made from the dried blossoms in boiling water, and sometimes combined with other herbs, is a pleasant tonic which is also taken as a cure for indigestion, bronchitis and whooping-cough. It is good for the nerves and also as a sedative. It relieves headache, neuralgia and nausea, and is used as a mucus-clearing medicine. A salve is made to heal fresh wounds, ulcers and sores, and clover-head poultices are sometimes used to help cancer patients.

Dried clover heads, mixed with coltsfoot leaves, are smoked as herbal tobacco. The flowers should be gathered in summer, dried in the shade on clean paper, and hung in paper bags (not polythene) in a dry place. Try making the following pleasant country wine.

Red clover wine

2qt (2l) flowers
4qt (4.5l) boiling water
3 lemons
2 oranges
4lb (1.8kg) white sugar
1oz (28g) yeast on toast

Pour boiling water over the flowers and leave until lukewarm. Slice oranges and lemons, add sugar and yeast on toast. Put all together in a bowl and leave for 5 days, stirring twice each day. Strain, and leave for another 5 days. Bottle and leave for

10 days, leaving corks loose. Finally cork, and leave for at least a month.

COLTSFOOT

Tussilago farfara

A HERB OF VENUS

A perennial herb, coltsfoot is native to Europe, America and the East Indies. It is commonly found in Britain in moist clay soils and on railway embankments.

Resembling a small dandelion on a straight

COLTSFOOT, as illustrated in Mattioli's *Commentarii*, 1554.

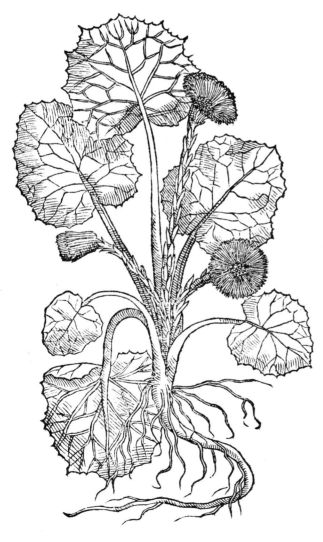

COLTSFOOT, from William Woodville's *Medical Botany*, 1832.

purplish-scaled stalk, this sturdy little plant grows to a height of 6–8in (15–20cm) and is leafless in spring and flowerless in summer. The appearance of its bright yellow flowers in February and March has earned it the country name of son-before-father, a name shared with the crocus.

This humble little flower, for its commercial value rather than its beauty, reached medicinal stardom when it became the apothecary's sign and was painted on the doorposts of their shops.

The generic name *Tussilago* comes from cough-wort or cold-wort, in accordance with the Latin *tussis,* a cough, which refers to its use as a remedy for coughs, colds and hoarseness. The hoof-shaped leaves with their under surface of thick white felt, which seldom appear before April or May, have merely added to the name of coltsfoot those of foal-foot, horse-hoof, asses-foot and bull-foot. The leaves give a greenish-yellow dye which turns to a clear green if copperas is added.

Coltsfoot was a simpler's plant, collected for the sake of its many and various uses, but it should not be introduced into the herb garden for it will take possession and will be impossible to eradicate. The cottony down under the leaves was collected and dipped into a solution of saltpetre for tinder, before the introduction of matches. The down of its seeds was used for the stuffing of pillows in the Highlands.

Coltsfoot tea, made of 1qt (1l) boiling water on 2 handfuls of leaves, sweetened with honey, is an old and tried remedy for coughs and colds, catarrh, asthma and pleurisy. Another recipe for the same purpose was an infusion of 1oz (28g) coltsfoot leaves, 1oz (28g) fennel, ¼oz (7g) fresh ginger root with honey.

Culpeper recommended 6 handfuls of fresh coltsfoot, 2 of hyssop, 2 of maidenhair fern and 2 of liquorice root, to be boiled in 4pt (2.2l) spring water until only 1pt (550ml) remains.

A decoction of the crushed leaves was prescribed for insect bites, ulcers, swellings and burns. The flowers should be collected as soon as they open, and the leaves collected when they reach full size.

Mixed with yarrow and rose-leaves, coltsfoot is now given for asthma. A coltsfoot lotion helps to heal cuts, and the bitter juice is used in medicinal beers and jellies. Coltsfoot rock or lozenges, made with treacle or brown sugar, should be kept in the cupboard for winter coughs and bronchitis. It is used with yarrow and meadow-grass as an additive for tonic baths.

It is in its use as a tobacco for asthma sufferers that coltsfoot is best known. According to Pliny, it had been known and used as a tobacco from ancient times, even in his own day, the fume of the burning weed being inhaled through a reed. Dioscorides mentioned its use by the Greeks: the smoke was swallowed and the patient sipped a little wine between each inhalation. Gerard said that 'the fume of the dried leaves taken through a funnell or tunnell, burned upon coles, effectually helpeth those that are troubled with shortness of breath, and fetch their winde thick and often'.

Today, the leaves are gathered in June and July, and hung in small bunches to dry in a warm place for the herb tobacco and cigarettes that are still prescribed for asthma patients. The powdered leaves are used in herbal snuff for clearing nasal passages and for headaches.

COMFREY, on the left, with Daisy in this illustration from an early 16th-century English herbal and bestiary. Several plants of the Compositae family are called daisies: the one in this illustration is the common daisy, *Bellis perennis*.

COMFREY
Symphytum officinale

A HERB OF SATURN UNDER THE SIGN OF CAPRICORN

A perennial of the Borage family, native to Europe, comfrey was taken to North America in the 17th century, where it later escaped from gardens and became naturalized.

Monks grew comfrey in their physic gardens, and the seed was sold by the early nurserymen for medicinal purposes, which gave the herb the classification of *officinale*. Its various names of knitbone, boneset, bruisewort and healing-herb are an indication of man's faith in its virtues. It is not as a bone-mender that it should be regarded, however, but as a healer of bruised over-lying tissues. 'Drink a strong decoction of comfrey with bread and butter, for an inward bruise' was the advice of Dr Parkins in 1826. The rootstock, which has a sweetish taste, is the part most frequently used in medicine, and its uses are many, varied and safe. A decoction of comfrey is valuable as a medicinal mouthwash or gargle for throat inflammation or hoarseness, and for bleeding gums. Made into a cold compress for eye

injuries, it is soothing and healing. The warm pulp applied as a poultice relieves gout, inflammations of all sorts, wounds, sores and insect bites. It has been used for lung complaints and dysentery.

At one time comfrey was a favourite herb in cottage gardens, but today it is seldom cultivated. The plant has egg-shaped bristly leaves and flowers that are scorpioid in form; the latter grow in one-sided pairs that taper to a small end-bud in a curve which resembled, in our ancestors' eyes, a scorpion's tail.

Comfrey flowers may be yellowish-white, greenish-pink or dull purple and appear from late April to the end of August. They grow to a height of 2–3ft (60–90cm), often by the riverside or in damp meadows. Although rough-leaved, the plants are relished by cattle. They are rich in gum-mucilage and sugar, and are a valuable fodder which has earned them the name of pigweed in certain parts of Britain.

For an astringent bath, simmer a decoction of sage, milfoil, nettles and comfrey for 10 or 20 minutes and add to the bath water. A wine-glassful of comfrey tea, preferably made from the fresh leaves, is good for digestive troubles and bronchitis. A decoction made of 2 parts comfrey and 1 part knotgrass, is given for stomach ulcers; a teaspoonful is taken in ½ cupful water.

Few people today think of using comfrey in cooking, but it is an excellent substitute for spinach or other green vegetables, and may also be used to flavour cakes. It can be blanched by earthing up and eaten as asparagus. Our grandmothers used it in fritters and often added it as flavouring to pumpkin-pie. The leaves may be dried and powdered, and stored in glass-topped jars.

Buttered comfrey greens
several handfuls washed and shredded young comfrey leaves
½ cup boiling water
2tbsp butter

Put shredded leaves into boiling water. Return to the boil, cover and cook until tender, about 10 minutes. Drain, add butter and toss well. Serve with minted new potatoes and boiled bacon or ham.

CORIANDER, depicted in *Tacuinum Sanitatis, c.* 1385. Coriander seeds and the oil derived from them are used in the flavouring of curries and liqueurs.

CORIANDER
Coriandrum sativum

UNDER THE DOMINION OF SATURN

An annual plant of the Carrot family, coriander is native to southern Europe and the Middle East, and is cultivated in North and South America, Britain and the Mediterranean area for its aromatic seeds. It is common in the Holy Land, where the plant was used for culinary and medicinal purposes. It is mentioned more than once in the Bible, and likened to the manna that the Lord provided for the children of Israel: 'and it was like coriander seed, white; and the taste of it was like wafers made with honey'. Coriander is also cultivated in France, Germany and Russia. The German and Russian seeds are the richest in oil, but the English are the finest in flavour. They are sometimes used in pot-pourri.

It may well have been one of the first herbs to be used in cookery, for more than 5,000 years ago the Chinese ate the boiled roots and used the seeds for flavouring. It was, and is still, used by Egyptians, Indians and Arabs with meat, curries and

soups, and Arab women take it for easing labour pains. Both Pliny and Cato mention the use of coriander, and it reached Europe, as so many useful herbs and spices did, by way of the Romans.

In the Middle Ages coriander seeds were put into the popular drink hippocras, so-called from the strainer through which it was pressed. Hippocrates invented the strainer, a sort of woollen bag through which the cordial was filtered. He also used coriander for medicinal purposes. Hippocras was a feature of Tudor weddings and other royal junketings.

Coriander is an attractive plant grown in the herb garden, but it needs plenty of sunshine. Growing to about 2ft (60cm), it has white or pinkish-mauve flowers and parsley-like leaves, and the whole plant is strongly aromatic. Seeds should be sown in April, but they are slow to germinate. It can also be grown as a pot plant. The seeds are used in the making of gin, and are still cultivated in Essex for that purpose. In the garden it is a good bee-plant, and grows well in the company of anise, dill, mallows and chervil. It should be harvested at an early stage of ripening.

It was once a witches' plant, and appeared as an aphrodisiac in *The Arabian Nights*. Strangely, it has an unpleasant smell until the seeds ripen. This then changes to a pleasant aroma, and was probably regarded as proof of its magic qualities.

Medicinally the seeds serve as an antispasmodic and carminative appetizer, but are little used except as a flavouring for other medicines. Richard Brook, in the *Cyclopaedia of Botany*, gave the following recipe for the once-famous honey water.

Honey-water

Take of Coriander seed .... 8ozs.
Lemon peel, fresh,
Nutmeg,
Sorax, } of each .... ½oz.
Benzoin,
Vanilla, ... 3 drachms.
Alcohol, ... 3 pints.

After infusing them for 24 hours, distil, and add, if it be thought requisite, a small quantity of essence of amber and of musk. It is reckoned cephalic, nervine, paragoric, and cosmetic: the dose about ½ an ounce.

In cookery, Gerard mentions that 'coriander seeds well prepared and covered with sugar as comfits, taken after meat, helpeth digestion', and on Victorian and Edwardian dinner-tables dishes of small, knobbly, pink and white roughly sugared little objects containing these aromatic seeds were served. They were also to be found in boxes of mixed chocolates. The seeds make a pleasant variation in the following recipe.

Courgette and coriander salad

1–1½lb (450–680g) courgettes
6tbsp olive oil
½pt (275ml) water
2 sprigs fennel
2 sprigs thyme
1 bay leaf
2tbsp lemon juice
½tsp coriander seeds
2 stalks celery

Wash and split lengthwise young courgettes. If larger, slice them. Put all other ingredients in a saucepan, bring to boil and add unpeeled courgette pieces. Bring to boil again, reduce heat and simmer for 20–25 minutes, until just soft. Leave until cold, and then take out courgette pieces and put on a serving dish. Strain liquid into clean pan, bring to boil and cook uncovered until reduced to about half original volume. Strain over courgettes and leave until cold. Good with cold chicken or fish, or as a starter.

COSTMARY

Tanacetum balsamita

A PLANT OF THE MOON, UNDER THE DOMINION OF JUPITER

A perennial grown in ancient Egypt, costmary was introduced into our gardens from southern Europe for the brewing of ale, before hops were used. It has long, narrow, pale green leaves, with finely toothed edges and small, bright yellow button-flowers, not unlike those of tansy, that open only when the sun shines in June and July. The whole plant has the faint odour and taste of mint, pleasanter and less harsh than that of tansy, to which it is allied. It is a rare herb, which does not set seed in Britain, but plants can be bought from a herb nursery. It is suitable for the middle of the border, and should be covered for protection against frost in winter. The plant should be harvested when starting to bloom, and dried quickly away from the light.

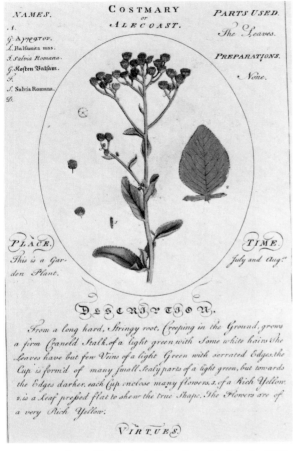

COSTMARY, from Sheldrake's *Botanicum Medicinale*, 1759.

Physicians in the Middle Ages prescribed costmary for indigestion, dysentery, ague and loss of weight. The bruised leaves were rubbed on insect bites and stings, and a lotion was made to remove head lice. It was also used as a strewing herb, and costmary flowers and lavender would 'lye upon the toppe of beds, presses, etc. for sweet scents and savours'. It was also used instead of sage in cooking, and in the brewing of sage ale, and in 'salades and sawces, for which purpose it is excellent, for it yeeldeth a proper taste and savour'.

In the USA it was a favourite spring tonic known by the colonists as Sweet Mary tea. Throughout eastern Massachusetts it was carried to church in a nosegay with southernwood and other aromatic herbs to enjoy during the long sermons.

A costmary tisane, infused for 15–20 minutes, helps catarrh. To avoid a metallic taste infusions should be made in a china teapot or an enamel saucepan. Equal amounts of dried costmary and powdered orange peel are a pleasant addition to China tea.

Costmary is dedicated to St Mary Magdalene, the patron saint of fallen women, from the legend that its scent was the balsam with which the penitent Mary washed Jesus' feet. In the past it was known as *herba-sancta,* balsam-mint and maudlin-wort. Alecost, another English country name, refers to its use in the brewing of ale, beer and negus. The US names of tongue-plant and beaver-tongue presumably arose from its sharply edged leaves. In a more Christian spirit it was known as Sweet Mary and bible-leaf, because it was so often used as a book-mark mounted on coloured card and left its sweet scent between the pages.

Both Gerard and Culpeper speak of it as common in their day. 'This is so frequently known to be an inhabitant in almost every garden, that I suppose it needlesse to write a description thereof.' Culpeper regarded it as 'An especial friend and help to evil, weak and cold livers'.

COWSLIP
Primula veris

A HERB OF VENUS, UNDER THE SIGN OF ARIES

One of the best loved flowers once common in the English countryside, the cowslip is becoming more valued as it becomes more rare. Richard Brook, at the beginning of the 19th century, wrote: 'It were useless to attempt a description . . . for the man who does not know them well will certainly neither buy nor read an Herbal.' Today, the green rosettes of wrinkled leaves, from which rises a slender stalk crowned by honey-scented pale gold chandeliers, are not so commonly seen.

Cowslips are members of the Primula family, perennials that grow only occasionally on clay soils, but bloom plentifully in chalky meadows in May and June. They were believed to be the favourite flower of the nightingale, which, it was said, haunted only the places where cowslips flourished.

Because the flowers were thought to resemble a bunch of golden keys that would presumably open the gates of heaven, they were given the names of Peterkeys, Peterwort and Peterkin, and were dedicated to St Peter. In some parts of the country they were called Our Lady's keys, and the keys of heaven.

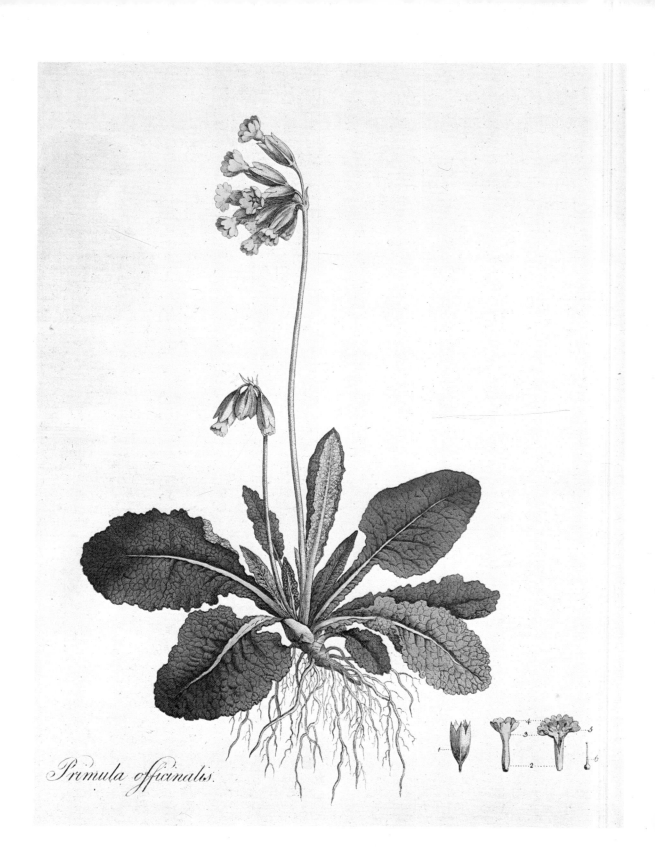

Primula officinalis.

COWSLIP, from Curtis' *Flora Londinensis*, 1817.

The old herbalists had great faith in the curative properties of the cowslip in cases of palsy and all paralytic ailments, for which it earned the name of palsywort or *Herba paralysis* — an unlovely name for the lovely flower of Shakespeare and Milton. These frail flowers were expected to cure or alleviate 'vertigo, false apparitions, phrenzies, falling sickness, palsies, convulsions, cramps, pains in the nerves'.

When Edward Hulme wrote and illustrated the series of Familiar Wild Flowers at the turn of the century, he lifted forever the burden of sickness that these fairy flowers had so long been forced to carry: 'We can only conclude that the herb must either have sadly lost its efficacy in these later days, or men their faith in its powers, for the tide of human misery rolls on as though the cowslips no longer dotted in their thousands the verdant meadows, or the breezy slopes of the rolling downs. Any health-giving properties they possess will probably rather be found in the search for them than in any more formal application.'

We may still trust in Parkinson, however, who said that with the juice of cowslips 'divers gentlewomen knew how to clense the skinne from spots or discolourings, as also to take away the wrinkles thereof and cause the skinne to become smooth and faire'. Culpeper agreed that 'our city dames know well enough the ointment or distilled water of it adds beauty, or at least restores it when it is lost.'

The young leaves and flowers were once made into salads, and used for pot-herbs and in puddings, tarts and creams. John Evelyn's recipe for pickled cowslips is simpler than most of his time. It comes from *Aceteria,* 1699.

Pickled cowslips

Pickt very clean; to each Pound of Flowers allow about one Pound of Loaf Sugar and one Pint of White Wine Vinegar, which boil to a Syrup, and cover it scalding hot.

Cowslip tea is a country cure for migraine, insomnia and general debility, and a glass of cowslip wine, being 'drank at night Bedward, causes sleep and rest'. A decoction made from the boiled rootstock is good for rheumatism and gout. For the making of the best of all country wines, women and children used to be employed in the fields in pulling the cowslip pips or peeps for 6d to 8d a gallon. No doubt farmers' wives and other lucky country dwellers may still be able to make cowslip mead and cowslip wine from the following or similar recipes.

Cowslip mead

To every gallon (4.5l) water allow 2lb (900g) honey. Boil for ¾ hour, skimming well. Take 1pt (550ml) of the liquor and slice into it 1 large lemon, then pour the remainder into an earthenware bowl and put in 1gal (4.5l) cowslip heads. Stir well, cover, and set in a warm place for 24 hours.

Stir in the lemon liquor, 2 sprigs of sweet brier and ¼oz (7g) yeast, dissolved in a little of the honey. Let it work for 4 days, then strain into a cask. Keep in a cool place for 6 months, then bottle.

Cowslip wine

Pare the rinds very thinly from 1 lemon and 1 orange, halve the fruit and press out the juice. Put this with the rinds into a tub or earthenware pan, and pour on 4qt (4.5l) boiling water in which 3lb (1.3kg) loaf sugar has been simmered for ½ hour. Skim well. When the liquid is lukewarm, stir in 4qt (4.5l) fresh cowslip pips and 2tbsp yeast, and leave the vessel covered with a cloth for 3 days, stirring twice a day. Strain the liquid off and pour nearly all of it into a cask, leaving the bung loose until the working has stopped. Fill up with the liquor kept for this purpose, and bung up close. Leave undisturbed for 3 months. A little brandy, although not necessary, will greatly improve it.

CUCKOO-PINT

Arum maculatum

UNDER THE DOMINION OF MARS

The only British representative of the huge Arum family, which has nearly 1,000 members, cuckoo-pint is a perennial, growing in moist and shady places, among bushes and in the wild garden. The rootstock, which is poisonous when fresh but edible when cooked and dried, is brown outside and white within. The arrow-shaped leaves are also poisonous. They are glossy, with warning blotches of brownish-red or purple. The pale green spathe, partially enveloping the spadix, appears in April and May. In autumn, nothing remains but a cluster of bright scarlet berries on a short stem, which seems to bear little connection with the handsome sculptured 'lily' that preceded it. These too contain dangerous poison.

A TRAVELLING COUNTRY APOTHECARY as depicted in an 18th-century French print by Oldendorp, now in the possession of l'Ordre Nationale des Pharmaciens, Paris

CUCKOO-PINT, illustrated here by J. F. Miller, 1770.

The plant gives off a strong smell of carrion, and is fertilized by carrion flies. Dioscorides wrote in *Materia Medica*, '. . . and they say that the smell thereof after ye withering of the flowers, is destructive of embryo newly conceived.'

Cuckoo-pint appears to be the earliest English name of *A. maculatum*. It is of Anglo-Saxon origin and derives from *cucu*, lively, and *pintle*, the penis; the latter associated it firmly with its use as an aphrodisiac and love philtre, an association endorsed by the *Doctrine of Signatures*. If any doubt remains, another popular name, wake-robin, has a similar derivation — *wake* from the same Anglo-Saxon source as *cucu*, and *robin* from the French *robinet*, cock.

Jack-in-the-pulpit (given in the USA to another, but related plant, *Arisaema triphyllum*) describes the position of the spadix within its sheath. There are over one hundred country names for this plant, but only one other can be accounted for here. Lords and ladies was probably a more acceptable nursery name, for the plant's inflorescences may be purple or white, and we tell our children that the 'lords' are the purple and the

'ladies' are the white. *Maculatum* means 'spotted', and refers to the leaves, which are often blotched with the colour of dried blood.

During Elizabeth I's reign, a starch was made of the roots; uncoloured it was applied to hair and beards, and red, yellow or purple was used to stiffen clothing. The yellow starch was probably coloured with saffron. A cosmetic powder was also prepared, similar to that used by the French and known as Cyprus powder, or *poudre de Cypres*. Mixed with rose-water the starch was also made into a face lotion to whiten the skin, which would account for the chalky appearance of women's skin in Elizabethan portraits. Gerard wrote that 'the most pure and white starch is made of the roots of the Cuckow-pint; but most hurtfull to the hands of the Laundresses that hath the handling of it, for it choppeth, blistereth, and maketh hands rough and rugged and withall smarting'.

Cuckoo-pint once flourished in the Isle of Portland, and tubers were collected in May and June for the making of starch. It was also sold in chemists' shops as Portland arrowroot, or Portland sago, for the making of a sort of gruel, said to be nourishing for sick people. A sweet called Portland pudding was made for George III on his visits to the island but the recipe has since been lost. The whole plant is intensely acrid, and the preparation requires pulping and elaborate washing before it is fit for food.

As well as starch, the tubers were used as a substitute for soap. Culpeper says that the people around Maidstone in Kent used both the herb and the tubers for this purpose, and there are later reports that the whole plant was soaked, crushed into a paste, and used for the washing of linen.

Theophrastus said that the roots were 'sweet and good for fractures'. It was a known remedy for gout, and an emulsion was made for rheumatic pains. Culpeper was cautious: 'Authors have left large commendations of this herb you see, but for my part, I have spoken neither to Dr. Reason nor Dr. Experience about it.' Cuckoo-pint is now regarded as a useful homoeopathic plant, but should not be used without medical advice.

fort Jungen's!

[67]

DANDELION, as seen in Jean Bourdichon's *Hours of Anne of Burgundy* from the 16th century.

DANDELION

Taraxacum officinale

UNDER THE DOMINION OF JUPITER

This plant might have been made welcome in the herb garden but for its over-enthusiastic although fabulously beautiful method of seed-dispersal. Gardeners may consider that the best means of getting rid of such an unwelcome visitor is to dig it up on sight and eat it, either in a salad or cooked as greens. Be certain, however, that every portion of the root is eradicated, or it will turn up again before the year is out. It is this quality of being able to flower throughout most of the year that makes it a valuable bee-plant. If the sight of this cheerful interloper is too offensive, another method is to cover it with an up-turned flower-pot and blanch it, whereupon the plant, having lost much of its bitterness, is welcome as a winter salad resembling endive.

It is a perennial plant, native in Britain and spread widely through most of the northern hemisphere, and is known by many names, not all of them polite. Dandelion, from *dent-de-leon,* is possibly a Norman name referring to the sharply toothed leaves. Sloping jaggedly towards the root

as they do, the leaves have a strangely upside-down appearance. It is called devil's milk pail and devil's milk plant from the milky juice in its leaves and stems which is used to remove pimples and warts. So effective as a diuretic is this herb that it is known by such names as piss-a-bed, pee-a-bed and mess-a-bed in the USA and in Britain, and *pis-en-lit* in France. In some country districts mothers would give their children dandelions to smell on May-day to inhibit bed-wetting for the next year. The reputation of the plant as 'a sovereign remedy against swooning and passions of the heart' gave it the name of heart-fever-grass in Ireland.

Writing of the approach of spring in US public parks in 1911, Alice Morse Earle described the appearance there of the dandelion gatherers. 'It is always interesting to see, in May, on the closely guarded lawns and field expanses of our city parks, the hundreds of bareheaded gayly-dressed Italian and Portuguese women and children eagerly gathering the young Dandelion plants to add to their meagre fare as a greatly-loved delicacy. They collect these greens in highly-coloured handkerchiefs, in baskets, in squares of sheeting; I have seen the women bearing off a half-bushel of plants; even their stumpy little children are impressed to increase the welcome harvest, and with a broken knife dig eagerly in the greensward. The thrifty park commissioners, in dandelion-time, relax their rigid rules, KEEP OFF THE GRASS, and turn the salad-loving Italians loose to improve the public lawns by freeing them from weeds.'

The French proved their enthusiasm for the dandelion by slicing the roots and eating them as well as the leaves, with bread and butter, and the leaves were sold in the markets in France. Even Betsey Prig, that loyal friend and 'frequent pardner' in healing of Sairey Gamp in *Martin Chuzzlewit,* was known to enjoy 'a trifle of the Herb called Dandelion'.

Culpeper thought highly of the dandelion: 'You see here what virtues this common herb hath, and that is the reason the French and Dutch so often eat them in the Spring; and now if you look a little farther, you may see plainly without a pair of spectacles, that foreign physicians are not so selfish as ours are, but more communicative of the virtues of plants to people.'

The plant is favoured by lovers, too, for the 'round downy blowbal', as Gerard calls it, can be used to send messages of love if blown in the direction of the loved one.

Dandelion was once included in the pharmacopoeias for its value in the treatment of dyspepsia.

It is used for arthritis to disperse the acidic deposits in the joints. It is laxative and tonic, and kidney and liver complaints as well as skin diseases respond to infusions of the leaves and roots. For a blood purifier take 1 part dandelion roots, 1 part nettle leaves, with 2 parts elder shoots and 2 parts primrose flowers and leaves, steeped in boiling water. For a liver prescription try 2 parts dandelion root and 2 parts speedwell, with 1 of chicory flower and 1 of woodruff. The juice pressed from the leaves and taken in milk or water is an excellent tonic. The root contains latex, and the whole plant gives a good magenta dye.

No wonder that an English traveller visiting the Botanic Garden of Sydney in the 19th century found himself 'ardently coveting the possession of a glorious dandelion, which classically labelled "Leontodon taraxacum" occupied one of the high places of the exhibition, and was treated as an illustrious foreigner'.

Its uses in the kitchen are well known if not well followed. The leaves chopped and cooked with butter and cider-vinegar or lemon are excellent. The sun-dried or oven-dried roots, ground and roasted, make an acceptable caffeine-free coffee. They can also be used for dandelion beer or stout, or dandelion tea. Dandelion stout was offered for sale at 2d a bottle in the north of England in Victorian times. In the USA the settlers mixed the young leaves with hops in the making of beer.

Dandelion wine

3qt (3l) freshly picked flower heads
3lb (1.3kg) sugar
1oz (28g) yeast
1lb (450g) raisins
1gal (4.5l) water
rind and pulp of 2 lemons
rind and pulp of 1 orange

Put the flowers (with no stalks) into a large bowl. Bring the water to the boil, pour over the dandelions and leave covered for 3 days, stirring each day. On the third day, add the sugar and the rinds only of the lemons and orange. Turn all into a pan and boil for one hour. Return to the bowl and add the pulp of the lemons and orange. Leave until cool and then add yeast. Let it remain covered for 3 days, when it will be ready to strain, and put into bottles. The bottles should not be quite filled, and the raisins should be equally divided amongst them. Do not cork until fermentation ceases. If the wine is made in May or June, it will be ready for Christmas.

DILL
Anethum graveolens

UNDER THE DOMINION OF MERCURY

A hardy annual herb dill is native to southern Europe and western Asia, North and South America, and southern Russia. It was introduced into Britain from the Mediterranean countries. The plant resembles fennel, with similar feathery leaves, which reach 2–3ft (60–90cm). The yellow flowers are borne on flat terminal umbels, from July to September, followed by quantities of flat fruits, which resemble the ribbed seeds of caraways. It is a useful bee-plant, and a good companion to coriander, chervil and mallow. It also grows well with cabbages, although not with carrots.

Dill was familiar to Dioscorides and to Pliny. Galen said that 'Dill procureth sleep, wherefore garlands of Dill are worn at feasts' — an odd remark. The name dill is derived from a Saxon word meaning to lull, for which purpose it has been used for generations of babies. Dill water, still the mother's standby, is obtained by distillation of the fruits. The village chemist used to sell 'a pennorth of dill' to harrassed mothers for wailing infants, and no better soothing medicine can be supplied. It is good for flatulence and indigestion in adults also.

With true medieval inconsistency, it was regarded as both a witch-plant and an anti-witch plant. It was a valued ingredient in a witch's cauldron when she mixed a love potion for some credulous lad or lass. And yet it was hung at doors and windows against the 'evil eye', and more than one poet wrote of 'the vervain and the dill, That hindreth witches of their will'.

For centuries dill was grown in the garden among the worts and cooked as a pot-herb, and the young and rather sharply aromatic leaves used in salads.

Travelling in New England in the 17th century, John Josselyn made a list of plants that prospered or failed in the new land: 'Coriander, Dill, and Annis,' he wrote, 'thrive exceedingly.'

Although grown in gardens for culinary purposes, dill is raised for medicine and for the perfuming of soap in East Anglia and a few other regions of England. The seeds are sown in April, in open sunny conditions, and mown in the autumn, when the plants are dried in small stacks. The fruits are then beaten out on to canvas sheets, and harvested for the oil which is used medicinally as *anethi fructus*.

DILL, from an English manuscript herbal from about 1100 now in the possession of the Bodleian Library, Oxford.

Chewing dill seeds cures halitosis and drinking dill tea for an upset stomach or for hiccups may at the same time help insomnia. Dill in hot milk is recommended to quieten the nerves.

In cookery, the principal use of dill is for pickling, in sauerkraut, sauces for fish, salad dressings and dips. Addison wrote in the *Spectator* that he was 'always pleased with that time of year which is proper for the pickling of dill and cucumber'.

From the *Receipt Book of Joseph Cooper*, cook to King Charles I (1640):

To pickle cucumbers in dill

Gather the tops of the ripest Dill, and cover the bottome of the vessel, and lay a layer of Cucumbers, and another of Dill, till you have filled the vessel within a handful of the top, then take as much water as you think will fill the vessel, and mix it with Salt, and a Quarter of a Pound of allom to a gallon of water, and poure it on them, and press them down with a stone on them, and keep them covered close.

For that use I think the water will be best boyl'd and cold, which will keep longer sweet, or if you like not this pickle doe it with Water Salt and White Wine Vinegar, or (if you please) pour the Water and Salt on them scalding hot, which will make them ready to use the sooner.

John Evelyn in *Acetaria, A Discourse of Sallets* (1669), gives the following recipe.

Dill and colly-flower pickles

Boil the colly-flowers till they fall in Pieces; then with some of the Stalk and the worst of the Flower, boil it in a part of the Liquor till pretty strong. Then being taken off, strain it; and when settled, clean it from the Bottom. Then with Dill, gross pepper, a pretty quantity of Salt, when cold add as much vinegar as will make it sharp, and pour all upon the Colly-flower.

Dill seeds are used in bread, cakes and as a flavouring in cream cheese. Here is a simple, cheap and enjoyable supper dish.

Jacket potatoes with cream cheese and dill

Scrub several large potatoes, one for each person, and if possible spear each on a metal meat skewer, for even and economical cooking. Beat up a carton of cream cheese with chopped dill. When the potatoes are done, split them lengthwise, and fill the split with the cream cheese and serve.

ELDER

Sambucus nigra

UNDER THE DOMINION OF VENUS

The elder is native to many parts of the world. It is the tree of myth and magic, dedicated to Thor, sacred to gipsies, an emblem of sorrow and death, and yet called 'the medicine chest of the country people'. In 1644 a book entitled *The Anatomie of the Elder,* which was entirely devoted to the tree, claimed that every part of it had medicinal value.

Now one of the remaining beauties of the English countryside, the elder still adorns waste ground and ruined buildings. Yet it is largely ignored and its virtues are forgotten. Country people used to strike the leaves of fruit trees and vegetables with elder-boughs, to distract insects, and farm carts were drawn by horses whose bridles were decorated with sprays of elder-flowers to keep away the flies. Farm horses surrounded by troublesome flies now have almost disappeared, but elder-flowers are dried and

ELDER, with elderberries on the left,
as illustrated in G. C. Oeder's *Flora Danica*.

powdered for use as an insecticide, and an infusion made to dab on human skin to keep off mosquitoes.

The flowers which Gerard described as growing in 'spoky rundles' smell like dusty hedgerows, bringing the scents of late August forward to early May. Still-rooms in May would be heaped with flowers — infusions for toilet waters, distillations for elder-flower vinegar, crocks full of florets waiting to be made into elder-flower tea or elder-flower champagne, all marking the passage of spring into summer. The good housewife had probably been working hard even earlier, before the flowers had appeared, filling her larders with pickled elder-buds and elder-shoots — possibly

she had her own special receipt for primrose-flower and elder-bud ointment.

In August, those branches that had so far eluded her reach, would be heavy with the red-stemmed black berries needed for flavouring the early apples, and for tarts and elderberry wine.

Gerard described other uses: he said that from these berries 'is pressed a purple juice, which being boiled with allom and such like things, doth serve very well for the Painters use'. He also knew that the seeds were good for 'such as are too fat and would fain be leaner, if they be taken in a morning to the quantitie of a dram with wine for a certain space'.

In winter boys busied themselves with making

skewers, combs and toys, shoemakers' pegs and other small articles of turnery. In days long past, the stems with the pith removed had been made into pipes and flutes, and into a triangular stringed instrument called a sambuca, which had given the tree its name of *Sambucus*. Men used the wood for the making of fences, forgetting the mysteries of witchcraft which frightened simple folk into believing that it was unwise to make furniture of elder-wood; it may have been the suspicion that Christ's cross had been made of elder-wood, or that it was the tree on which Judas had hanged himself 'for despeyr' that gave man the uneasy feeling that a wood so tainted was best left alone.

Elder-flowers and berries have been gathered for pomades, cosmetic ointments and hair dye ever since the Romans used the juice for this purpose. Indeed, Pliny had little reason to say, as he did, that an elder-berry was 'all skin and bones'. It is still agreed to be one of the best cosmetics either the countryside or the shop has to offer.

The flower heads gently simmered for 45 minutes in the melted contents of a jar of vaseline make an excellent hand cream. Six tablespoonfuls of elder-flower water, with one teaspoonful of glycerine, one teaspoonful of rectified spirit, and half a teaspoonful of fluid ammonia, is a cheap and reliable hair-setting lotion. The flowers mixed with yoghurt and used as a facial mask help to bleach freckles and remove wrinkles. A head of flowers in a muslin bag hung under the hot tap may be used for a refreshing bath.

Elder trees are cultivated in Kent for the making of elderberry wine and to colour raisin wine, and the so-called 'British wines' and 'clarets', 'Bordeaux' and 'tawny port'. As the berries possess valuable medicinal properties, these additives and colourations are beneficial.

The old country cure of a mug of spiced elderberry wine and a piece of toast might go down well as a nightcap today, and another old favourite, cider and elderberry wine in equal parts, is worth trying. The northern Britisher drank hot elderberry wine laced with rum as a cold cure.

Until the end of the 19th century hot elder wine was sold in the London streets on cold winter days and nights, and a comforting beverage it must have been to travellers and workers. It was served from a handsome copper or brass urn, erected on a pedestal, with a lid ornamented with brass mouldings. The wine was kept boiling by means of a charcoal fire.

An infusion of elderflower and sage, with lemon juice, vinegar and honey is still effective as a gargle; and elderflowers and peppermint sweetened with honey make a soothing drink for a cold if taken hot. Dried elderflowers kept in a caddy of China tea give special pleasure to those who appreciate delicately flavoured teas.

Elderberries give a soft blue or lavender dye with an alum mordant, and purple with chrome mordants. In the past the berries were used to make ink. They were also used with copperas, vinegar and alum to stain paper blue.

The heads of the flowers, gathered fresh from the tree and inspected carefully for black-fly, will if dipped into a thin batter, fried and lightly sugared make a delightful sweet.

On consulting any cookery book of the past, one is likely to find a recipe for a syllabub, for it was a favourite delicacy of the 18th century. This one, although it contains no elderflowers, has slipped in on the strength of its charm.

Syllabub under the cow

Take a large china bowl — a punch bowl is most suitable for the purpose — put into it half a pound lump sugar, the strained juice of a lemon, a pint of sherry, a glassful of brandy and ¾ pint of cream beaten up with white of egg.

Stir the mixture briskly for a minute or two, and put a dozen ratafias into it. Take it to the dairymaid and let her milk the cow into the bowl until it is quite full. Put it away, and let it remain untouched till the following day. Grate a little nutmeg on the top and serve.

Should a cow not immediately be available, a more realistic but still enjoyable recipe is:

Gooseberry and elderflower syllabub

1lb (450g) green gooseberries
¾pt (400ml) water
8 heads of elderflowers
2dssp sugar
¾lb (340g) sugar
2 glasses sweet white wine
juice of 1 lemon
½pt (275ml) whipped cream

Make a syrup with sugar and water and when boiling drop in gooseberries and simmer gently until tender. Add elderflowers tied in muslin during last 5 minutes of cooking. Strain and cool. Mix 2 glasses wine with 2 glasses syrup, add 2dssp sugar and lemon juice. Leave covered in cool place for a few hours. Fold gently into cream and leave overnight in refrigerator. Serve in tall glasses with sponge fingers.

ELECAMPANE
Inula helenium

UNDER THE DOMINION OF MERCURY

A perennial of the Daisy family, elecampane is native to many parts of Europe and in China, Manchuria, Mongolia and Korea. It was introduced to, and cultivated in New England by the settlers, and has since become naturalized in the eastern USA, where it grows wild along the roadsides. It has been cultivated in Holland, Switzerland, Germany and France for its essential oil, once used in the flavouring of absinthe. This splendid plant was eaten in ancient Rome as a vegetable, and described by Dioscorides as a medicinal herb. According to Pliny, 'the best Elecampane is that which groweth in the Island of Helena'.

Elecampane has a long history in British monastery physic gardens. It was a much valued simpler's plant, gathered for the apothecaries who used every part of it as powder, ointment, syrup and infusion.

It is occasionally found in Britain in moist places, but is more often seen in cottage gardens. It has wrinkled leaves, bright green on the upper side and grey beneath, full of netted veins. Its yellow flowers, which appear in June and July, are a little coarse, but nevertheless it is a handsome plant for the back of the herb garden, where it may grow to a height of 5ft (1.5m). It is sweet of scent and bitter of taste, and the whole herb is covered with silken hairs. The long brown seeds which ripen in August are carried on the wind by downy sails. The entire plant has a pungent odour.

It was named *helenium* or *elenium*, 'of the lamentable and pitifull teares of Helena, Wife to Menelaus, when she was violently taken away by Paris into Phrygia, having this herbe in her hande'. As we should expect from the herb of Helen, a lotion was made for the complexion.

Elecampane was used by the Elizabethans in a candied confection like marzipan made of the ground roots with eggs, salt, sugar, saffron and other spices. In medicine it was recommended for a quaintly assorted trio of ills — convulsions, contusions and hip-gout. Gerard thought highly of it 'for them that are bursten and troubled with cramps', and he also believed it to be 'good for shortnesse of breath, and an old cough, and for such as cannot breathe unlesse they hold their neckes upright'. Culpeper said that 'the roots and herb beaten together and put into new ale or beer and daily drunk, is good for the eyesight'. Through the ages, elecampane has been an old village remedy for numerous ills — whooping-cough, bronchitis, lung diseases, kidney troubles and diarrhoea. Elecampane lozenges were sold by druggists in England, and various carminative preparations containing elecampane could be bought in Europe. The plant contains inulin, a powerful antiseptic and bactericide, which may be used in surgical dressings. It is also a well known medicine for horses.

A medicinal tea made of ¼oz (7g) of each of elecampane, cherry bark, angelica-root and liquorice root helps to relieve hay fever, asthma and coughs.

Elecampane oil is used for catarrh, whooping-cough and bronchitis. It is good for kidney troubles and, as an ointment for massage, for the treatment of rheumatic pains.

The whole plant is sold in a dried form in most Chinese herb shops. The scent of the dried root, after it has been kept for some time, is reminiscent of orris. The leaves, bruised and steeped in wine together with wortleberries, produce a rich blue dye.

EYEBRIGHT
Euphrasia officinalis

UNDER THE DOMINION OF THE SUN AND THE SIGN OF LEO

An annual herb, eyebright is native to Europe and western Asia, and naturalized locally in the USA. It grows in meadows, on mountains, and by the sea, and may be found in English lawns, gathering part of its nourishment from the surrounding grass. It has square leafy stems, and two-lipped red or purple and white flowers, spotted with yellow and streaked with black, the whole giving it an alert and intelligent look that has earned it the name of eyebright, and a place in the *Doctrine of Signatures*. The 16th-century herbalist William Coles, a strong believer in the *Doctrine*, said this combination of colours gave it the appearance of a blood-shot eye and so indicated its use as a cure for eye diseases. For this reason it became known also as Ocularis and Ophthalmica.

Formerly the herb had been called Euphrosyne, after one of the Graces, who typified gladness and mirth, and indeed it *is* a cheerful looking little flower. Later, this name was corrupted to Euphrasy, and from this came its generic name *Euphrasia* and the specific *officinalis*, which refers to its use by apothecaries.

ELECAMPANE, from *Flora Medica*, 1829. The simplers found this an ideal plant, for every part of it could be put to some medicinal use.

Coles believed that even the birds used it for the benefit of their nestling's eyesight. He also said that 'if the herb were put into beer, as wormwood and scurvy grass are, when tunned, it would work wonders . . . making old men to read small letters without spectacles that could hardly read great ones with their spectacles before'.

Culpeper too said that the 'distilled water of eyebright, taken inwardly in wine or broth, or dropped into the eyes, helpes all infirmities of the eyes, that cause dimness of sight . . . it also helpeth a weak brain or memory. This tunned up with strong beer . . . or the powder of the dried herb mixed with sugar, a little mace and fennel seed, and drunk; or eaten in broth; or the said powder

(*right*) FENNEL, shown in a French 19th-century engraving from an original by P. Naudin, now in the possession of the Bibliothèque Nationale des Arts Décoratifs, Paris.

made into an electuary . . . hath the same powerful effect'. He was certain that 'if its uses were properly understood, spectacle-makers would be ruined'.

This tiny plant belongs to the Foxglove family. It is a valuable bee flower, and has a three-lobed lower lip, patched with yellow on the centre lobe; both lips are mapped with honey-guides to assist the bees in their visits.

The herb is bitter and astringent, containing a tonic which is equally good taken in white wine at night, or as early morning tea. Infusions and poultices are made for coughs, colds, sore throats and catarrh. For an infusion, use a heaped tea-spoonful of the fresh herb in boiling water. A

EYEBRIGHT, as portrayed by Turpin for Chaumeton's *Flore Medicale*.

Turpin. P.   Dubois sculp

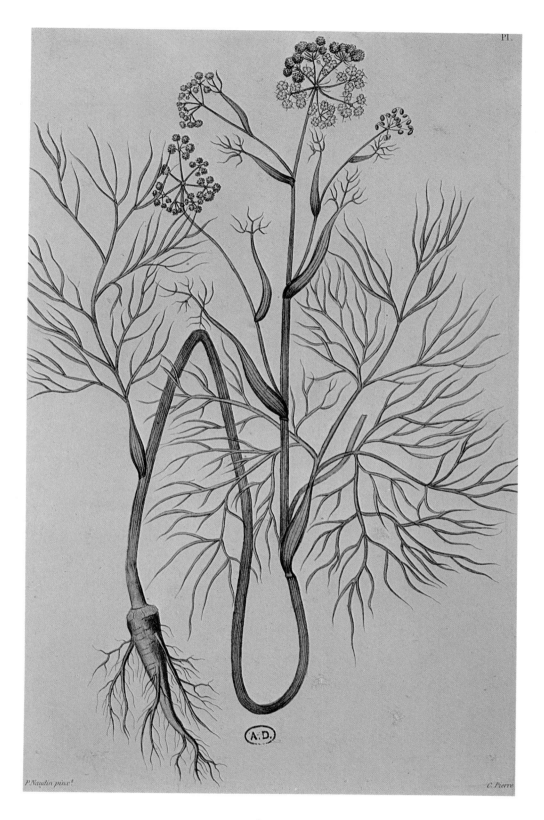

P. Naudin pinx.

C. Pierre

decoction of the dried herb is steeped in a cup of water for 5 minutes. A tincture may be combined with rose-water. As an eye-wash, a teaspoonful of the tincture should be mixed with boiled and slightly salted water, and used three times daily. The plant must be gathered in flower and cut off just above the root. It is used in homoeopathic medicine. It is also one of the ingredients of British herbal tobacco.

The conserve and wine made of eyebright were famous.

Conserve of eyebright

Take Eye-Bright in July with the white flowers; strip them from the stalks, chop them small and take one pound and a half of sugar; then set it in the sun and stir it well oftentimes about, — this is the conserve of Eye-Bright — very commodious for the eyes; it sharpeneth also all dark sight; it dryeth the brains of all cold and superfluous humours, strengtheneth the liver, expelleth yellow jaundice, and the ague that proceeds from an unclean stomach.

FENNEL

Foeniculum vulgare

A HERB OF MERCURY, UNDER THE DOMINION OF VIRGO

A perennial herb of the Carrot family, fennel is native to southern Europe, the Mediterranean shores and Asia Minor. It is cultivated and sometimes grows wild in the USA. In England it is naturalized, or perhaps escaped from gardens, and is found in north Wales along sea coasts and river banks, south and east England, especially on chalk, and most frequently, in Devon and Cornwall. It is a tall and rather handsome herb, reaching a height of 4–6ft (1.2–1.8m), with bright yellow flowers which bloom from April until October, and dark green or bronze feathery leaves. The whole plant is strongly aromatic. It should be harvested when starting to bloom, and the seeds when they are just turning brown.

Fennel is an ancient medicine, mentioned in Anglo-Saxon herbals. It is used for jaundice, flatulence (particularly in babies), hiccups and as a laxative. It is one of the constituents of gripewater. It is taken for shortness of breath, and for those feeling 'choosy' it 'takes away the loathings which oftentimes happen to the stomachs of sick and feverish persons'. In the 16th century it was a

FENNEL, from *Tacuinum Sanitatum*, c. 1385, in the possession of the Bibliothèque Nationale, Paris. The stems of the variety of fennel *Foeniculum vulgare dulce* are cultivated in some parts as a vegetable.

weight-watchers' herb, 'much used in drink or broth ... to make those lean who are too fat'. According to Gerard, 'Fennel seed drunke assuageth the pain of the stomach and wamblings of the same'.

An excellent eye-wash is made with 1 teaspoonful fennel seeds to ¾pt (400ml) water: 'Of Fennel, Roses, Vervain, Rue and Celandine is made a water good to cleare the sight of eine.'

An infusion is good for the memory and for people recovering from strokes. Usually only the seeds are used, but both seed and root are required for fennel oil, which is taken on a lump of sugar for flatulence. The seed boiled in milk and strained is a pleasant digestive. 1–3 drops of fennel oil in 1 tablespoonful honey is good for coughs.

Fennel is good for cosmetic purposes: to smooth out wrinkles, an infusion of the seed is combined with honey and yoghurt; as a skin softener it is combined in a lotion with elderflowers and rose petals; or as a hair rinse, for which 1oz (28g) of the dried herb is steeped in 1pt (550ml) boiling water, cooled, strained and used as a final rinse after shampooing. The oil is also employed commercially in perfumes.

For cookery fennel has been grown since Roman times as a pot-herb and a garnish. Elizabethan cooks coated the seeds with sugar and they were eaten like coriander seeds. Another confection was made by dipping them in white of egg and orange-flower water, sprinkling them with white sugar and drying them before a fire. The stems were tied in bunches, boiled like asparagus and served with butter and vinegar, or the young stalks peeled and eaten like celery. Like celery too, they were earthed up and blanched for salads. The young roots were boiled in salted water and a little vinegar, and served with melted butter. Chopped leaves flavoured sauces, soups and salads, and the dried seeds were used in pickles and marinades, and as a flavouring in cakes.

Today it is most frequently eaten with fish, or in egg and cheese dishes. The roots may be cooked like parsnips, with the fibrous core removed if necessary. In whatever way it is used, fennel will add a slight flavour of anise, and a sprig or two is pleasant with stewed gooseberries.

Fennel vinegar

Take a screw topped glass jar into the garden or the wild, and pack it three-quarters full of the leaf-tops. Slightly warm a bottle of wine vinegar and fill the jar with it. Cover with waxed paper before screwing on the top, to prevent rust.

Florence fennel, or sweet fennel, *F. dulce*, has swollen, delicately flavoured stems which are delicious cooked as a vegetable, and served with white sauce, or fried in butter. Thinly sliced and mixed with a French dressing it is a welcome accompaniment to cold chicken. *F. dulce* is the best for the garden, although the seed is slightly more difficult to germinate. It requires a sunny open position.

Stuffed mackerel with fennel sauce

Clean a large mackerel, or one small mackerel per person. Split and remove backbone. Fill with equal quantities of fennel (*F. vulgare*) and parsley. Season with pepper and salt, and oil it on both sides. Grill or bake, and serve with fennel sauce.

To make the sauce, strip leaves from their stalks, wash and put into a pan of boiling water with a little salt added. Boil for 3 minutes. Mince finely. Put in a sauce boat and pour on some melted butter, mix gently and serve.

FEVERFEW, illustrated here from Chaumeton's *Flore Medicale* after an original by Turpin.

FEVERFEW
Pyrethrum parthenium

A PLANT OF VENUS

A hardy perennial herb, feverfew is both cultivated and grows wild in many parts of the world. It was introduced into Britain from south-east Asia, and was grown in most physic gardens in the 16th and 17th centuries.

The stems are hard and round, with sharply divided yellow-green leaves, and its small white daisy flowers bloom in June and July. The whole plant is strongly aromatic and exceedingly bitter. It grows on poor soil and waste land, but still finds a corner in most cottage gardens. It is generally dispersed, but is inclined to grow singly, and is nowhere abundant. Gerard described the flower as 'a small pale of white leaves set round about a

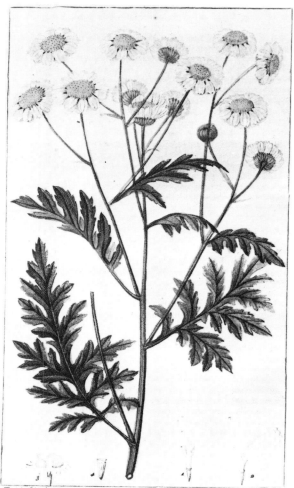

Turpin Pinx.   Lambert Sculp.

yellow ball or button'. He added that 'it joyeth to grow among rubbish'. It was a favourite simpler's plant, and was cried in the London streets.

Here's fetherfew, gillie flowers and rue,
Come, buy my knotted marjoram, ho!

Bacon recommended it 'for windowes and pots'. Its name of feverfew comes from its older name, febrifuga, given for its usefulness in allaying fevers; more frivolously it was called flirtwort, bachelor's buttons and devil daisy. It is thought to be the *parthenium* of Dioscorides, and ranks with chamomile and tansy, to which it is closely allied in its medicinal virtues. It is also known as featherfew.

It is related to the ox-eye daisy and the corn-marigold, and in the garden to pyrethrums and chrysanthemums. Like pyrethrum, feverfew is used in insecticides, which explains why bees avoid the plant. A tincture applied to insect bites and stings gives relief, or sprayed on the skin it acts as a repellent.

It is a woman's plant, for 'Venus commands this herb, and hath commended it to succour sisters . . . and to be a general strengthener of their wombs, and remedy such infirmities as a careless midwife has there caused. If they will but be pleased to make use of her herb boiled in white wine, and drink the decoction, it cleanseth the womb, expels the afterbirth, and doth a woman all she can desire of an herb. And if any grumble because they cannot get the herb in Winter, tell them, if they please, they make a syrup of it in Summer.'

Culpeper's summer syrup was taken for winter coughs, and may still be made from feverfew and honey.

It was prescribed as an antidote against narcotic poisoning and was also considered a valuable poultice herb, with cooling and analgesic properties. In powdered form, it was taken for vertigo, and was used in the treatment of piles. The distilled water was employed as a general cosmetic lotion, and to remove spots.

FIGWORT

Scrophularia nodosa

UNDER THE DOMINION OF VENUS

A perennial plant, figwort is native to Britain and the USA. It is common in woods and ditches, and other damp, shady places.

This unlovable plant has a quadrangular stem which has earned it the odd name of carpenter's square. Its knobby rootstock made it an obvious cure, according to the *Doctrine of Signatures*, for the 'fig' or piles — hence the name figwort — and for varicose veins. Since it was believed to have cured the 'King's evil', it was also called the scrofula plant, of the family *Scrophularia*, and *nodosa*, knotty rooted. The Romans knew it as *cervicaria*, because they said that it cured neck diseases.

It has dark green or purplish-brown sharply toothed leaves, and small dark purple-green or brown flowers in terminal panicles, blooming from June to October. Hard, brown pointed heads contain the seeds. It is deciduous, and grows to a height of 2–4ft (60–120cm). The whole herb is collected in June and dried.

Various superstitions have grown around the figwort, and Gerard noted that 'divers doe rashly teach that if it be hanged about the necke, or else

(*left*) FIGWORT, as depicted by G. Spratt for *Flora Medica*, 1829. The name 'figwort' is applied not only to *Scrophularia nodosa*, shown here, but also popularly to the other *Scrophularia* species, all of which share a characteristic pungent aroma. They are of the same family as foxgloves.

132

FOXGLOVES provide us with the valuable drug digitalis. The variety illustrated here, the purple foxglove from Curtis' *Flora Londinensis*, 1817, is the one commercially grown today for the purpose of extracting the drug.

Digitalis purpurea

[79]

carried around one, it keepeth a man in health'. It was also proof against the 'evil eye', and with St John's wort it was first smoked in fires on St John's eve and then hung in houses and barns against witches. It was used in Wales as a cure for swellings, boils and burns, either as an ointment or merely by binding a fresh leaf around the affected part. The ointment was made for winter use when the fresh herb was not available. A standard infusion of the whole plant sweetened with honey is now used for eczema, rashes and bruises, scratches and small wounds, and for removing freckles.

Although it is bitter tasting and smells unpleasant, the root is edible; it was the only nourishment of the garrison of Rochelle during the whole of the siege by Cardinal Richelieu in 1628. The French have since called it by the honourable name of *herbe de siège*.

FOXGLOVE

Digitalis purpurea

UNDER THE DOMINION OF VENUS

A familiar biennial, foxglove is found wild in the English countryside, particularly along the steep hedge banks of Devon and Cornwall. It may be found naturalized along the Pacific coast from British Columbia to California, and in many places in Europe. It is cultivated in India.

It was first mentioned by Dr Turner in the reign of Queen Mary. 'There is an herbe that groweth in Englande, and specially in Norfolke, about ye cony holes in sandy ground, and in divers woodes, which is called in English Foxgloue. It hath a long stalke, and in the toppe many floures hanginge downe like belles or thumbles.' These 'thumbles' grow in a graduated one-sided spire, pinkish-purple and occasionally white, freckled inside and each tube ending in a pouting turned-down lower lip. They bloom in July, and later develop into small hard brown pepper-pots, from which the tiny seeds are efficiently dispersed.

Although Gerard stated firmly that foxgloves 'are of no use, neither have they any place amongst medicine, according to the Antients', they were recommended by the other herbalists of that time for dropsy. They also used foxglove boiled with honey and water 'to scourge and cleanse the chest'.

The foxglove was finally given its important place in medicine by Dr William Withering, whose work *Account of the Foxglove,* was published in 1785, after ten years' work. Some seeds were sent by Dr Withering to a colleague in the USA. Since then it has been used for the valuable heart drug *digitalis,* which is its chief contribution to the *Pharmacopoeia.* It must be remembered, however, that foxgloves contain a deadly poison. In Ireland it was called dead man's thimbles, in reference to its poisonous qualities, and Culpeper summed it up neatly: 'The operation of this herb, internally taken, is often violent, even in small doses: it is best therefore not to meddle with it, lest the cure should end in the churchyard.'

It seems that weak doses, inadvisable as they might be, are not necessarily fatal, for in *Times Telescope* for 1822 a writer states that 'women of the poorer class in Derbyshire indulged in copious draughts of foxglove-tea, as a cheap means of obtaining the pleasures of intoxication'. It may, if nothing worse, cause headaches, nausea or rashes in some people. Unless you are a doctor or a chemist, then, it is safer to leave the foxglove alone and merely regard it as part of the folklore of the countryside, where it has earned such names as fairy-fingers, fairy-gloves and ladies'-glove from the appearance of its flowers.

Welsh housewives used to make a black dye from its leaves with which they painted crossed lines on the stone floors of their cottages. This was probably done to keep witches away and may have derived from a superstititon held in the Middle Ages that it was an anti-witch plant.

In Kent, a less controversial use was made of the foxglove: the hardened stalks were used for making parasol handles.

GARLIC

Allium sativum

DEDICATED TO MARS

A bulbous plant of the Onion family, garlic is so ancient that its origin cannot be traced, but it seems to belong most happily to the Mediterranean countries. It was first cultivated in England in 1548, but it is now naturalized. For those who can bear its pervasive smell, it is an important and almost daily accompaniment to cooking. It is also a valuable medicine. The bulb is composed of numerous bulblets, known as 'cloves', enclosed within a papery skin. The curious straggly whitish flowers are also partially enclosed in a spathe. Ramsons, the wood garlic, with leaves like those

GARLIC being collected; an illustration from *Tacuinum Sanitatum, c.* 1385.

of lily of the valley and white starry heads of blossoms, is the beauty of the family, but grows in solitude.

Garlic was known to the Chinese in 2000 BC and has been used medicinally by them ever since. Pliny says that divine honours were paid to garlic: the Egyptians placed it among their deities, and no Egyptian priest was permitted to eat it. In one of the Egyptian pyramids an inscription states that 100,000 men were employed on its construction, and these ate garlic, leeks and onions to the value of 1,600 talents of silver. It was one of the staple foods of Egypt where it grew in great abundance.

Galen's description of garlic as the rustic's theriac, or antidote to poison, has become happily translated into poor man's treacle. It is supposed to be strongly aphrodisiac (only between consenting garlic eaters?).

It was believed to have magic properties, and was carried as a talisman in China, Japan, Greece and Turkey. German miners took it with them into the mines as a charm against evil spirits. In country districts it was put in the stockings of children suffering from whooping-cough. More

sensibly, the bruised cloves were mixed with lard and used as a liniment for the same purpose.

Superstition may be dead or dying, but garlic continues to be used in the treatment of diarrhoea, dysentery, ague, rheumatism, colitis, scurvy and high blood pressure. Research is going on in many countries on the use of garlic in the treatment of cancer, and in the prevention and treatment of coronary heart diseases. Chopped garlic may be taken in beef broth or in warm milk, or swallowed as capsules and tablets which leave no odour on the breath. Its use in cooking has rapidly spread since World War II, and small bunches hang in most modern kitchens.

Brazilian liver and rice

1lb (450g) lambs' or calves' liver
1 clove garlic (crushed)
¼pt (137ml) cider-vinegar
steamed rice
2 large onions
pepper
vegetable oil for frying

GINGER appears on the right of this illustration from the 16th-century French work by Platearius, *Livre des Simples Medecines.* The plant in the centre is snakewood, while that on the left is turmeric.

Slice liver thinly and marinade overnight in vinegar, garlic and pepper. Slice onions and fry in hot oil until brown. Take out and keep hot while liver is lightly fried on both sides. Remove liver and pour strained vinegar into pan. When it is almost boiling, add liver. Arrange liver on the steamed rice with onions, pour sauce over and serve.

GINGER

Zingiber officinale

Said to be native to Asia but cultivated in many parts of the Tropics, ginger has been one of the most important trade items of the Far East since antiquity. It was taken to the USA by the Spanish explorers at some time during the 16th century and naturalized soon after. In about 1600 it was introduced into England as a stove exotic by Lord Zouche, traveller and plantsman, owner of a famous garden in Hackney, and friend of Gerard.

'Ginger is most impatient of the coldnesse of these our Northerne regions, as my selfe have found by proofe, for that there have beene brought unto me at severall times sundry plants thereof, fresh, greene, and full of juice, as well from the West Indies, as from Barbary and other places; which have sprouted and budded forth greene leaves in my garden in the heate of Summer, but as soone as it hath beene but touched with the first sharpe blast of Winter, it hath presently perished both blade and root.' That was indeed unfortunate, for Gerard was well aware of its uses and properties. 'Ginger, as Dioscorides reporteth, is right good with meat in sauces and otherwise in conditures, for it is of a heating and digestive quality.'

Hippocrates used it as a medicine, but the Romans valued it for its culinary properties, and its strong aromatic pungency caused it to be added to almost any dish in medieval Europe. *Zingiber* is the ancient name used by both Greeks and Romans.

To the Chinese also it was extremely important; and they would take a small quantity in boiling water as a tea for dyspepsia and loss of appetite. It was also drunk before breakfast.

The valuable creeping rhizomes are known as the 'race'. The likeness of the rhizomes to the convolutions of the human digestive system caused the inclusion of the ginger plant in the *Doctrine of Signatures,* and not for the only time, the *Doctrine* has been proved correct.

Ginger is described as 'black' or 'white'

GINGER, from William Woodville's *Medical Botany*, 1832. Widely cultivated in many parts of the world today, this perennial has many and varied uses: as a condiment; as a flavouring for culinary purposes and in such delicacies as ginger marmalade; and in the treatment of stomach upsets — to name but a few.

according to whether it is peeled or unpeeled. The white, when dried without being scalded, is thought to be the best. Green ginger is the root before drying. It has two kinds of stem, one bearing the leaves, the other the flowers, small and in shape like an orchis, purple, white and yellow. They are traditionally worn by Hawaiian dancers, their *leis* being a combination of jasmine, carnations, gardenias and ginger lilies. The plant grows to a height of 3–4ft (90–120cm).

Ginger is obtainable in crystallized or powdered form. Ginger tea is soothing at the onset of a cold, or for a sore throat. Taken hot it promotes perspiration. It is taken for diarrhoea, sickness, toothache and gout. Raw and crystallized ginger is a pleasant breath sweetener. In the East it is regarded as an aphrodisiac.

In cookery its uses are many and varied.

Lemon ginger syrup

Bruise 4oz (113g) whole ginger and put in a saucepan with 1qt (1l) water and the thinly peeled rind of a lemon. Bring to the boil, and simmer for ¾ hour. Strain, measure, and to every pint (550ml) liquid allow 1lb (450g) sugar and the juice of a small lemon. Put the liquid, sugar and lemon into a saucepan, and boil for 10 minutes, skimming well.

When cold, bottle and seal for storage. Take 1tbsp syrup in a tumbler of boiling water with a slice of lemon on top.

Ginger shortbread

2 breakfastcups flour
8oz (226g) butter
1 small tsp bicarbonate of soda
1 breakfastcup moist brown sugar
2tsp ground ginger
pinch of salt

Mix dry ingredients with moist brown sugar. Work in butter until the whole resembles breadcrumbs. Spread evenly on an oiled baking tin, press down firmly and bake in moderate oven for ¾ hour. Cut into fingers or wedges while still warm in the tin. Remove when cool.

GINSENG

Panax ginseng (Asia)
Panax quinquefolia (North America)

Asiatic ginseng is a native of the mountainous forests of northern China. It has been and is esteemed by the Chinese as an omnipotent herb, and has given rise to many legends, one of which is that it grows only where lightning has struck a clear stream. It has also commanded higher prices than any other medicinal plant. It is regarded as the elixir of life, mild enough to give a baby for colic, and yet allaying fatigue, staying the infirmities of age, increasing mental capacity and prolonging life. It was also the Chinese answer to the mandrake, for its man-shaped roots were believed to cure all the ills of man — or 'gin' in Chinese. The word *Panax* comes from the Greek, *panakos,* a panacea. The prices which these roots fetched depended on the resemblance, and, as in European countries, obliging sculptors could always be found to assist nature in this respect.

P. ginseng is a low perennial herb of the Ivy family, bearing umbellate green flowers on a round purple stalk, about 1ft (30cm) high. The plant grows for 6–7 years before it reaches maturity, and the roots are then harvested. During its growth ginseng root extracts so many minerals, nutrients and valuable trace elements from the soil that the soil is exhausted and needs at least 10 years to recover.

Owing to its popularity ginseng was becoming rare in China during the eighteenth century, when a similar plant, *P. quinquefolium*, was found to be growing in Canada. A consignment was shipped to Canton by the Jesuits in 1718, and a boat load followed from Boston in 1773. Owing to its scarcity, it sold for many times its weight in silver. There was no such dramatic outcome when Peter Collinson introduced it into England in 1740.

GINSENG, as represented by Turpin in Chaumeton's *Flore Medicale.*

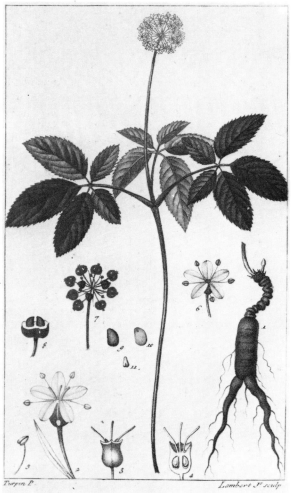

Fig. 3.

Fig. 1.

Fig. 2.

(*left*) GINSENG roots depicted in an 18th-century coloured engraving from Buchoz's *Plantes de la Chine*. It is little wonder that the orientals considered ginseng rather as the equivalent of our western mandrake.

GINSENG of the Chinese variety, *Panax ginseng*, from a German 18th-century engraving, showing the various parts of the plant. The dried ground roots of both this and the North American variety, *P. quinquefolius*, can be infused to make a tranquillizing tea.

The American ginseng, closely related to the Asiatic, and once a wild plant, is now cultivated, although the cultivated plant is considered less efficacious than the wild. It has little or no domestic usefulness, but for years it has been a major American export to China and other countries in the Far East. In the USA it was used only in a few skin ointments, but there are signs, both in the USA and Britain, of increasing interest in the medicinal properties of the plant.

The Russians also are doing scientific work on the ginseng, and they claim that it is effective for insomnia, neurasthenia and general debility, as well as for diabetes and anaemia. Russian cosmonauts have been given it during their space flights.

The fame of ginseng, born of the conjunction of lightning with clear water, is still spreading. Now, having abandoned its bifurcated form, ginseng may be obtained in health food stores in convenience packs of Chinese herb prunes for constipation, and ginseng teabags for almost everything else. Its stimulating effect has led to its being marketed as a legal marijuana substitute.

GOLDEN ROD

Solidago virgaurea

A PLANT OF VENUS

A perennial herbaceous plant, golden rod appears to belong rather to the New World than the Old. Out of 125 species, only two or three occur outside North America. Golden rod is the official state flower of Alabama, Kentucky and Nebraska. The various *Solidago* species vary from 3in (7cm) to 10ft (3m), and all contain a sap from which Thomas Edison at one time hoped to make a rubber substitute. The *Solidago* native to Britain has narrow lance-shaped, slightly toothed leaves, and its numerous tiny golden daisy flowers are carried in panicled racemes on tall stems from July to September. Its heavy, sticky pollen is transported by insects, and not by the wind, and so it is no enemy to those who suffer from asthma and hay fever — in fact it has been held to be good for both ailments.

It is a magic plant, for where golden rod grows secret treasure lies hidden. If it springs at the house door the inmates may look for unexpected fortune. In proper hands, it will act as a divining rod, and discover hidden springs of water.

Since *Solidago* was valued for medicinal purposes, the dried plants were imported and sold by herb women in the London markets during Elizabeth I's reign, for at this time no one had discovered that the plant was growing wild in Hampstead woods. Gerard was first to point this out: 'I have knowne the dried herbe which came from beyond the sea sold in Bucklersbury for half a crowne an ounce. But since it was found in Hampstead wood, even as it were at our townes end, no man will give half a crowne for a hundred weight of it; which planely setteth forth our inconstance and sudden mutabilitie esteeming no longer of anything how pretious soever it be, than whilst it is strange and rare.' Sixty-five years later, the Reverend Thomas Fuller evidently thought that the point might well be embroidered in his *History of the Worthies of England*, saying that 'when golden rod was brought at great expense from foreign countries, it was highly valued; but it was no sooner discovered to be a native plant, than it was discarded'.

GOLDEN rod, as shown in an illustration by G. Spratt for *Flora Medica*, 1829.

Not only was this golden weed valued in England for its medicinal qualities, but people began to realize what a handsome plant it was in the garden: a golden Adonis in summer, and still handsome when grey in autumn. William Cobbett wrote in *The American Gardener* in 1816, 'A yellow flower called the "Plain-weed", which is the torment of the neighbouring farmer, has been above all the plants in this world, chosen as the most conspicuous ornament of the front of the King of England's grandest palace, that of Hampton Court, where, growing in a rich soil to the height of five or six feet, it, under the name of "Golden Rod," nods over the whole length of the edge of a walk, three quarters of a mile long and, perhaps, thirty feet wide, the most magnificent perhaps, in Europe.'

The name *Solidago* means 'makes whole'. It helps to heal wounds and at one time was called woundwort. In America it was known as blue-mountain tea, from the pleasant aromatic tea made from it. This was also popularly spoken of as bohea tea, from the fashionable 18th-century beverage, a name already given to both the finest black China tea and to the poorest. Another common name is Aaron's rod.

Golden rod is carminative, antiseptic, a good tonic, and allays morning sickness. The pulped leaves, stalks and flowers are good for staunching blood, and may be useful in cases of gangrene and tetanus. The American Indians used a lotion of its flowers for bee-stings. It gives a yellowish-tan dye with alum, and with a chrome mordant an old gold.

HEMLOCK

Conium maculatum

A PLANT OF SATURN

A handsome biennial, hemlock is found in waste places and moist soils in many parts of Europe. It has been introduced into North and South America. One of the Umbelliferae, it is related to parsnip, carrot, celery, fennel and parsley. It has a smooth stem, blotched with red or purple, and legend says that the spots signify the mark of Cain, which was put upon his brow after he had murdered Abel. The leaves are a dull green colour, ferny and elegantly divided. Umbels of minute white flowers appear from June to August and like so many poisonous plants, it has a fetid smell. Culpeper said that it stops 'lustful thoughts', and

no doubt it does, since it is likely to put an end to *all* thoughts! Domestic animals and insects avoid it, although the song thrush makes a meal of its seeds without disaster.

It is commonly known as poison parsley, poison root, poison snakeweed, devil's flower and bad man's oatmeal. Germans regard it as belonging to the infernal regions, and Russians call it the satanic herb.

Hemlock has a dark history, for it was the execution cup of ancient Greece. In Rome it was mixed with opium and taken by philosophers weary of life and dreading the infirmities of old age. Dioscorides said that it was so poisonous that 'whosoever taketh of it into his body dieth remediless, except the party drank some wine before the venom hath taken the heart'.

Early books on magic suggested dipping the sorcerer's black handled knife into the blood of a black cat mixed with hemlock juice before tracing the magic circle in which to stand before calling up demons. 'Root of hemlock, digg'd i' the dark' was considered the most potent when used at night.

The powerful narcotic drug called *conium* which hemlock contains, comes from the dried unripe fruit. In medieval times it was discovered that a drop of this juice on a piece of sweet pastry might be taken once a day as a preventative against cholera. It was also used as a remedy for hernia, pleurisy, epilepsy, fainting and double vision.

Conium is sedative and antispasmodic, and is used *under medical advice* as an antidote to other poisons. As an inhalation it is prescribed for bronchitis, whooping-cough and asthma. Culpeper says: 'If the root thereof be roasted under the embers, wrapped in double wet paper, until it is soft and tender, and then applied to the gout in the hands and fingers, it will quickly help this evil.'

HEMP

Cannabis sativa

A PLANT OF SATURN

An annual herbaceous plant, hemp is indigenous to northern India, southern Siberia and the western parts of Asia. It is thought that it may be native to Europe as there are records of its growth for nearly 2,600 years. According to Herodotus (born 484 BC), the Scythians, who lived in Europe north of the Danube bordering the Black Sea, used hemp, although the Greeks were scarcely acquainted with it at that time. However, it is

Plate 30

HEMLOCK, shown in a late 18th-century plate from William Curtis' *Lectures in Botany*.

possible that the Scythians may have introduced the plant from central Asia and from Russia, when they migrated westward in about 1500BC, a little before the Trojan War. It has been cultivated in Africa, Turkey, Italy, Spain, Persia, Egypt, the East Indies, the USA, Canada, France, Denmark and Sweden. It was in cultivation in England by 1626.

This plant of the Nettle family may grow to any height from 3 to 18ft (1 to 5.4m), according to climate and conditions. It has rough, hairy, angular branched stems with opposite palmate leaves consisting of five to seven narrow, coarsely serrated leaflets. The upper side is dark green,

ANAGYRIS.

HEMP, *Cannabis sativa*, widely cultivated not only for the narcotic drug but also for its oil and fibres. The illustration to the right is from Mattioli's *Commentarii*, 1554. The illustration below is a late 19th-century copy of a mid 14th-century original showing hemp fibres being carded and spun in England: presumably the fibres had been imported.

HEMP, on the left, and hops, from an English *Herbal and Bestiary ABC*
from the early 16th century. The hop plant, *Humulus lupulus*,
is cultivated worldwide, the female inflorescences being used in the
making of beer.

although the underside is lighter, rough and furrowed. Male and female flowers grow upon separate plants. Male plants are more slender and delicate than the female and the male flowers grow near the top of the stem in clusters, each bearing nine or ten small green blooms. The fibres composing the bark are finer and more elastic than those of the female. Male plants grow faster than the female and about 6in (15cm) higher to enable the farina of the stamina to be diffused on to the pistil of the female. The female stem is topped by tufts of large leaves and the small ash-coloured fruit grows on its stem. The male plants are pulled in the beginning of July, but the female plants are not pulled until four or five weeks later, when they have ripened their seeds.

Pliny said that the root, juice and other parts possessed wonderful medicinal virtues, which he regarded as more useful than the manufacture of cordage, which had been used for shipping more than 200 years BC.

It was woven into the hangman's rope for the first time in 1532, and earned the names of gallowgrasse and neckweede. More happily, it was made into stout cloth for country people, which was known as hempen home-spun; this name has been transferred to the wearers, as when, in *A Midsummer Night's Dream*, Puck appears among the rustics saying,

What hempen home-spuns have we swaggering here,
So near the cradle of the fairy queen?

The spinning of hemp and flax was part of the housewife's lot, as Sir Anthony Fitzherbert in his *Boke of Husbandrie*, 1523, says: 'And thereof may they make sheets, broadcloths, towels, shirts, smocks, and such other necessaries, and thereof let thy distaff be always ready for a pastime, that thou be not idle.' The fibres of hemp are longer and coarser than those of flax. The huckaback towels that hung on rollers behind our great-grandmothers' kitchen doors were still being made of coarse hemp fibre, and so were the doormats and the shepherds' smock-frocks, with their wonderfully elaborate self-coloured embroidered gathering, that took the name of smocking. In past ages in China, not only was hemp used for cloth and cordage, but its long fibrous canes were brandished over a sick man's bed to drive away the evil spirits that were believed to haunt him.

Hemp seeds yield an oil which the Russians use in cookery, and which was used in Britain in the making of paints and varnish. The seeds are good and nutritious food for poultry, and are mixed with other seeds for cage birds. Where hemp is found growing wild in Britain, it is likely that the seed has been dropped by birds. For a time hemp was cultivated in Dorset, Somerset, Suffolk, Norfolk, the Lincolnshire Fens and Yorkshire, but never extensively; although Defoe, in his *Tour Thro' The Whole Island Of Britain* records many hundreds of acres of hemp in Norfolk in 1727.

Its hallucinatory properties were known to primitive peoples, and with civilization came the belief that nepenthes, Homer's magic potion with the power to make unhappy mortals forget their grief, was indeed hemp. The narcotic qualities lie in the leaf, and thus it was called 'the Leaf of Delusion'. It was thought dangerous to sleep in a field of hemp. The word 'assassin' is said to come from the savagery arising from the use of hashish, a derivative of hemp.

In growing, the plant has been found to have the remarkable property of destroying all surrounding weeds, and it has been used as a ground-cleanser for this purpose. It also keeps away the cabbage white butterfly and its caterpillars.

Culpeper had a number of medicinal uses for hemp. A decoction of the seed, he suggested, 'stayeth bleeding at the mouth, nose or other places, some of the leaves being fried with the blood of them that bleed, and so given them to eat', and to help them, it is hoped, to a speedy recovery.

Although hemp may be used in the treatment of rheumatism, influenza and colds, dropsy, pleurisy, catarrh, jaundice, asthma, diphtheria, and many lesser ills, it is variable and unstable, and is regarded as unreliable. In the past it has been well thought of for the relief of migraine and neuralgia, and ironically, as an aid to withdrawal from alcohol and opiates. The restrictions now placed on the usage of cannabis have resulted in the slowing down of its employment in medicine, and it should on no account be taken without professional advice.

HENBANE
Hyoscyamus niger

A PLANT OF SATURN

A biennial, henbane is found widely throughout central and southern Europe, and naturalized in the USA and Brazil. It is not considered to be a true native of Britain, but it occurs fairly frequent-

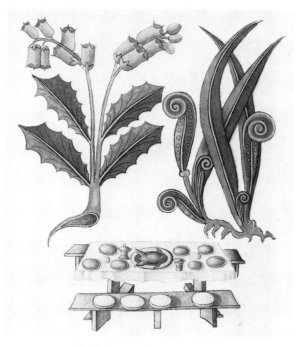

HENBANE, on the left, and hart's-tongue, from an early 16th-century English manuscript. From henbane, an ill-smelling and poisonous herb, can be derived the dangerous narcotic alkaloid poison hyoscyamine, a major source of the drug atropine. Hart's-tongue, *Scolopendrium vulgare*, is a fern which gains its name from the shape of the fronds.

ly, probably having in the first place escaped from old herb gardens. It now frequents graveyards, ruined buildings and abandoned chalk quarries, and fortunately is less common than it was in Culpeper's day. His description of its habitat does little to improve the image of this unattractive plant. 'Henbane delights most to grow in Saturnine places, and whole cart loads of it may be found near the places where they empty the common Jakes, and scarce a ditch is to be found without it growing by it.' It is not surprising, therefore, to hear that it belongs to the potentially dangerous Nightshade family, to which belong the potato, tomato and tobacco — and belladonna.

Most suitably henbane was believed to be a witches' plant, and was one of the ingredients of sabbat ointment with which they smeared themselves before flying off on their ungodly revels. It also furnished one of the ingredients of their love potions. The plant has thick, soft woolly leaves which lie on the ground, and a root like a parsnip. Both stems and foliage are covered with long, clammy hairs, and even to touch the plant is unpleasant, for its leaves transfer their nauseous smell to the fingers. When burnt, the plant crackles and sparkles in an ominous manner.

The flowers are a dingy yellow, pencilled with purple veins, usually displaying a purple eye in the centre. They grow in one-sided clusters in June, and these develop into two-celled capsules enclosed in the calyx, containing dark grey seeds that resemble poppy seeds. The plant is poisonous to poultry, hence the name henbane.

The medicinal uses of henbane are ancient. Both Dioscorides and Celsus prescribed it in the first century, and in the Middle Ages it was used on a sponge as an early anaesthetic. Operations under these conditions could be extremely hazardous, since the patient was likely to wake up during the proceedings, for it was not known how long the effects of the narcotic would last.

The old healers believed that a seeded branch of henbane resembled a jaw with teeth, and thus, according to the *Doctrine of Signatures*, it was used for those suffering from toothache. Anodyne necklaces, made of the root, were given to babies to wear during teething, and it was smoked by country people as a cure for toothache. Like belladonna, an extract was used by oculists for dilating the eyes. Today, tinctures and drops are sometimes prescribed for ear-ache, but it is a drug to be used only under medical direction.

HEPATICA

Anemone Hepatica species

The hepaticas, *H. acutiloba*, *H. americana* and *H. nobilis*, are native to the USA, Canada and parts of Europe. In Britain hepatica is better known as a garden plant, *Anemone Hepatica*. In most countries they are all called liverwort or liver-leaf, because the lobed leaf was supposed to resemble the shape

HEPATICA, or liverwort, rather simplistically depicted in *The Grete Herball*, 1529.

(left) HEPATICA, from G. C. Oeder's *Flora Danica.*

of the liver. The name hepatica comes from the Greek, *hepatikos*, of the liver, and was adopted by the *Doctrine of Signatures* for this plant which was believed to be the cure for all liver diseases.

English liverwort, *Peltigera canina*, is a lichen of an entirely different family, but with the same reputation as a remedy for liver complaints, although it was also regarded as a cure for rabies. It was first recommended against rabies by Mr Dampier, brother of the famous circumnavigator of that name, and was adopted into the *London Pharmacopoeia* in 1721.

The English liverwort was also known as the ash-coloured liverwort, and was pronounced by Culpeper to be under the dominion of Jupiter and the sign of Cancer. Sir John Hill did his best to clear up a confusing situation in his book *Eden, or a Compleat Body of Gardening*, in 1757. 'All the Old Writers name it; and its common title is Hepatica, or *Hepatica nobilis*. Our English Herbalists have translated their Names into Liverwort, and Noble Liverwort; but the Gardener preserves the Latin Term *Hepatica*.'

In *A Modern Herbal* (1976 edition) Mrs Grieve has the liverworts clearly divided as Liverwort, American, *Anemone Hepatica*, and Liverwort, English, *Peltigera canina*, and says that it is the lichen, the ash-coloured liverwort, that is 'held in esteem as a remedy for liver complaints'. The former, American liverwort, Mrs Grieve quotes as 'an innocent herb which may be taken freely in infusion and syrup. It is a mild remedy in disorders of the liver, indigestion, etc'.

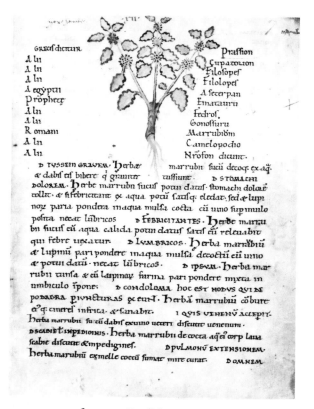

HOREHOUND, from an English manuscript dated about AD 1100 in the possession of the Bodleian Library, Oxford.

for this companionship, it supplied a valuable if evil tasting medicine for gout. An infusion of equal parts of black and white horehound and betony is good for rheumatism.

HOREHOUND, BLACK

Ballota nigra

A PLANT OF MERCURY

This dismal looking poor relation of *Marrubium vulgare* also has its useful qualities, although its name *Ballota* comes from a Greek word meaning 'rejected', because cattle refused to eat it.

It grows to a height of 3–4ft (90–120cm) has branched stems and dusty-looking hairy leaves, and dull purplish-red flowers which appear from June to October. It is a plant of towns and villages, settling near houses and travelling with man. Black horehound may be found wherever the English colonist has settled, even as far from home as the sheep-rearing stations of Australia. In return

HOREHOUND, WHITE

Marrubium vulgare

An herbaceous perennial, white horehound is native to many parts of Europe, including Britain, where it flourishes particularly in Norfolk and Suffolk. It is naturalized in the USA. It is a homely, woolly-looking plant, with greyish-green crinkly paired leaves, clothed in felty white hairs. Its tiny white two-lipped flowers bloom from June to September, making it an attractive plant for the herb garden. It has a pleasant musky scent. It was known to the Egyptians who dedicated it to Horus.

Walahfrid Strabo, the squint-eyed monk, grew it in his physic garden in 842, and wrote in his *Hortulus*:

HOREHOUND, from Mattioli's *Commentarii*, 1554.

*A precious herb, though biting
And sharp on the tongue where it tastes so unlike
its scent: for whereas the scent is sweet, the taste
Is not sweet at all.*

Horehound was once cried in the streets of London. Horehound cough-drops were sold by the itinerant traders who wheeled their stalls full of their home-made stock-in-trade on barrows to their stands. One had his stand in Holborn, where he sold his cough cures in the form of sticks or drops. Horehound, coltsfoot and other herbs lay in a dried state on the stall, as well as a few bottles of the mixture. The horehound sticks were a halfpenny each, neatly wrapped in paper. His cry was, 'Long life candy! Candy from herbs!'

The plant had many domestic uses: handfuls of the felty leaves were used by dairymaids to wash out the milk-pails; the dry calices made wicks for clay lamps; and the stems were floated on oil for nightlights.

Many cottages in East Anglia grew horehound in their gardens for the making of beer, as well as syrup of horehound for coughs and colds. Boiled with woodsage and sugar it made a cooling drink, woodsage beer, which was drunk by the men at harvesting. Horehound candy was made by housewives for catarrh, and horehound tea was brewed from the fresh leaves in boiling water, flavoured with honey. In Wales an infusion of the chopped leaf was used internally and externally for eczema and shingles. In the American countryside horehound was gathered to make medicine for throat and lungs, and horehound tea was taken as a laxative.

Its uses are fewer today, but it is a pleasant flavouring for cakes and candy, and it is still used in the USA for cough-drops. The tops of the young shoots are gathered by herbalists for dyspepsia, jaundice, croup, asthma and bronchitis.

HOUSELEEK

Sempervivum tectorum

UNDER THE DOMINION OF JUPITER

A mysterious plant with an ancient history, houseleek is native to the mountain ranges of central and southern Europe, and of the Greek Islands. It grows plentifully in Tenerife, covering the steep cliffs and rocks near the sea. The Greeks employed it as a love philtre and many centuries ago it was introduced into Britain, where it was grown on cottage roofs as a guardian against lightning and fire. Thus it was grown in the days of Charlemagne, King of the Franks and Emperor of Rome, who ordered that every householder in the empire should grow houseleeks on his roof. It was then called Jupiter's beard in the hope that Jupiter would recognize the compliment and withhold his lightning. So it has grown for 2,000 years. Today it is also grown as a pot-plant, as in Rome it was once grown in vases outside houses.

The light green leaves grow directly from the fibrous rootstock in rose-like tufts, sharply pointed and full of juice. Gerard described them as 'fat, well-bodied ... an inch long or somewhat more, like little tongues, very curiously minced in

L. *Sedum maius*
G. *Joubarbe*
A. *Houfleeke*
Ge. *Hauswurtz.*

HOUSELEEK, from Crispin de Pas' *Hortus Floridus*, 1614.

with cream it may be applied to relieve the discomforts of vaccination. It is healing in cases of erysipelas and ringworm. Houseleek juice mixed with honey is prescribed for the mouth condition 'thrush', and an ointment is made from the plant for ulcers, burns, scalds and inflammations. In large doses it may be emetic and purgative.

HYSSOP
Hyssopus officinalis

A PLANT OF JUPITER, UNDER THE SIGN OF CANCER

A perennial herb, native to southern Europe, hyssop was introduced into Britain by Gerard in about 1596, and later into the warmer parts of the USA. Its sturdy stems are square, branched and downy, woody at the bottom, and growing to about 2ft (60cm). The leaves are long, elliptical, deep green and grow in pairs. The flowers, rose-coloured to bluish-purple, appear from June to September. The whole plant is powerfully scented and pungent to taste. It belongs to the Mint family. It is a pleasant, clean and orderly plant, admirably fitted to its early purpose of edging the Tudor knot-gardens. Old mazes, too, were sometimes set with hyssop, but although it is perennial and evergreen it is best regarded as an annual, since it is not entirely hardy.

When John Parkinson finished his much loved book, *Paradisi in Sole Paradisus Terrestris*, 1629, and began on his herbal, *Theatrum Botanicum*, an immense work of 1,748 pages, he chose hyssop as the first herb of 'The First Tribe': 'From a Paradise of pleasant Flowers I am fallen (Adam like) to a world of profitable Herbes and Plants, namely those Plants that are frequently used to help the diseases of our bodies: in which world or sea of Simples, I have propounded to my selfe this methode; to distribute them in sundry Classes or Tribes that so neere as may be, and is most convenient, shall be sorted out those severall Herbes — Plants that are fit for each Tribe, that so they may be found in one place together: and first of the *Hisopes.*'

He gave a short description of fifteen different varieties — but the virtues of only one — which may be safely used until the true hyssop is known. By the 'true hyssop' he meant the hyssop of the Bible, the herb of Moses and the herb of David, for David said, 'Purge me with hyssop, and I shall be clean; wash me, and I shall be whiter than snow'.

The hyssop of Scripture was a purification

the edges'. The rosy star-like flowers, on stems that are covered with scaly leaves, are believed by some to be unlucky, and are cut off as soon as they appear in June and July. The plant spreads neatly, by offsets, and even in time of drought its succulent leaves seem to contain all the nourishment it requires. It is considered unlucky to pull it up.

Houseleek seldom seems to die, hence its name *Sempervivum*. Sengren, another ancient name, means evergreen. It is less easy to find a reason for its popular Dorset name, welcome-home-husband-though-never-so-late (or-drunk). *Sempervivum* was taken to the New World, and was probably an easier passenger than most plants. John Josselyn reported in 1672 that 'it prospereth notably'.

Medicinally, it was used for St Anthony's fire, shingles, gout, and as a vermifuge. It was pulped and applied to the skin for rashes and inflammations, and as a wart- and corn-remover. The juice was also dropped into eyes and ears, and sometimes boiled in milk and the strained milk given to reduce a fever. Nettle-stings, mosquito-bites and bee-stings respond to its cooling juice, and mixed

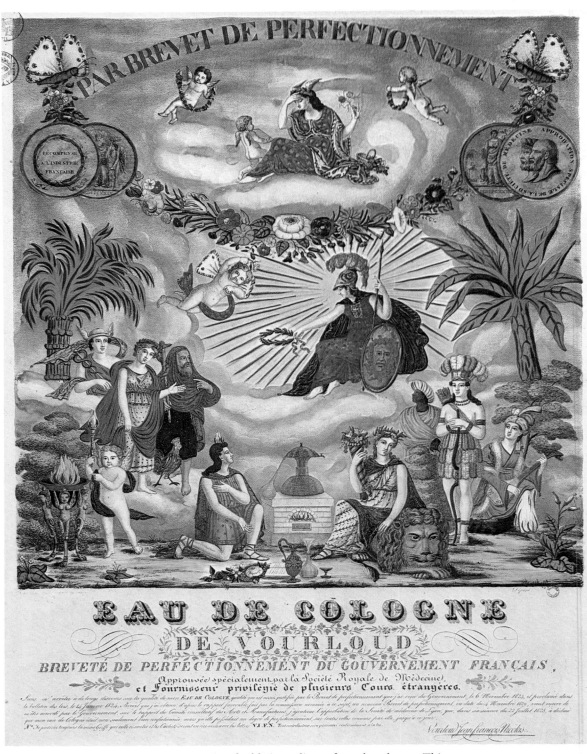

HYSSOP is an invaluable ingredient of eau de cologne. This
advertisement, dating from about 1820, extols the virtues of
Vourloud's eau de cologne, recommended for its guarantee of
perfection.

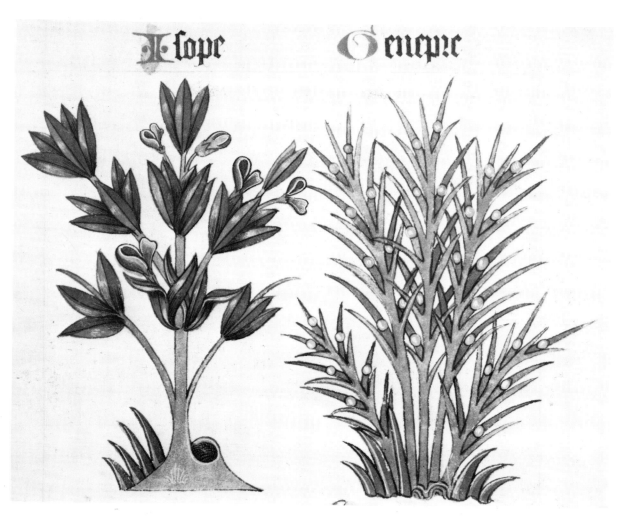

Ffope   Genepre

HYSSOP, on the left, and Juniper, from an early 16th-century manuscript. Originally cultivated for medicinal purposes, hyssop is now used primarily in the kitchen. Junipers are evergreen trees and shrubs of the genus *Juniperus*; illustrated here is the common European species *J. communis*, whose pungent-tasting berries yield oil of juniper, whose best known use is in the manufacture of gin.

herb, used in cleansing lepers and leprous houses, and the arguments over the true biblical hyssop have lasted unresolved for centuries. It was used for the consecration of Westminster Abbey — no doubt a ritual cleansing ceremony.

Parkinson also said that hyssop was used 'of many people in the Country to be laid unto cuts and fresh wounds, being bruised and applyed eyther alone, or with a little sugar'. It was homely, safe and available, and much used in the domestic medicines of the people, as 'more easy for the parson's purse and more familiar for all men's bodies'. It·was familiar, too, in nosegays and as a strewing herb, and it was cried in the London streets.

The butterflies loved it, the bees loved it (hyssop honey is delicious and contains all the medicinal properties of the herb), above all the people loved it. To improve their complexions they were told to drink six spoonfuls of the juice of hyssop in warm ale in a morning and fast. They drank hyssop tea, and tied it into muslin bags and dipped it into boiling water for black and blood-shot eyes. The hot vapours were taken by a funnel in at the ears 'to ease inflammations and the singing noise of them'. They anointed each other's heads with its oil to remove lice.

Herbalists today use hyssop to relieve catarrh and reduce mucus, to clear the chest and to calm the nerves. For these purposes, a strong infusion mixed with honey and oil of almonds is good. It helps to regulate too high or too low blood-pressure, and it is safe enough to give to children for coughs.

Though not a cooking herb, its flowers are used to decorate salads, and it is employed in the making of Chartreuse and Benedictine. It is also a valuable component of eau de cologne.

The following is an old receipt from *The New London Family Cook.*

Queen Elizabeth's cordial electuary of hyssop

Boil a pint of the best honey; and having carefully taken off all the scum, put into this clarified liquid a bundle of Hyssop which has been well bruised before being tied up. Let them boil together till the honey tastes strongly of the Hyssop — then strain

JIMSON WEED, Jamestown weed or thorn apple, as depicted in *Flora Medica*, 1829. From this poisonous annual can be derived, as from henbane, the dangerous narcotic hyoscyamine.

the Honey very well and add a quarter of an ounce of pulverised liquorice root and the same of aniseed with half the quantity of pulverised elecampana root and angelica root and a pennyweight each of pepper and ginger.

Let all boil together for a short time and stir well — then pour into gallipots and stir till cold. Keep covered for use and whenever troubled with straightness at the stomach, or shortness of breath, take some of the electuary, which will very soon give relief.

JIMSON WEED
Datura stramonium

An annual plant, jimson weed is found on waste ground, in pastures, gardens and roadsides all over

JOE PYE WEED: an engraving by David Weber after Foster, 1819.

[98]

LAVENDER being sold on the streets of London: a watercolour, dated 1806, by W. M. Craig.

North and South America, and in many other parts of the world. It is rare in Britain.

The root is large, white and divided, and the stem thick, erect and smooth. The leaves, which are dark green above and lighter green beneath, are irregularly toothed, large and pointed. The beautiful white or violet trumpet-shaped flowers, which bloom from June to September, are followed by prickly green capsules containing many black seeds. The leaves produce a nauseating odour, while the flowers are sweetly scented but dangerous to smell, as giddiness may result. The flowers open in the late afternoon and are visited by moths which effect pollination. In exchange for this service, caterpillars feed on the plants unharmed, despite the fact that the whole plant is poisonous to humans and animals. At night, the leaves rise to protect the delicate flowers.

Jimson weed belongs to the Nightshade family and possesses the same virtues and dangers as belladonna. It is believed that the priests of Apollo at Delphi made use of its narcotic properties to assist them in their prophecies.

The plant is a native of India, where its properties were understood. Dancing girls drugged wine with the seeds in order to rob their victims, and they became so familiar with the effects that they could make a man mad for as long or as short a period as they wished, in the knowledge that the victim would have no memory of what had occurred. The Indians know this plant as drunkard, deceiver, madman and fool-maker.

There are six varieties in the USA; the popular name derives from Jamestown, Virginia. According to settlers' accounts of the period, newcomers gathered the tender shoots in spring, and boiled them for pot-herbs. Some soldiers in the district ate the new vegetables, became wildly intoxicated and committed all kinds of outrageous extravagances. After their recovery, they had no memory of what had occurred.

For good or ill Britain may put the responsibility firmly on the head of Gerard for the introduction of this dangerous plant, which he obtained from his friend Lord Zouche. He made good use of it in surgery, and recommended boiling it with hog's grease as a salve for 'all inflammations whatsoever, all manner of burnings or scaldings, as well of fire, water, boiling lead, gun-pouder, as that which comes by lightning'. The first experience came from Colchester, where 'Mistress Lobel a merchant's wife there being most grievously burned by lightning, and not finding ease or cure in any other thing, by this found helpe and was perfectly cured when all hope was past'.

Jimson weed (also known as thorn apple) is now known to be antispasmodic, anodyne and narcotic, with the same properties as belladonna. Medicinal cigarettes and pipe tobacco have been made of it for sufferers from asthma, or it can be ground and used as an inhalant. It must never be used except under medical direction. Its common names of mad-apple, devil's-apple and stinkweed are warning enough.

JOE PYE WEED
Eupatorium purpureum

A North American perennial, Joe Pye weed is found in moist woods and meadows, where it likes to grow along streams. Its woody rootstock produces white-pithed stems which are tall and graceful and streaked with purple. These grow from 3 to 10ft (1 to 3m) high. The leaves are thick textured, rough above and downy beneath, with sharply serrated edges. The flowers appear in loose terminals of white, pink to purple, magenta and crimson in August and September.

The plant has received its genetic name *Eupatorium* from Mithradatus Eupator, King of Pontus, and its common name from Joe Pye, a New England Indian medicine man. Joe Pye was famous for his cures of typhus and other fevers with his decoctions made from this plant.

Learning from the Indian women, who bathed their ailing children in an infusion of the root, white settlers gathered it and used it for all kinds of medical purposes. Its astringent and diuretic properties made it a dependable medicine for rheumatism, backache, neuralgia, dropsy and all kinds of urinary disorders. It was also called gravelroot, for its use in the treatment of this latter condition.

LAVENDER
Lavandula vera

A PLANT OF MERCURY

An evergreen perennial, lavender is a shrub of the Mint family, native to the Mediterranean coast, and cultivated in France, Italy and England. It is now grown for perfume in Australia.

In spite of its Mediterranean origins, lavender seems to belong in its very essence and its cool blue-grey undertones to the cloudier skies of English gardens. It belongs to the cottage garden

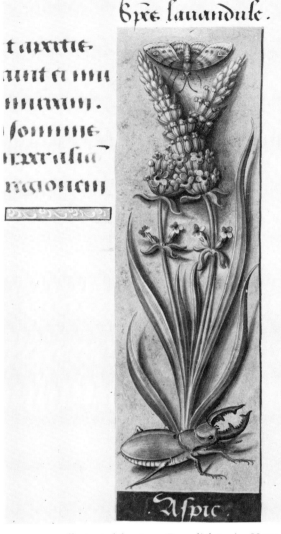

LAVENDER, illustrated by Jean Bourdichon in *Hours of Anne of Burgundy*, a French 16th-century work now in the possession of the Bibliothèque Nationale, Paris. There are a number of species of lavender (genus *Lavandula*), all of which seem to be blessed with wholesome qualities.

as surely as it belongs to the formal garden and this unobtrusive plant, magnificently responding to grey English days, still produces the finest lavender in the world — although perhaps less abundantly than in the past.

L. vera, the common English lavender, grows 1–3ft (30–90cm) high. A decorous and puritan plant, it has crooked, many branched stems and numerous erect, broom-like spikes composed of whorls of bluish-violet, strongly scented labiate flowers that bloom from June until September.

Spike lavender, *L. spica*, is a coarser, broad leaved variety, found in the mountain districts of France and Spain. Together with *L. stoechas*, it produces a dark green oil which is used with turpentine in the making of fine varnishes and lacquers, for painting on porcelain.

Dwarf lavender, more compact and with flowers of deeper colour, is more suitable for borders. There is also a rare white lavender, which Queen Henrietta Maria grew in her garden at Wimbledon.

In a book entitled *New England's Rarieties Discovered*, John Josselyn reported that 'lavender is not for the climate'. Nevertheless, in a Boston newspaper of 30 March, 1760, lavender was advertised for sale.

The Romans used lavender to perfume their baths — hence its name which is derived from *lavare*, to wash. It was one of the herbs dedicated to Hecate, the goddess of witches and sorcerers, and to her two daughters Medea and Circe. In spite of this, it was used to avert the 'evil eye'.

Lavender water is one of the oldest English perfumes. Its earliest mention is in the work of Abbess Hildegarde, who lived in the 12th century and who described the strong odour and many virtues of the plant in a chapter entitled '*De Lavendula*'.

William Langham in *The Garden of Health*, 1579, found many uses for lavender. 'Smell often to it to comfort and cleare the sight. Boyle it in water and wett thy shirt in it and dry it again and weare it ... Shread the herbe with the flowers and distill it and drinke two ounces of the water to helpe giddinesse of the head and rub the head all over with it and let it dry by itself ... Seathe Lavender in water and temper thy wine therewith and also make a syrope with the said water and use it against swooning and to comfort the heart.'

In 1387, cushions stuffed with 'lavende' were made for Charles VI of France. A recipe for lavender water written about 1615 directs the distilling of the flowers with canella (wild cinnamon), wallflowers, galingall (*Cyperus longus*) and grains of paradise in water.

A recipe of the Stuart period for 'A Sweet-scented Bath', lists the following: 'Roses, Citrus flowers, Orange flowers, Jasmine, Bays, Rosemary, Lavender, Mint, Pennyroyal, and Citron peel, each a sufficient quantity, boyle them together gently, and make a bath, to which add Oyl of Spike 6 drops, Musk 5 grains, Ambergrease 3 grains ... Let her go into the Bath before meat.'

'Lavender is almost wholly spent with us,'

wrote Parkinson, 'for to perfume linnen, apparell, gloues and leather and the dryed flowers to comfort and dry up the moisture of a cold braine.'

Not only was it placed between linen in the housewife's press, to perfume the sheets and prevent moth, but it was strewn on the floors of houses and churches to keep off the plague. On St Barnabas' day the churches were decked with garlands of roses, box, woodruff and lavender.

Gerard said that a conserve of the flowers with sugar was good for migraine, faintness, and 'the panting and passion of the heart . . . if the quantitie of a beane be taken thereof in the morning fasting'.

Culpeper gave a recipe containing flowers of lavender, horehound, fennel and asparagus root, with a little cinnamon, for 'giddiness and turning of the brain' — although it is unlikely that anyone would be willing to uproot their asparagus, even in such a good cause.

Lavender heads soaked in brandy or gin was once an acceptable farmhouse restorative. By the 18th century the English House of Yardley had a flourishing soap and perfumery business in London, and their famous lavender water was a great commercial success.

But when the bees were busy in the Mitcham lavender fields and harvesters wore a sprig of lavender under their hats to guard against headaches in the hot sun, time went slowly by. The days are past when the flowers were cut by hand, loaded into wheelbarrows, turned and shovelled into furnaces for distillation, and women sang in the streets;

Come buy! Come and buy my sweet lavender!
Only two bunches for a penny!

The lavender fields of Mitcham are now lost beneath suburbia, but no doubt some corners of small gardens are still fresh and sweet with a plant or two. London street names remain such as Lavender Hill, Lavender Street, Lavender Lane and Lavender Sweep. Lavender has found wider skies in Lincolnshire, Norfolk, Suffolk, Cambridgeshire and Kent, for it is still needed for soaps, lotions, bath liquids and shampoos. Much is exported to the USA, where it is still known as Mitcham Lavender.

Oil of lavender is used for a number of medicinal purposes.

LIQUORICE, shown above as illustrated in the English 16th-century work *Herbal and Bestiary ABC*. The picture shows also, on the left, ivy, *Hedera helix*, a popular climbing plant both outside and inside the home.

LIQUORICE, as illustrated in *Tacuinum Sanitatum, c.* 1385.

LIQUORICE

Glycyrrhiza glabra
G. lepida

UNDER THE DOMINION OF MERCURY

A perennial shrub, liquorice is native to south-east Europe and south-west Asia; it also grows in northern China and Mongolia. It was introduced into Britain by the Black Friars in the 16th century and later was cultivated extensively in the Pontefract district of Yorkshire. The plant is very deeply rooted, and penetrates to a depth of 3–4ft (90–120cm). It has a woody rootstock, wrinkled and brown on the outside and yellow within, which has a sweet taste. The leaves are composed of three to seven dark green leaflets. Yellowish-purple or white bean flowers bloom from June until August, giving place to flat smooth pods containing hard round seeds.

It was cultivated around London in about 1560 and later in Godalming in Surrey and Worksop in Nottinghamshire; the extensive and important liquorice grounds in Pontefract were not worked until the end of the 17th century. It was cultivated in Italy and Spain, and exported to America for sweetening tobacco. The type known as Spanish liquorice usually comes from Italy.

Gerard grew it in his garden in Holborn, and so did Parkinson, who in his garden book places it among 'such herbes as are of most necessary uses for the Country Gentlewomens houses'.

For the making of liquorice, the roots were macerated and boiled, and the resulting liquid concentrated into a solid extract. It was rolled into long cylindrical sticks and used for many medicinal purposes, and by brewers in the manufacture of porter. In medicine it was sold as liquorice powder, liquorice water and in the form of troches — little flat cakes — sometimes impressed with the name of the place where they were made. These were generally referred to as Pontefract cakes, and resembled nothing so much as mourning seals for black-edged envelopes.

Pontefract cakes and liquorice 'bootlaces' are obviously regarded as extremely palatable by the young; but the worst injustice ever inflicted on innocent childhood was the forcible administration of a 'black draught' of the same herb reinforced with cascara for the doubtful benefit of the child's health.

Liquorice was a favourite medicine with ancient physicians. Dioscorides knew of it as *Glycyrrhiza*, from the Greek meaning a sweet root. Culpeper recommended 'the fine powder of Liquorice blown through a quill into the eyes that have a pin and web (as they call it)'. Presumably he meant a cataract. He added, more acceptably, that 'the juice in distilled Rose-water, with some gum-tragacanth, is a fine licking medicine for hoarseness, wheezing, etc'. Another old recipe for that purpose was for liquorice boiled with maidenhair and figs.

American liquorice, *Glycyrrhiza lepida,* was an old country remedy for earache, for which the leaves were steeped and the liquid used as ear-drops. The fresh roots were chewed for tooth-ache, and the boiled roots given for fevers. For some time past it has been successfully used in the treatment of peptic ulcers.

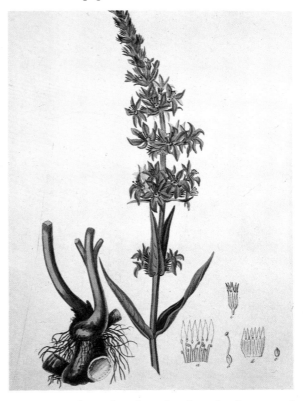

LOOSESTRIFE, shown here in a plate from Stephenson and Churchill's *Medical Botany*, 1834.

LOOSESTRIFE, PURPLE

Lythrum salicaria

A HERB OF THE MOON

A perennial herb purple loosestrife grows in many parts of the world, including Belgium, France, Holland, Germany, Spain, central Asia, North

America, Britain and Australia. Almost as handsome as the foxglove, and of a somewhat similar purplish-red, it is a pity that it is a stranger to our gardens, while the yellow loosestrife, an entirely unrelated plant, is common to many.

Purple loosestrife frequents damp and marshy waterside places, reaching about 4ft (120cm) from a thick branched root. The plant is slender rather than bushy, with stems sharply angled, ordinarily four-cornered but sometimes hexagonal. The leaf is similar in shape to a willow leaf, from which it gets its country names of purple willow strife and willow-lythrum. It is sometimes called red Sally, again referring to the willow, and to its specific name of *salicaria*. The leaves, which are a clear fresh green, with an under-surface somewhat greyer due to the slight downy hairs which cover them, contain tannin. They have been used in the preparation of leather. The spires of purplish-red flowers elongate with their development in June and July. The seeds are small and brown.

The Loosestrife family is abundant in the American tropics, but *L. salicaria*, has been described by Harold Modenke as 'a welcome European immigrant which has found our swamps and wet meadows much to its liking and now rewards us for our hospitality with blazing masses of colour which are so showy as to attract the attention even of persons ordinarily oblivious to the beauties of nature'. Modenke's description of the dense colonies in which it grows, and its flowers of ½in (1cm) across in thick spikes, makes it clear that this immigrant, like so many others in that hospitable continent, is now very much at home.

Purple loosestrife is astringent and tonic, and was used in Europe to treat fevers. In Ireland, where it also flourishes, it was used as a medicinal herb for diarrhoea, dysentery and the healing of wounds.

It is a herbalists' plant, and ever since Culpeper said 'neither do I know a better preserver of the sight when 'tis well, nor a better cure of sore eyes, than Eyebright taken inwardly and this used outwardly', eyebright and purple loosestrife have been used as a lotion for the eyes. ½oz (14g) of the herb steeped in ½pt (275ml) boiling, slightly saline water for 30 minutes and strained before use, is recommended. It is also used as an ointment for ulcers and sores, and as a gargle for quinsy.

LOVAGE
Levesticum officinale

RULED BY THE SUN AND UNDER THE SIGN OF TAURUS

A native of southern Europe and Asia Minor, lovage is a perennial that grows wild on the sea-coasts of Scotland and northern England, and may be found fairly commonly in other parts of Britain, at river mouths and among the ruins of monasteries.

Lovage resembles angelica in flavour and scent and, like angelica, has stems which may be crystallized. The short thick rootstock is hot, aromatic and biting. The small pale yellow or white flowers appear in compound umbels in July and August.

Once popular in herb gardens, it is seldom seen today, but is well worth growing for its use in medicine and cookery, and for the beneficial effects it seems to have on nearby plants as an insect repellent. It can, however, grow to considerable heights, reaching 6–10ft (1.8–3cm). Culpeper said: 'It is usually planted in gardens where, if it be suffered, it groweth huge and great'. It is propagated by seeds or root divisions.

It is carminative, with diuretic properties, and a decoction was used for the treatment of ague. Distilled water of the herb for jaundice and quinsy was considered beneficial, and it was used as a gargle. 'If Saturn offend the throat,' wrote Culpeper, 'this is your cure ... Half a dram at a time of the dried root in powder taken in wine doth wonderfully warm a cold stomach.' Lovage tea was taken for rheumatism.

It could be used as an eyewash, or as a cleanser of oily skins. 'The leaves bruised, and fried with a little hog's lard, or laid hot to any blotch or boil, will quickly break it.' It also cleared spots and freckles. As a cold cure the fresh seeds were taken steeped in brandy and sugar or honey.

'This herbe for hys sweet savoure if used in bathe' is perhaps the first mention of lovage as a bath additive. It comes from *The Gardeners Labyrinth*, 1577, by Thomas Hyll. Today for a cleansing and refreshing additive use dry lovage or the green herb hung in a muslin bag beneath the hot tap, or mixed with chamomile, peppermint, rosemary or elderflower.

In the Shetland Islands lovage was eaten cooked or as a salad, although perhaps a little strong for our palates. The Highlanders used to eat it first thing in the morning to preserve them from infection throughout the day. They also chewed it instead of tobacco. The Germans peppered their meat dishes with the hot seeds.

It is good in soups and stews and the young leaf-tops may be shredded in salads. Formerly the stems were blanched like celery and eaten as a vegetable. The seeds were used as a flavouring for biscuits. Rural inns commonly served lovage cordial in the last century, and it is still sometimes possible to order a lovage and brandy.

To candy lovage

Cut the young stems in April. Boil until tender, drain, scrape gently and dry in a cloth. Lay in a syrup previously prepared, cover and leave for three days. Heat, but do not boil, and leave in a slightly warmed oven to dry.

MADDER could, according to Philip Miller's *Method of Cultivating Madder*, 1758, be pounded in a pounding house of this design.

MADDER
Rubia tinctorum
R. peregrina

A HERB OF MARS

Madder belongs to a large and complex family, the Rubiaceae, and is of wide distribution. In Britain, the wild madder, *Rubia peregrina*, may be found on the Isle of Wight, in Somerset, Devon, Cornwall and south Wales on cliffs and downs near the sea; the plant is now rare. *R. tinctorum*, the cultivated madder, was known to the Greeks and Romans in both medicine and dyeing. It was mentioned by Dioscorides as a valuable dye plant and is still the best vegetable source of red.

It is a shrubby plant, with square, angular and toothed stems, and leaves that resemble a large bedstraw. These leaves are dusky green and whorled, rough and prickly on the lower surfaces and margins. The flowers, which do not appear until the second or third year, are inconspicuous, small and yellow, with a strong and peculiar smell. Two juicy berries, closely joined, contain

LOVAGE, from G. C. Oeder's *Flora Danica*.

With the growth of the textile industry in England during the 14th century, woad and madder were being supplied to London by Frankfurt agents. The cultivation of madder was first introduced into England by Gerard, but it was subsequently found to be cheaper to import the plant. Philip Miller thought this was unfortunate, for, as he said, 'it will thrive here as well as any country in Europe; and the consumption of it is pretty large; for I have been informed that we pay upwards of £30,000 annually for this Commodity, which might be easily sav'd to the Nation, were it cultivated here'. It was imported mostly from Holland and Flanders, either as the dried root or freed from bark and pith, and ground. By 1754, cultivation in England was almost at an end, except in small quantities for medicinal use.

The chief value of madder as a dye-plant is the wide range of colours that can be obtained, according to the mordant used: it ranges from lilac to black and from pale pink to garnet; it produces crimson-red in cold water or spirit, and a rich brown in hot water. It successfully dyes cotton, silk and wool, although not so good for linen. It responds better to hard water than soft. It has been of great use to painters, especially for reproducing flesh tints in miniatures.

Madder has given many of the rich hues to oriental rugs, and middle-eastern dyers have performed strange wonders with cow-dung and madder to produce a fiery Turkey red. So richly pigmented are the roots that the spent madder in a calico works is reported to have yielded one-third of the original strength of colour. It makes the bones and teeth of animals who feed on it a strong red, and the beaks and claws of birds also become dyed. It is therefore useful to doctors in the study of bone growth.

In medicine it is a mild tonic and has astringent properties. It was once used for treating dropsy. The root was boiled in wine or water for palsy, jaundice and sciatica, and for treating inward and outward bruises. The leaves and roots were beaten and applied externally to remove freckles and other skin blemishes. It is seldom used today except for colouring purposes and for research. Madder formed one of the principal ingredients of an old Welsh recipe which follows on page 108.

the seed. The roots run very deeply into the ground and have a black bark or rind; the inside is reddish and semi-transparent, with a yellow pith. These roots are dug for use after the third year, when they are dried in ovens or kilns. They grow best in sandy soil.

Although madder may have been gathered in the fields and used in dyeing long before cultivation was considered, it was known as a commercial plant during Pliny's lifetime. That knowledge of dyeing and use of mordants had already reached a high degree of skill can be seen in the dyers' shops unearthed at Pompeii. Madder was also used in the dyeing of leather, and from parts of Asia Minor alum was exported to Europe for the dye trade. It was cultivated in medieval France and became naturalized there.

MADDER depicted in a striking illustration from Philip Miller's *Method of Cultivating Madder*, 1758.

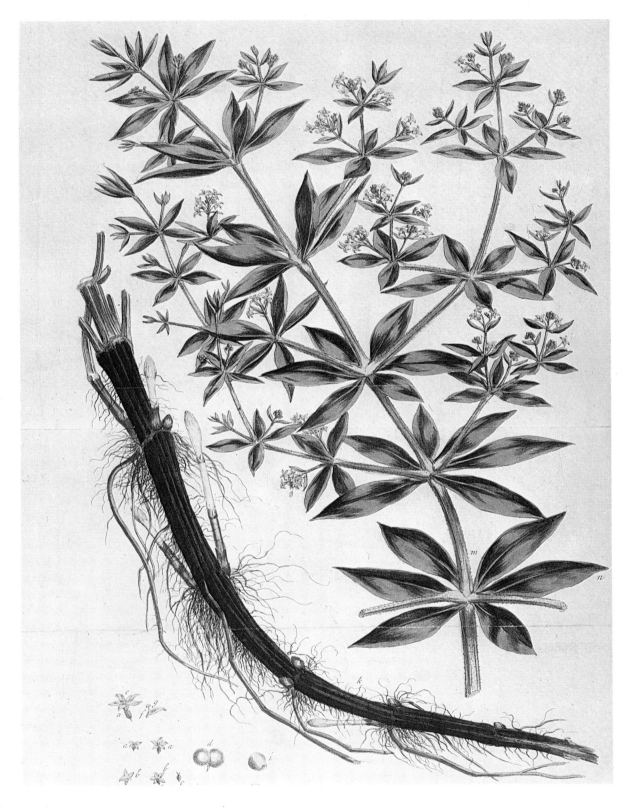

A potion prepared by divine authority for the help of a wounded man, which will be discharged by the wound, and heal it from within without fail

Take the Tansy, sprigs of hemp, red nettles, raspberry, red cabbage, plantain, avens, and madder (of the last as much as of all the rest). Pound them well in a mortar, boil in strong ale, strain, and let it be drank in the night warm, and in the morning cold.

A red cabbage leaf should be applied to the wound, and nothing more, in order to cure the patient.

If you collect the above ingredients in the month of May, or at furthest at midsummer, pound in a mortar, making into small pills and drying without much wind or sun, you will be able to have them at hand when they could not otherwise be had. It is better even to keep what is needful, and then they may be bruised in ale and used as above directed.

MANDRAKE
Mandragora species

UNDER THE DOMINION OF MERCURY

The oldest known narcotic plant, native to southern Europe and the Mediterranean areas, where there are six known species, this belongs to the Potato family, which includes some of the most poisonous plants. It was probably introduced into Britain in the 11th century, for it was known to the Anglo-Saxon leeches who were skilled in medicine and wort-cunning.

It is perennial and deep-rooted, penetrating the ground to a depth of 3–4ft (90–120cm). The root is brown and frequently bifurcated — no doubt the cause of its highly coloured history. The plant has several large dark green leaves; these grow upright when young, but when fully developed lie flat upon the ground. The white or pale purple bell-shaped flowers develop into round and fleshy yellow berries.

At first mandrake appears to have been used in medicinal rather than magical practices. Hippocrates reported that 'a small dose in wine, less than would occasion delirium, will relieve the greatest depression and anxiety'. Theophrastus stated in 230BC that 'the leaf mixed with meal is useful for wounds, and the root for erysipelas. When scraped and steeped in vinegar it is also used for gout, for sleeplessness and for love potions. It is administered in wine or vinegar. They cut little balls of it as of radishes and making a string of them, hang them in the smoke over must.'

Dioscorides recorded its use as an anaesthetic during operations, and Pliny said that 'for this last purpose with some people the odour of it [the wine] is quite sufficient to produce sleep'. The root was put under pillows for insomnia. As an anaesthetic mandrake proved disastrous, as the surgeon could not know for how long it was safe to operate.

The roots, which contain starch, were left to rot (for sixty days, according to some prescriptions) after which they were considered fit to eat or made into a sort of gruel. As a poison it was concealed in tastier foods, and for this purpose it was used by both Lucrezia and Cesare Borgia. The leaves were infused for a potent tea. Both produced an initial excitement, followed by torpor.

The shape of the root and the excitement

MANDRAKE, from *Tacuinum Sanitatum*, *c.* 1385. One of the most famous of all herbs in myth and legend, mandrake is a member of the Potato family. It has a poisonous root which can be pounded for use as an emetic, although such a practice is dangerous in amateur hands.

produced by its drug, including a quickening heart-beat, dizziness and high temperature, gave it an aphrodisiac reputation. Larger or repeated doses might cause delirium, coma and death.

It was believed to be a mystic plant by Eastern races, not only aphrodisiac but with the power to remove sterility. In this capacity it was mentioned in *Genesis*, when both Leah and Rachel conceived after eating mandrake. The smell of the fruit differs considerably according to the locality in which it grows, which is why it has been described as both pleasant and unpleasant. The ancient Greeks referred to the fruit as apples of love and the Arabs called it devil's apples.

Traditionally, it was one of the plants of Circe, who turned men into swine by the sole use of herbs. Its use in demonology and witchcraft was surrounded by elaborate ritual which concerned its growing as well as its uprooting. It was believed 'never or very seldom to be found growing naturally but under a gallowes, where the matter that has fallen from the dead body hath given it the shape of a man ... the uprooting must be performed, (with the assistance of an unfortunate dog) at midnight, within three magic circles performed by a sword, and with strict attention to the direction of the wind.' The emerging mandrake finally appeared uttering groans and shrieks.

Since it was believed that whoever uprooted a mandrake would die, it was found expedient to dig all around the root and at this delicate stage of the operation to tie a rope from the root to the tail of a dog. A piece of meat was then thrown just out of reach of the dog, and the mandrake gatherer adroitly retreated. The dog, having leaped upon his last meal, like a prisoner to his final breakfast, died at sunrise, and the mandrake was successfully retrieved.

At the trial of Joan of Arc, the Maid was accused of being in possession of a manikin mandrake, which she was supposed to have carried in her bosom as a means of acquiring wealth by witchcraft.

It is hardly necessary to say that the demand for these fertility-producers became greater than the supply and other roots, such as briony and flag, were carved and manipulated into the desired manikins and sold for large sums. Ingenious mandrake-forgers went to the lengths of sowing grains of barley or millet in those areas where they wished hair to grow, and then replanting the figures, to be dug up again when the hirsute crop had satisfactorily sprouted. Not only mandrakes but womandrakes were pictured in the manuscripts of the 12th, 13th and 14th centuries; even as late as 1648, John Parkinson wrote that there were both mandrakes and womandrakes. In the time of Henry VIII these artificial mandrakes were sold in boxes, and no doubt gave satisfaction to many eager purchasers. If not required for furthering procreation, these versatile roots could be turned to humbler uses, and eaten to cure indigestion.

By the beginning of the 16th century doubt was creeping in, and herbalists were writing of the mandrake's medicinal properties and casting doubts on its magical ones. 'The rynde of ye roote of mandrake is principally good for use in medicine, the fruyte next, And thirdly ye leaves', it was stated in the *Grete Herbal* of 1526. But by 1551 William Turner, Dean of Wells, who was also a Doctor of Physick, was saying that 'the rootes which are counterfeited and made like little puppettes and mannettes which come to be sold in England in boxes with hair such as a man hath, are nothing else but foolish feined trifles and not natural. For this they are so trimmed of crafty thieves to mock the poore people withall and to rob them of both their wit and their money'.

Superstitions die hard. By 1800 mandrakes had been demoted to parlour mantelpieces, where they were still cherished as talismandrakes. They also figured in Gothic novels and horror stories.

Once an ingredient of witches' brews and fertility potions, mandrake, after a somewhat rakish past, has now been reinstated by homoeopaths in a new role for the treatment of coughs, asthma and hay fever.

MARJORAM
Origanum species

UNDER THE DOMINION OF MERCURY AND THE SIGN OF
ARIES

A perennial of vigorous growth, marjoram is native to the Mediterranean regions, Asia and North Africa. It is wild in Britain, particularly in the chalky counties of the south-east. It is cultivated in the USA where the state of Oregon is so called because marjoram, or *Origanum*, grows there in great abundance.

It has a creeping rootstock, square stems which are downy and purplish, with opposite ovate leaves and purple two-lipped flowers; the latter bloom from July to October. It is a member of the Mint family and frequents chalky and limestone downland pastures.

It was cultivated by the Greeks, who believed

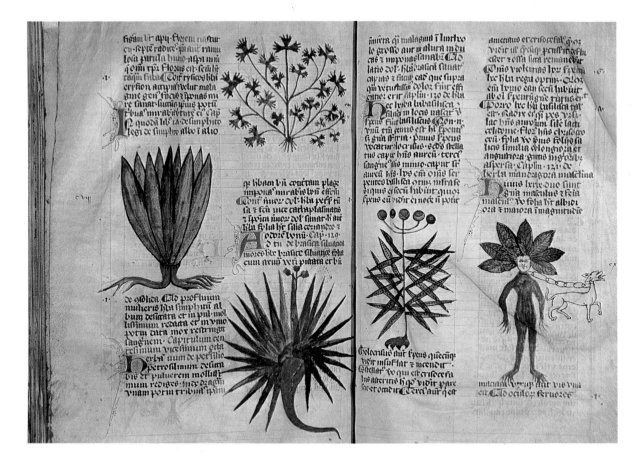

MANDRAKE has always been connected with the human form because of the bifurcate nature of its root, reminiscent of the lower half of the human body. In this French 14th-century manuscript version of Dioscorides' *De Materia Medica* are illustrated both male (*above*) and female (*right*) mandrakes — reflecting a superstition which might have annoyed Dioscorides himself.

MARJORAM, from *Tacuinum Sanitatum, c.* 1385.

MARJORAM, from an English manuscript dated about 1100 in the possession of the Bodleian Library.

that Aphrodite had created it. They called it joy of the mountains. Theophrastus wrote an interesting account of the plants used for perfumes in his time; he said that sweet marjoram had the lasting scent that women required, although it caused headaches. The perfume was made from the roots and tinted pink with the juice from roots of alkanet and krona. Both Greeks and Romans crowned young married couples with marjoram.

O. vulgare is the only marjoram used in medicine, and from this are derived the sweet or knotted marjoram, *O. marjorana*, winter marjoram, *O. heracleoticum*, and *O. onites*, pot marjoram, all of which are used to flavour salads, soups and fish. It seems it was *O. marjorana* that was cried in London streets: 'Come buy my knotted marjoram, ho!'

Marjoram has the unusual distinction of being not only a bee-plant, but a bear-plant and a cow-plant as well. In the Prologue of Beaumont and Fletcher's play *The Knight of The Burning Pestle*, the playwrights say: 'Where the bee can suck no honey, she leaves her sting behind; and where the bear cannot find origanum to heal his grief, he blasteth all other leaves with his breath'. As for the cows, marjoram is known as both a good cow feed to prevent abortion and as nourishment after successful calving.

Gerard says that marjoram, like basil, should be watered in the middle of the day rather than in the morning or evening as most plants are,

cr111·

Uascitur locif cultif
herba origanū
fimo & melle ad
mifce puluerē & faci
bibat maqua ca

ic uepref & frutices.
mpuluere mollif
terrid decocta·
ef crocifcof & da ut
bida· fanabitur.

although he gives no reason for this preference.

Parkinson valued it highly. 'The sweete marjeromes are not only much used to please the outward senses in nosegaies, and in the windowes of houses, but also in swete powders, swete bags, and swete washing waters, but are also of much use in physicke, to comfort the outward members and parts of the bodie, and the inward also.'

Before hops were used in brewing, marjoram provided the bitter flavour in beer and ale. Like hops, the bruised leaves were also used to fill small pillows to encourage sleep. Almost every druggist kept a good supply of dried marjoram in stock for use in sweet-bags, for even to smell marjoram, it was thought, kept folk in good health. The young tops were used to dye cloth purple, and linen reddish brown. It was a strewing herb, and marjoram in a delicate mixture with other herbs was Elizabeth I's favourite scent. Like balm, it could be used to polish furniture — no wonder that villagers gathered large quantities of marjoram which they tied up in bunches and hung in their cottages to dry for winter use.

Our ancestors were very particular in their bastings and dredgings, as will be seen by the following quotation from *May's Accomplished Cook*, 1665: 'Equal quantities of dried marjoram, lemon thyme and sweet basil mixed with breadcrumbs sprinkled over the joint.'

Marjoram even played a part in death for powdered marjoram was used to scent winding-sheets and comforted the bereaved, for to find marjoram growing on a grave meant that the lost one was happy.

Marjoram oil relieves rheumatic pains and is nature's remedy for insomnia, indigestion, dropsy, jaundice, toothache and headaches. A bag of the leaves and flowers plunged in boiling water and squeezed out makes a soothing poultice. It is used in ointments and salves, in liniments and lotions. Marjoram wine is strongly antiseptic. An infusion of the flowers prevents sea-sickness. It is an excellent tonic if used as a bath additive. In New England it was cultivated and drunk as a herb tea.

In cooking, it was enjoyed by the Romans in sauces for their meats, and it is still a popular flavouring in Italian food. Dried marjoram is found in most English kitchens today, ready for use in stuffing, soups and stews, as well as egg and cheese dishes and salads — in which, of course, the fresh herb is preferable. Chopped in melted butter it makes a delicious garnish for vegetables, or powdered it adds a pleasant flavour if sprinkled on pork, veal or lamb before roasting. As the flavour is strong very little is required. The following recipe made with finely chopped fresh marjoram leaves makes a good accompaniment for any stew.

Marjoram dumplings
2oz (56g) self-raising flour
1oz (28g) shredded suet
1tbsp marjoram
pinch of salt
enough cold water to make a dough

Mix all ingredients together and with floured hands form into small round balls for stew, or tiny ones for soup. For stew the dumplings are best steamed separately, but for soup the tiny balls may be dropped in and cooked in the soup.

MAYAPPLE
Podophyllum peltatum

A perennial plant of the Buttercup family, mayapple is native to the USA. It is abundant in damp and shady woods where its unbranched stems grow 1–2ft (30–60cm) high from horizontal poisonous rootstocks, carrying handsome, shiny lobed leaves. The basal leaves are rolled up into a twisted spear, which frequently impales last year's dead leaves, and carries them a foot or so into the air. The leaf then unfurls its green umbrella. The flowering stems emerge from different rootstocks and a solitary waxen white or creamy nodding flower with a nauseous smell appears in about May, followed by a yellowish egg-shaped fruit, the size of a small lemon. The root and leaves are acrid and poisonous, but the pulp of the fruit contains active medicinal qualities.

Apart from being known as ducksfoot and hogapple, it is also called the American mandrake, although it is unrelated to the European mandrake. Mayapple or mandrake was listed in old American pharmacy handbooks as a cure for rheumatism, and unfortunate children were dosed with it as a good purge or emetic for summer diarrhoea. A powerful remedy for kidney troubles was made from the roots of mayapple and Jacob's ladder, *Polemonium reptans*, boiled together; and a root tea treated liver complaints. It is said the Indians used it for suicidal purposes. It must be treated as dangerous and not used without medical advice.

It is probably best to regard mayapple as merely a decorative water plant.

T. 24.

Turtur Caroliniensis.
The Turtle of Carolina.———

Anapodophyllon Canadense &c.

MAYAPPLE, often called mandrake in North America although it bears no
relation to the true mandrake, as illustrated in Mark Catesby's
Natural History of Carolina, 1731. The bird is a Carolina thrush.

MEADOWSWEET

Spiraea ulmaria

UNDER THE DOMINION OF VENUS

A perennial common in Europe, eastern USA and Canada, meadowsweet grows in the deep meadows and stream-banks of Britain on clay soil, where it beautifies the countryside, and makes its presence known by its unmistakable sweet-almond perfume. It is very suitably known as honeysweet in the USA, where it escaped from cultivation.

Meadowsweet was one of the plants held sacred by the Druids. It was once a favourite wedding herb, hence its country name of bridewort. At weddings it was not only made into garlands for the bride and posies for the bridesmaids, but was also strewn along the way to church and in the church itself. It was also known as meadow-maid, queen-of-the-meadow, pride-of-the-meadow and mead-wort — a plant to flavour mead.

It was a favourite strewing plant in Tudor times, and Parkinson wrote that 'Queen Elizabeth of famous memory did more desire it than any other sweet herbe to strew her chambers withal'. Gerard, too, wrote of it with love. 'The leaves and floures of meadowsweet farre excelle all other strowing herbs for to decke up houses, to strawe in chambers, halls and banqueting houses in the summer time, for the smell thereof makes the heart merrie and joyful and delighteth the senses.'

A member of the Rose family, meadowsweet grows from 3–4ft (90–120cm) and has much-divided leaves which are dull green on the upper side and whitish and downy underneath. The leaves are rough to the touch like those of the ash, or crumpled and wrinkled like the elm — hence the specific name *ulmaria*. In July and August, on stems of pale green or reddish purple, densely packed heads of tiny five-petalled creamy flowers open and these give way to crooked and cornered seeds. The flowers contain prussic acid and can cause ill effects when placed in an enclosed room. The scent of the leaves is entirely different from that of the flowers, and both flowers and leaves are used in herbal medicine.

A decoction of meadowsweet and copperas was used as a black dye. Medicinally, it is taken for the treatment of diarrhoea and enteritis in an infusion of 1oz dried flowers and leaves to ¾pt (400ml) boiling water. This may also be given for gout, rheumatism, arthritis and influenza. It is rich in vitamin C.

A decoction is made with white wine to be taken in doses of 1–2tbsp, or, drunk as a beverage, it is good for clearing the complexion. Distilled in water it was used as an eye lotion.

In the past the root has been ground and used as a substitute for flour. It was roasted as a vegetable and drunk as tea.

The bitter astringent leaves were used with borage to flavour the old drink known as cool tankard, and, according to Culpeper, 'a leaf hereof, put into a cup of claret wine, giveth it a fine relish'. Meadowsweet beer was an old country beverage.

Meadowsweet beer

2oz (56g) each of meadowsweet, betony, raspberry leaves and agrimony. Boil in 2gal (9l) water for 15–20 minutes. Strain and add 2lb (900g) white sugar to each gallon (4.5l) of strained liquid and the juice of a lemon. Bottle when nearly cool.

MINTS

Mentha species

ALL THE MINTS ARE UNDER THE DOMINION OF VENUS

The most common and useful of the many mints found wild or cultivated are *M. piperita*, the peppermint; *M. viridis*, or *M. spicata*, the garden mint used in cooking and known as spearmint; *M. pulegium*, or pennyroyal, used in medicine; and *M. citrata*, from which a sweet-smelling oil is extracted, reminiscent of bergamot. All yield fragrant oils by distillation.

Mint derives its name from Mintha or Minthe, the daughter of Cocytus. Mintha was loved by Pluto, and when Persephone discovered that her husband was unfaithful, in her jealous rage she transformed the unfortunate girl into the herb that has since borne her name. In later times, mint was dedicated to the Virgin Mary. The Jews strewed the floors of their synagogues with mint so that its clean and aromatic perfume scented the place as they entered to worship.

PEPPERMINT

Peppermint is native to Britain, and in the USA it is a naturalized escape from gardens. It is perennial, mostly cultivated, but found wild in moist soil in many parts of Europe. Its square branching stem is reddish-purple, with dark green serrated leaves. The small purple flowers on terminal

MINT: an illustration from *Tacuinum Sanitatum*, *c.* 1385, describing the mints.

spikes appear from July to September, reaching 2–4ft (60–120cm).

Medicinally, its oil is used in pharmaceutical preparations and medicines demanding a masking flavour. Peppermint tea is taken for indigestion, headaches, vomiting and insomnia. It is used as a bath additive for general aches and pains, or as a salve for massage. It is a pleasant and stimulating substitute for tea or coffee. Three to four drops on a cube of sugar may be taken for indigestion.

This species contains menthol which has a hot and aromatic flavour, afterwards causing a sensation of cold in the mouth. A cordial is marketed known as peppermint water.

It is grown commercially in south and east England, and harvested in August when it begins to flower. The leaves are distilled to obtain oil of peppermint, or menthol. As a flavouring, it is employed in confectionery, chewing-gum and dentifrices.

SPEARMINT

Spearmint was thought by the ancients to be 'a good Posie for Students oft to smell' and it was used, as we might well use it today, to scent the bath water. The plant has wrinkled bright green leaves with finely toothed edges, and pinkish-lilac flowers arranged in whorls in the axis of the upper leaves, forming slender tapering spires. It is known that it was used very early in cooking for Pliny says that 'the smell of mint doth stir up the minde and the taste to a greedy desire of meat'. At one time it was taken in powdered form after meat as a digestive. It is still perhaps the most popular flavouring in the world and the most important herb grown commercially.

This is the only mint that Culpeper described, except for a short reference to horse-mint, and its curative rather than its culinary purposes concerned him. It is hard to imagine anything more delightful for an ailing female than Culpeper's prescription. 'I have frequently cured and healed

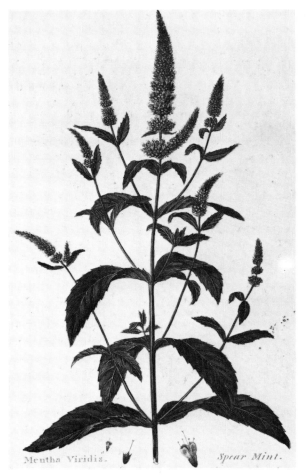

SPEARMINT, from W. Sole's *Menthae Britannicae*, 1798.

many young ladies of weak, delicate, relaxed and consumptive habits of body, by ordering them to go with the maid a milking for a few mornings, and take with them a new laid egg beaten up with a large table spoonful of Rum, and a little Spear Mint cut small, to which add about a tea cup full of new milk from the cow; these being beaten all together in a basin and drunk in the field, together with the addition of the morning air, have done wonders.'

Mint julep

Put a dozen young sprigs of mint into a tumbler. Add a tablespoonful of castor sugar, half a wine-glassful of brandy and the same of peach brandy, and then fill the tumbler with ice. Even with the substitution of lemon juice and dry ginger ale for peach brandy, mint julep might have won Culpeper's approval.

Buttered mint cauliflower and bacon

Break the cauliflower into florets and steam until cooked but slightly crisp. Chop mint and mix into 2tbsp melted butter. Pour over cauliflower and serve with curled rashers of streaky bacon.

PENNYROYAL

Chiefly used for medical purposes, pennyroyal was known by the Romans as *pulegium* from its reputed power to drive away fleas. This ancient reputation has been retained in its present specific name. It was popularly known as pudding-grass since it was used as a stuffing in hog's puddings. It is the smallest mint, having prostrate quadrangular stems and flowers that grow in whorled clusters rising in tiers; the blooms vary from reddish-purple to lilac-blue and flower in July and August.

It was once gathered by simplers from damp ground bordering streams and pools 'on a common at Mile End, near London' and 'besyd hundsley [Hounslow] upon the heth beside a watery place', and by roadsides and ditches all the way from London to Colchester.

Its flavour is more pungent and less agreeable than those of the other mints, which caused Parkinson to write, 'The former age of our great-grandfathers had all these pot herbs in much and familiar use, both for their meats and medicines, and therefore preserved themselves in long life and much health: but this delicate age of ours, which is not pleased with anything almost, being meat and medicine, that is not pleasant to the palate, doth wholly refuse these almost, and therefore cannot be partaken of the benefit of them'.

Mentha Pulegium — Pennyroyal.

PENNYROYAL, from W. Sole's *Menthae Britannicae*, 1798. The North American plant also called pennyroyal is in fact of a completely different genus, but *Hedeona puleigioides* also provides an extract with medicinal uses.

Even so, it was used for toothache, headache, colds, sores, cramp, colic and stomach pains. Pliny recognized its medicinal properties for, in his *Natural History*, he mentioned forty-one remedies to be obtained from mint and twenty-five from pennyroyal. It was grown in cottage gardens wherever the situation was sufficiently moist, and highly valued as lotions for skin diseases and insect bites. Pennyroyal has sudorific, carminative and sedative value and is still taken as a herbal tea. The following receipt comes from a cook-book of 150 years ago.

To distil pennyroyal water

Get your penny-royal when it is full grown, and before it is in blossom, then fill your cold still with it, and put it half full of water, make a moderate fire under it, and distil it off cold, then put it into a bottle, and cork it in two or three days time, and keep it for use.

DOCTORS meeting in the drug distillery of the *jardin des plantes*
at Versailles, from an engraving by Le Clerc.

AN ENGRAVING coloured in watercolours dating from 1636 showing the
jardin des plantes at Versailles. The
garden was originally established by Louis XIV as a zoo, and later
expanded to include, among other things, this botanical garden.

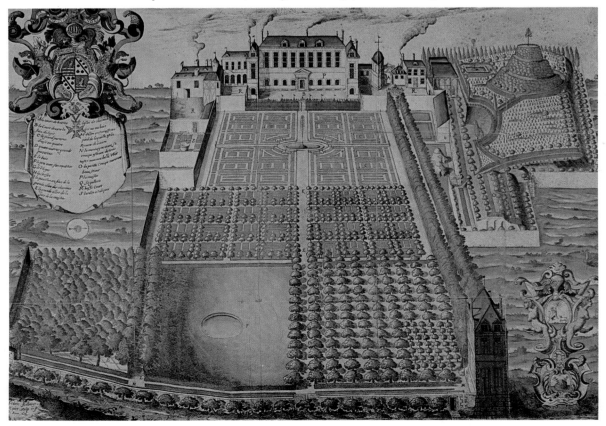

LEMON MINT

M. citrata has variegated leaves of dark green striped with lemon, with a delicious and lasting perfume similar to that of bergamot.

Lemon mint was used in the making of perfume by the Greeks, and in powdered form was sprinkled in their bedding to scent the body completely and with lasting effect. Pliny recommended poets and philosophers to wear coronets of mint, for the excellent reason that 'it exhilarates the mind and is very proper'.

MONKSHOOD

Aconitum napellus and species

A perennial native to Europe and northern Asia many varieties of monkshood grow in India and China, and a few of a limited distribution in North America. It is only a rare native in parts of Britain, and cultivated on a small scale in west Suffolk and Hertfordshire for the drug *aconiti radix*. Belonging to the Buttercup family, all of the genus contain poison in varying degrees, and one, *A. ferox*, which grows in Nepal and the Himalayas, is considered the most virulent poison in India.

The plant is tall, with five to seven lobed leaves which are dark green on top and pale green underneath. The midnight-blue flowers appear in long irregular racemes from June to August. It frequents damp woods and shady hedgerows, but it is also a favourite cottage garden plant. A yellow-flowered variety grows in Lapland.

Gerard's description is not pretty. 'The symptoms that follow those that doe eat of these deadly Herbs are these; their lippes and tongue swell forthwith, their eyes hang out, their thighs are stiffe, and their wits are taken from them.' He gives an antidote to the poison, made from the flies that feed upon it in great numbers. The composition consisted of 'two ounces of *Terra lemnia*, as many of the berries of the Bay tree, and the like weight of Mithradate, 24 of the flies that have taken their repast upon Wolfes-bane, of honey and oile Olive an sufficient quantitie'.

Philip Miller, in *The Gardeners Dictionary*, 1754, having stated that monkshood was to be found in all old gardens, added that it should not be put in the way of children, 'lest they should prejudice themselves therewith'. He described the flower as 'resembling a Friar's Cowl, from where it had that Name: the Flowers of this Kind are commonly brought to Market in May, to furnish Flower-pots for Chimneys'.

MONKSHOOD, illustrated in *Pharmaceutisch Medicinisch Botanik*, 1828, by Daniel Wagner.

Since it was believed to have arisen from the foam dropped from the mouths of Cerberus, watch-dog of the Underworld, aconite was obviously destined from a seedling to become a witches' plant. It is therefore all the more surprising to learn that it was called dumbledore's delight, meaning bee's delight. In a garden list printed in Boston in 1828, it was called Cupid's car, a coy name for this murderous plant, which stemmed from the idea that beneath its hood it conceals a miniature chariot drawn by doves. The name wolfs-bane seems more appropriate since arrows used in wolf-hunting were tipped with it.

Aconite was believed to be the poison that caused Juliet's coma in the tomb. It was an ancient anaesthetic used by the Chinese in surgery.

The drug *aconiti radix* is used internally for fevers and externally to relieve rheumatism and neuralgia. It is extremely valuable as a pain-killer.

MULLEIN, from Crispin de Pas's *Hortus Floridus*, 1614.

MULLEIN
Verbascum thapsus

UNDER THE DOMINION OF SATURN

A hardy biennial of the Figwort family, mullein is native to Britain and many parts of Europe, Asia, North Africa and the USA. It frequents roadsides and waste ground, and arrives uninvited in gardens, where it is usually welcome.

The plant has a long divided root which grows deeply into the ground to support its considerable height — it may reach 8ft (2.4m). Its large leaves are covered with a white hairy felt. The flowers are carried in terminal spikes of pale yellow on a strong, fibrous woolly-covered stem, from June to September. The capsule that follows is oblong and separated into two cells which contain many small angular seeds.

Its known history begins with the Greeks and Romans, who used it for many domestic purposes. Pliny reported that figs do not rot if kept wrapped in mullein leaves. Its long stem dipped in wax was used to burn at feasts and funerals and in

L. *Verbascum*
G. *Bouillon*
A. *Mullein*
Ge. *Wulkraut*.

34

their homes. The Roman legions used it in their torches. The dark Roman women made a hair-wash of mullein flower steeped in lye to dye their hair blonde.

But mullein had a darker and more sinister side. Circe used it in her incantations and therefore it was the plant of all witches and sorceresses since it served to light them in their rites — hence the names hag-taper and pig's-taper. Yet if the leaves of this same plant were gathered when the Sun was in Virgo and the Moon in Aries they acted as a protection against sorcery. Ulysses took mullein to protect himself against the wiles of Circe.

Over the centuries its shady reputation was forgotten and mullein settled down to being an old household friend. Parkinson said that its stalks were dipped in suet to burn 'whether at funeralls or otherwise'. Henry Coles mentioned in his Herbal of 1657 that 'Husbandmen of Kent do give it their cattle against the cough of the lungs, and I, therefore, mention it because cattle are also in some sort to be provided for in their diseases', — it was called also bullock's lungwort.

The flowers were laid to dry in the sun and the oily substance they exuded was spread on linen and applied to the chest as a poultice for inflammation. The leaves made cooling applications to wounds. Dried leaves were smoked in pipes and cigarettes for asthma, or the root burnt and the fumes inhaled. The ashes were also made into soap to restore grey hair to its former colour. Mullein was a popular hair-bleach in the 19th century. It enticed the bees, it yielded a purple dye, and its leaves were made into candlewicks — hence its name candlewick plant. Culpeper said 'a decoction of the leaves hereof, and of sage, marjoram and camomile flowers, and the places bathed therewith, that have sinews stiff with cold or cramps, doth bring them much ease and comfort'.

It was cultivated in Ireland to supply local chemists and in their own homes people boiled the leaves in milk and drank it warm. Mullein, whether boiled in milk or infused in water, must always be strained through fine muslin or filter-paper to remove any hairs from its leaves or stem.

There are seven species of mullein, and today this accommodating plant is still used in herbal remedies. It is a good chest-herb for pneumonia, pleurisy, whooping-cough, catarrh and hay fever. A gargle is made whose analgesic effect is good for inflamed tonsils, and its emollient properties help to relieve piles. The crushed fresh flowers are said to remove warts. Fomentations of mullein and sanicle tea wrung out of a hot cloth are advised for any sort of inflammation.

MUSTARD, BLACK

Brassica nigra

UNDER THE DOMINION OF MARS

An annual, *Brassica nigra* is native to most of Europe and naturalized in North and South America. It is largely cultivated in Holland, Italy and Germany for its seed, as a condiment, and partly for its oil. In Britain it has been cultivated principally in Essex; and in the Isle of Ely, whenever foundations were dug, a crop of black mustard immediately appeared.

The plant has a branching angular stem, about 3ft (90cm) high, with alternate leaves and yellow flowers in terminal racemes; the flowers are smaller than those of white mustard. The seeds, about half the size of white mustard seeds, are brown or black. Black mustard may be distinguished from charlock by its smooth upper leaves.

For table mustard it is planted in March, thinned out in May, and harvested in midsummer when the seeds are ripening but the leaves green. Commercial table mustard usually consists of both *B. alba* and *B. nigra*, together with some wheat-flour coloured with turmeric.

Mustard is used medicinally for rheumatism, sciatica and neuralgia. The seeds may be chewed for toothache. Ground mustard used like snuff is good for clearing the head. The oil expressed from the seeds is used for medicinal purposes, and the cake that remains after the oil is expressed is used as cattle food.

For a mustard bath, steep 8oz (226g) mustard powder in 2qt (2l) water, and add to the bath. For a foot bath, use 4–6oz (113–170g) mustard powder in a bag steeped in warm water for 5 minutes. In cases of poisoning, a teaspoonful of mustard in a cup of boiling water should be drunk as swiftly as possible as an emetic.

Mustard plasters are good for pains and swellings, and to draw out splinters. 1 part mustard to 4 parts wholemeal flour is made into a paste by mixing with warm water. Spread immediately on to a cloth and apply to the injury. There is a danger of blistering if the plaster is left on too

AN 18TH-CENTURY French print of an apothecary laden with some of his traditional equipment: 1, a vase to keeep sleeping potions in; 2, all sorts of medicine canisters; 3, medicine bottles; 4, snakes; 5, spatulas; 6, syringe; 7, pitcher; 8, golden goblet from which to take medicine; 9, wallet for receipts; 10, portable stove; 11, mortar; 12, pestle; 13, an aloe; and 14, various simples.

Moutarde noire

MUSTARD, one of the world's most popular relishes, is prepared from the ground seeds of *Brassica nigra* mixed with vinegar and other flavourings. This illustration of the mustard plant is from *Phytographie Medicale*, 1821, by J. Roques.

long, but if the mustard and flour is mixed with egg-white instead of water, blistering will be avoided.

As a condiment, mustard is used in every household. The following recipe, written in 1755, is ascribed to the Reverend Sydney Smith.

To make a salad

Two boiled potatoes strained through a kitchen sieve,
Softness and smoothness to the salad give;
Of mordant mustard take a single spoon,
Distrust the condiment that bites too soon;
Yet deem it not, thou man of taste, a fault,
To add a double quantity of salt.
Four times the spoon with oil of Lucca crown,
And twice with vinegar, procured from town;
True taste requires it; and your poet begs,

The pounded yellow of two well-boiled eggs.
Let onion's atoms lurk within the bowl,
And scarce suspected animate the whole;
And lastly, in the flavoured compound toss
A magic spoonful of anchovy sauce;
Oh, great and glorious! oh, herbaceous meat!
'Twould tempt the dying anchoret to eat;
Back to the world he'd turn his weary soul,
And dip his finger in the salad bowl.

The following is from *The Cook's Oracle*, 1817.

A recipe for opulent epicures

Some opulent epicures mix their mustard with sherry or Madeira wine, or distilled vinegar, instead of horseradish water. The French flavour their mustard with Champaigne, and other wines, capers, anchovies, tarragon or elder vinegar, garlick, shalott, celery, and fine herbs, truffles, etc. etc.

MUSTARD, WHITE

Brassica alba

UNDER THE DOMINION OF MARS

An annual, white mustard grows both cultivated and wild in Europe, Asia and North Africa, and in many parts of the world.

It is believed to have been discovered by Aesculapius, and its properties and usages are much the same as those of black mustard. Mustard is one of the biblical herbs, and it has followed man, invading his grainfields wherever he has cultivated.

It is an erect plant, reaching about 1ft (30cm) in height. It bears yellow cruciferous flowers in July; these develop into long pods, carried horizontally, each tipped with a beak and containing four to six globular seeds.

During the reigns of Elizabeth I and James I, mustard was grown for its seed only which, pounded with vinegar, was eaten 'with any grosse meates, either fish or flesh'. It was used in medicine as snuff, 'as it marvelously amendeth the braine'. One can hardly believe that it was dropped into the eyes to improve the sight.

It seems mustard as a condiment went out of fashion. According to Parkinson in 1640, 'Our ancient forefathers, even the better sort . . . were not sparing in the use hereof . . . but nowadays it is seldome used by their successours, being accounted the clownes sauce, and therefore not fit for their tables.'

Culpeper thought highly of mustard as a cure for everything. 'Let such whose stomachs are so weak they cannot digest their meat, or appetite it, take of Mustard-seed a dram, cinnamon as much, beat them to a powder, add half as much mastick in powder, and with gum arabick dissolved in rose-water make it up into troches, of which they may take one of about half a dram weight an hour or two before meals; let old men and women make much of this medicine, and they will either give me thanks, or show manifest ingratitude.' He also found it valuable as a hair-restorer, for leprosy and lousy evil, 'and a crick in the neck'.

Cole said in 1657, 'In Gloucestershire about Teuxbury they grind mustard and make it into balls which are brought to London and other remote places as being the best the world affords.' Mustard balls were the form in which mustard was usually sold. The balls were sometimes mixed with honey and vinegar, and in Italy powdered dried lemon or orange peel was added.

It was not until the 18th century that a Mrs Clements of Durham invented a way of making mustard flour like wheat flour; and consequently made a fortune with her Durham mustard.

In 1825, the 2nd Marchioness of Bath published a little book of *Cottage Domestic Economy*, dedicated 'To the Cottagers of My Neighbourhood'. It contained:

Mustard

How to make it, and the advantage of not only saving *money* by so doing, but perhaps, your *life*.

Why *buy* this, when you can *grow* it in your garden? The stuff you buy is half *drugs*, and is injurious to health. A *yard square* of ground sown with common mustard, the crop of which you would grind for use, in a little mustard mill, as you wanted it, would save you *some money*, and probably save your *life*. Your mustard would look *brown* instead of *yellow*; but the former colour is as good as the latter; and, as to the *taste*, the *real* mustard has certainly a much better than that of the *drugs* and flour, which go under the name of mustard. Let any one *try* it, and I am sure he will never use the drugs again. The drugs, if you take them freely, leave a *burning at the pit of your stomach*, which the real mustard does not.

Today, the seedlings of white mustard, together with the seedlings of garden cress, *Lepidium sativum*, are grown as mustard and cress for salads and sandwiches. As mustard sprouts more quickly than cress, it should be sown four days later; both take about a fortnight to be ready for the table. Although it is easy to grow in the house or garden, most crops are raised under glass by specialist growers. White mustard leaves may be cooked as a vegetable or eaten raw in salads. The plant is grown also as sheep fodder, and for ploughing in for soil improvement.

NASTURTIUM

Tropaeolum majus
T. minus

An annual, nasturtium is native to South America and cultivated all over the world. It has tender, smooth sprawling or climbing stems, which may reach 10ft (2m) or more, with round, radially veined, alternate bright green leaves. The strongly scented red, yellow and orange flowers bloom from June to October. These are furnished with five sepals, the upper one having a long spur which looks more like a protective weapon than the honey-store it is. There are five irregularly shaped petals, two upper and three lower, and eight stamens. The fruits that follow are separable into three sections.

The name *Tropaeolum* means a trophy, and the plant was said to have arisen from the blood of a Trojan warrior, the flower symbolizing the golden helmet, and the round leaf the shield. The first European to publish a description was Nicholas Monardes, a physician of Seville: 'I sowed a seede which thei brought me from Peru, more to see his fairnesse than for any Medicinall vertues that it hath . . . It is a flower very beautiful, which doeth adornate the gardens.'

From Spain, this new plant made its way to France and Flanders, and thence to Britain. Gerard mentioned receiving seeds from France in 1597: 'The seeds of this rare and faire plant came from the Indies in Spaine, and thence into France and Flanders, from where I received seed that bore with mee both flowers and seed, especially those I received from my loving friend John Robin of Paris.' At this time it was known as Indian cresses.

Parkinson grew the plant in his garden and classified it as yellow larkes heels (larkspur) because of its spurred flower. He said 'the whole flower hath a fine small sent, very pleasing, which being placed in the middle of some Carnations or Gilliflowers . . . make a delicate Tussimussie'. Parkinson evidently went more for scent than colour in his flower arrangements. He described its 'very long trayling branches, interlaced one with another, very confusedly yet it doth not

NASTURTIUM, in a rather idealized illustration from an English 13th-century manuscript.

winde it selfe with any claspers about either pole or any other thing, but if you will have it close thereunto, you must tye it, or else it will lye upon the ground'.

It is antiscorbutic; John Evelyn claimed that the seeds were 'the most effectual and powerful Agents in conquering and expunging that cruel Enemy [scurvy]'. It was advised that 'patients to whom the nauseus taste of scurvy-grass is intolerable, may find a grateful substitute in Nasturtium', and so they did, until nearly the end of the 18th century, when it was discovered that either lemons or limes were even more effective.

Scientific investigation has proved that nasturtiums planted beneath apple trees and encouraged to climb into their branches help to protect the trees from woolly aphis.

Nasturtiums are powerfully antiseptic for both internal and external purposes; ½ teaspoonful of the fresh juice, or a tea made from the juice, is excellent for colds. It may be taken as a tonic to benefit the blood and the digestive system.

Its leaves are both tasty and health-giving in a salad or sandwich, and the flower-buds and unripe seeds may be used in sauces, pickles, and in place of capers in lamb stew. The flowers may be used together with the leaves and seeds to make an appetizing sauce.

Brown nasturtium sauce

½ beef stock cube with ½pt (275ml) water
3oz (85g) flour
2oz (56g) butter
2tbsp nasturtium seeds
1tsp nasturtium juice from leaves and flowers
1tsp chili vinegar
pepper and salt

Melt butter and dredge flour into the melted butter, shaking it above the heat until it has lost all taste of flour. Gradually stir in the beef stock, which should be at boiling point. Add nasturtium seeds, nasturtium liquid and chili vinegar. Return to stove and bring to boil. Serve.

NETTLE, STINGING
Urtica dioica

UNDER THE DOMINION OF MARS

An ancient prescription which may date from the Roman occupation of Britain runs thus: 'Take nettles, and seethe them in oil, smear and rub all thy body therewith; the cold will depart away.' There is a tradition that the variety of nettle *U. pilulifera*, known as Roman nettle, and now a rare plant, was introduced by the Roman soldiers, who believed that English winters were unendurable and brought the seeds from Italy so that they might have a plentiful supply with which to rub their bodies and thereby keep themselves warm. The rigours of the English winter seem not to have endeared the genus to the English people. And yet St Patrick blessed this unloved plant for

NETTLES of various species of the genus *Urtica* have useful culinary or medicinal properties. This illustration of a stinging nettle is from a picture by J. F. Miller, 1770

its services to man and beast, for the nettle has been put to more varied and useful purposes than almost any other herb.

The poet Thomas Campbell wrote a letter early in the 19th century saying, 'I have slept in Nettle-sheets, and I have dined off a Nettle-table-cloth. The young and tender Nettle is an excellent pot-herb, and the stalks of the old Nettle are as good as flax for making cloth. I have heard my mother say, that she thought Nettle cloth more durable than any other linen.' The thread with which these sheets and table-cloth were stitched may well have been made with nettle also. The German name for muslin, *Nessel-tuch*, or Nettle-cloth, proves that a finer material could equally well be woven. As late as World War I, nettle fibre was used to make army clothing. Ropes, sailcloth, sacking and the twine for nets were also made from the fibre of nettles for the fishing fleets, and in France it was used in making paper.

In 1596 Coghan wrote in *The Haven of Health*,

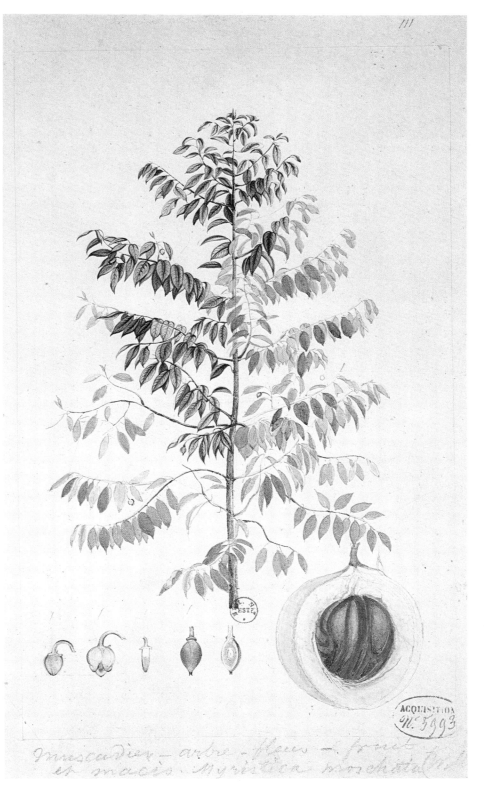

NUTMEG shown in a 19th-century French watercolour. The detail at lower right shows the fruit, the kernel of which is ground to give the spice nutmeg, and the covering of which provides mace.

'I will speak somewhat of the nature of Nettle that Gardeners may understand what wrong they do in plucking it for the weede, seeing it is so profitable to many purposes ... Cunning cookes at the spring of the yeare, when Nettles first bud forth, can make good pottage with them, especially with red Nettles.'

In the 17th century nettle porridge was a common dish in England, and a good cook was said to be able to make seven different dishes out of nettle-tops. Pepys wrote in his diary in February 1661: 'We did eat some nettle porridge, which was made on purpose today for some of their coming, and was very good.' Nettle soup and nettle pudding were common in Scotland; nettle pudding was made from a mixture of nettle-tops with cabbage, brussels sprouts or broccoli and rice, cooked in a muslin bag and served with butter.

Nettle beer was a pleasant country drink made of nettle-tops, dandelions, goosegrass and ginger, boiled and strained. Brown sugar was added, and while still warm a slice of toasted bread, spread with yeast, was placed on top, and the whole kept warm for six or seven hours. Finally, the scum was removed, a teaspoonful of cream of tartar was added and the beer was bottled. It was taken as a remedy for gouty and rheumatic pains, or simply for pleasure.

John Wesley was herbalist as well as preacher; the following recipe comes from his own book: 'Boil nettles till soft. Foment with the liquor, then apply the herb as poultice. I have known this cure a Sciatica of forty-five years standing.'

Culpeper said: 'This is also an herb Mars claims dominion over. You know Mars is hot and dry, and you know as well that Winter is cold and moist; then you may know as well the reason why Nettle-tops eaten in the Spring consume the phlegmatic superfluities in the body of man, that the coldness and moistness of Winter hath left behind.' He advised the taking of roots or leaves boiled, or the juice of either with honey and sugar for wheezing, short breath, sore throats and inflammation of all kinds. He considered a concoction of the seeds good for gravel and stone, and this treatment is still used today. It also 'killeth worms in children, easeth pains in the sides, and dissolveth the windiness in the spleen, as also the body, although others think that it is only powerful to provoke venery'.

Nettles were often used in London market gardens for packing plums and other plants with bloom on them, a practice known and written about in 1683 in Lawson's *New Orchard*. 'For the gathering of all stone fruit, as Nectarines, Apricots, Peaches, Pear-plums, Damsons, Bullas, and such like ... in the bottom of your large sives where you put them, you shall lay Nettles, and like-wise in the top, for that will ripen those that are most unready.' In many country villages the leaves were laid under cream cheese.

Today, it has been proved that the stinging-nettle helps neighbouring plants grow more resistant to disease. As a companion plant it increases the content of essential oils in neighbouring herbs, and stimulates humus formation.

Nettles were commonly used as a hair-conditioner in the 19th century, and are still in use for this purpose today. The hair tonic is made from a handful of young nettles simmered in 1qt (1l) water for 2 hours, and then strained and bottled.

A nettle tea is made for the treatment of haemorrhoids. The young nettle tops are boiled for 20–30 minutes in enough water to cover them, and a small amount of honey or sugar added as a sweetener if desired.

NUTMEG AND MACE
Myristica fragrans

The tree which produces both nutmeg and mace is native to the Banda Islands, the Malayan Archipelago and the Moluccan Islands, where it is also cultivated, as it is in India, Penang, the West Indies, Brazil and Réunion.

The nutmeg tree grows 20–30ft (6–9m) high, and has a greyish-brown smooth bark. The whorled branches produce alternate aromatic leaves, a dark green and glossy above and a pale green beneath. The male and female flowers, which are small, white and bell-shaped, are produced on different trees. The fruit, known as the nutmeg-apple, is about the size of a walnut, and consists of a thick fleshy covering containing a single nut. When the fruit opens the nut is seen to be enveloped in a red netlike covering, the arillus, which is the mace. The kernel is the nutmeg of commerce.

The trees are very fertile, bearing both flowers and the ripe fruit all the year round. A good specimen may yield upwards of 2,000 fruits a year. The tree will not bear fruit until it is eight or nine years old, after which it may continue for nearly a century.

It is said that the scent of the Nutmeg Islands is so powerful that birds of paradise become intoxicated. The mace resembles the nutmeg in its properties and they have similar flavours. The bark contains a red stain. An oil extracted from the nuts is called nutmeg butter or oil of mace, although it is obtained from the nutmeg itself, and not from the mace. When dried, the mace acquires a cinnamon-yellow colour, in single and double blades.

After gaining possession of the Molucca or Spice Islands, the Dutch strictly monopolized nutmeg and it was confined to a single island, the Island of Banda. The wood-pigeon, however, was the innocent means of thwarting this monopoly by disseminating the plant outside the manmade boundaries. The Moluccas were taken by the British in 1769 and the nutmeg was imported into Britain by the East India Company. Its cultivation then spread to Mauritius, Madagascar and some of the colonies of tropical America. The nutmeg tree was introduced into Britain by Sir Joseph Banks as an ornamental hot-house plant.

According to the *Doctrine of Signatures* nutmeg was used as a remedy for all mental ailments due to its 'resemblance' to the human brain. It became one of the most valuable commodities of the Orient during the Middle Ages on account of its many uses. Oil of nutmeg was used as an opiate.

To obtain nutmegs the outer pulpy coat was first discarded and afterwards the mace removed with a knife. The nuts were then placed over a slow fire and when the shell became brittle the nutmeg fell out. The mace was dried in the sun and then sprinkled with salt to preserve it. Commercial mace may be flexible or brittle, cinnamon yellow, in single or double 'blades', with a smell like nutmeg and a warm aromatic flavour.

Both nutmeg and mace are used for flatulence, nausea and vomiting, and have great digestive value. Powdered nutmeg is used in the composition of medicines and its oil is used to disguise the flavour of various unpleasant-tasting drugs. It is a mild narcotic, and sprinkled on the top of hot milk at bedtime makes a soothing drink. Our grandmothers often carried a little silver nutmeg-grater on their chatelaines to make nutmeg tea for a nightcap. Nutmeg brandy was also made as a soporific. 3oz (85g) grated nutmeg were put into a bottle of brandy, corked, and shaken once every day for a fortnight. After being left to settle, the liquid was poured off without disturbing the sediment. Ten drops in a glass of hot milk or water was the usual dose.

However, nutmeg is more often used for culinary purposes. Although it may be bought in powdered form, it is best used freshly grated on milk puddings, in cakes, biscuits, fish dishes, soups, sauces and pumpkin pie. Pumpkin soup, made with a few slices of cooked pumpkin and one chopped onion, blended with milk and a pinch of nutmeg is delicious. Mace may also be bought ground or whole. The flavour is somewhat similar, but stronger, so it should be used sparingly in pickles and chutney, fish and cheese dishes, creamed spinach, or potato mashed with plenty of butter.

Jugged hare with mace and peppercorns

1 hare or jointed portions of hare
4 peppercorns, 1 small blade mace and 1 bay leaf,
in a muslin bag
1 rasher bacon
2oz (56g) dripping
1 onion stuck with two cloves
1½pt (825ml) stock
1½oz (42g) blended flour
pepper and salt
1tsp red-currant jelly
1 glass red wine
forcemeat balls

Fry hare and bacon in dripping. When lightly browned, cover with stock, stir in blended flour, onion, seasonings and bag of spices. Cover and simmer in a moderate oven or on top of stove for three hours, or until tender. Before serving remove onion and spice bag, stir in jelly and wine, and reheat without boiling. Serve with forcemeat balls.

Mashed potato au gratin and nutmeg

1½lb (680g) potatoes
3oz (85g) grated cheese
butter
2 onions
1tbsp browned breadcrumbs
nutmeg
salt and pepper

Boil potatoes, then mash them with chopped onions. Add salt and pepper to taste, 2oz (56g) cheese and a sprinkling of nutmeg. Form into a pyramid on an oiled dish, and sprinkle with rest of cheese mixed with the browned breadcrumbs. Dot with butter and bake in hot oven until brown.

The following recipe is included for the fervent recommendation which accompanies it in *Apicius Redivivus: or The Cook's Oracle*, 1817. The proud inventor was Dr Kitchiner.

[127]

Tewahdiddle

A pint of table beer, a tablespoonful of brandy, 2 teaspoonsful of brown sugar, or clarified syrup; a little grated nutmeg or ginger may be added, and a roll of lemon peel.

Observation. Before our readers make any remarks on this composition, we beg of them to taste it; and if their palate does not differ very much from that of its inventor, they will find it one of the most delicious beverages they ever put to their lips.

PARSLEY

Petroselinum crispum (curly parsley)
Petroselinum satirum (Hamburg parsley)

UNDER THE DOMINION OF MERCURY

A hardy biennial of the Carrot family, parsley is native to north and central Europe, and particularly to Sardinia, where it is believed it may have originated. It has been used since ancient times — in fact it received the name *Petroselinum* from Dioscorides himself. Parsley was introduced into England in about the middle of the 16th century.

It is probably the most widely used culinary herb of any, and there are many varieties. Cooks and gardeners should never allow the white or greenish flowers, which appear from June to August, to develop, but herbalists depend upon the seeds for medicinal purposes. Parsley is grown by market gardeners for sale in either fresh or dried form, and oil, distilled from the fresh seeds, is used by druggists and also as a flavouring for liqueurs. The plant withstands winter conditions, but usually dies after its second season. The seed is sown early in the year, and it is said by some that after going down to the devil seven times it eventually appears. According to elderly British gardeners and also to American negroes, it is unlucky to transplant it from one garden to another, a superstition probably derived from the fact that it is a choosy herb which may resent interference and promptly die.

Parsley was too greatly venerated by the Greeks and Romans to be used as a culinary herb. For a Greek athlete, or a Roman poet, there was no greater distinction than to be awarded a chaplet of parsley. The dead were honoured too with a parsley garland hung about their tomb. The plant was dedicated to Persephone.

Although its former glories are now only a matter of garden history, parsley remains the prop and stay of the suburban kitchen garden and there are several cultivated varieties. There is a turnip-rooted parsley, which produces large and edible roots, and another which develops a parsnip-shaped form, both of which were sold in London markets in 1770. The seeds of these, or of similar varieties, are available today, and are useful in soups or stews.

Parsley piert, a wild plant unrelated to garden parsley, is highly regarded for all problems related to anaemia, rheumatism, sciatica, jaundice, tumours and boils. One of its chief uses was in the treatment of stone in the bladder, for which it was in ancient times given the name of parsley breakstone, or parsley pierce-stone, corrupted into parsley piert.

Culpeper described it as growing plentifully around Hampstead Heath, Hyde Park, and near Tothill Fields. 'It were good the gentry would pickle it up as they pickle up Samphire (and still do, in the coastal areas of Britain) for their use all the Winter. I cannot teach them how to do it; yet this I can tell them, it is a very handsome herb.'

The distilled water of parsley was familiar to nurses as a remedy to give their small charges when troubled with wind, which they called 'the frets'. When a newcomer arrived the first infant was told that his little brother, or sister, as the case might be, had been 'found in the parsley bed'. Just who was the author of this happy thought we shall

PARSLEY, from a 14th-century *Tacuinum Sanitatum* now in the possession of the Austrian National Library.

never know, but in 'Mr Gay's Receipt to Stew a Knuckle of Veal' it is clear that John Gay was familiar with the theory. The author adds to the veal

Some sprigs of that bed
Where children are bred,
Which much you will mend, if
Both spinage and endive,
And lettuce and beet,
With marygold meet.

A concoction of the crushed seeds was made for freckles, infusions were used as an eye-wash, and strong parsley tea was taken for urinary disorders. A hot fomentation made with flannels dipped in parsley tea is still thought good for stings and insect bites and for swollen glands. It is currently being used as a preventive herb against cancer. It is rich in vitamin C.

Parsley, as well as making one of the most modest, simple and pleasant sauces in the world, may be served in appetizing little balls as parsley butter.

Poached eggs and parsley sauce

Eggs
a little minced parsley
3–4 minced chives
2oz (56g) butter
grated bread
salt and pepper
sprig of parsley
glass of white wine

Put butter rolled in flour in a pan, with parsley, bread, chives, seasoning and wine, and let it boil for 2–3 minutes. Poach eggs, put them on individual dishes, and pour sauce over. Serve with green salad and brown bread and butter.

PEONY

Paeonia species

A HERB OF THE SUN, UNDER THE DOMINION OF LEO

A perennial, peony was believed by the ancients to be an emanation of the Moon, although declared by astrologer-herbalists to be a herb of the Sun. In its guise as a Moon plant, peony was given to lunatics to cure them of their madness. It was described as the first floral descendant of Paeon, a pupil of Aesculapius, the god of medicine. Some say the flower was handed to Paeon from the clouds of Mount Olympus by the mother of

PEONY, as depicted in *Ortus Sanitatis*, 1485.

Apollo and that, by its means, Paeon cured Pluto of a wound he had received at the hands of Hercules, and so the miraculous plant was given the name of peony.

The true wild peony, *P. corallina*, is a native of southern Europe, and in Britain is rare. It can be distinguished from the garden peony by its uncut leaves and single flowers of five to ten concave petals.

P. officinalis, which was brought to English physic gardens in the 16th century from Switzerland, has deeply divided leaves and full crimson flowers which appear in May. This variety was once thought to be the female peony, while the single-flowered *P. corallinus* was known to be the male.

Parkinson, in his *Theatrum Botanicum*, described a dubious character called *P. faemina promiscua*, the doubtful female peony, who seems unsuitable to be mentioned in his learned pages. She does not appear in later herbals.

Culpeper described the virtues of the male and female peony as seen through the eyes of a 17th-century herbalist. 'The root of the Male Peony, fresh gathered, has been found by experience to

PEPPER being gathered in the Kingdom of Quilon: an episode from the travels of Marco Polo illustrated in the 15th-century *Le Livre des Merveilles*.

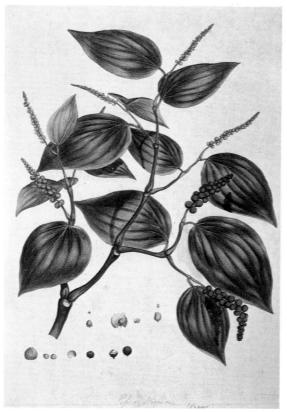

(*left*) PEPPER, *Piper nigrum*, as depicted in a hand-coloured etching by John Miller.

(*right*) PEPPER climbing around and up the trunk of an areca tree, a type of palm, as shown in a print by J. Charton, 1784.

POIVRE NOIR DU MALABAR MONTANT SUR UN ARECA.
Dessinée par J. Charton.

cure the falling sickness; but the surest way is, beside hanging it about the neck, by which children have been cured, to take the root of the Male peony washed clean, stamped somewhat small, and laid to infuse in sack for 24 hours at the least; and afterwards strain it, and take it first and last morning and evening, a good draught for sundry days together, before and after a full moon; and this will also cure older persons, if the disease be not grown too old, and past cure, especially if there be a due and orderly preparation of the body with posset drink made of betony, etc ... The Female is often used for the purpose aforesaid (Nightmares), by reason the Male is so scarce a plant, that it is possessed by few, and those great lovers of rarities in this kind.' What he failed to mention is that the entire plant is poisonous, and that it is essential to understand the plant's properties before prescribing it.

Garden peonies had the reputation of driving away tempests and witches, which is why they became so popular in cottage gardens, being usually grown close to the door.

Mrs Leyel, in *Herbal Delights*, gives a rare recipe using peony flowers.

Syrup of peony flowers

Take of fresh Peony flowers 1 pound, infuse them in 3 pints of hot water for the space of 12 hours, then let them boil a little and press them out, adding the like quantity of fresh flowers and use as the former up to 5 times, then add to the infusion 2½ pounds of loaf sugar and boil to a syrup.

It is known that peony seeds were eaten as a condiment and used to decorate creams in the same way that we use sliced almonds. It is evident, however, that the peony had no great appeal as food, although it seems to have been in use during fasting days, according to Piers Plowman, in a dialogue where a priest questions a poor woman: '"Hast thou ought in thy purs?" quod he, "Any hote spices?" "I have peper and piones [peonies]" quod she; "and a pounde garlike, a ferthynge worth of fenel seed, for fastyying dayes."'

Whatever its undoubted glories in the garden, as a medicinal herb the peony has lost face. By 1800, Richard Brook had made this plain in his *Cyclopaedia of Botany*. 'Most extraordinary virtues were formerly attributed to the peony, but they want proof in modern practice. It may be that the cultivated plant has not the same virtues as the wild one, as we know that many wild herbs of known virtue, lose the whole of their virtue when transferred into a garden.'

PEPPER
Piper nigrum

There are about fifty species of plants called peppers, many unrelated, consisting of herbs, shrubs and trees: see, for example, capsicum. A perennial, *Piper nigrum* is cultivated in the East and West Indies, Malay Peninsula, Malay Archipelago and Thailand. The best pepper comes from Malabar. It grows wild in India.

Black pepper is a climbing vine which will grow up to 20ft (6m) unless cultivated. It has smooth woody and jointed stems which lie on the ground unless supported. The leaves are dark green and heart-shaped and the white flowers grow in spikes, followed by berries which are at first green but ripen to red. They are collected just as they are turning red but before they are completely ripe. After being gathered and dried, the berries become black and wrinkled, and form the black pepper we use either whole or ground. White pepper is the same berry skinned by rubbing and washing. It is aromatic, pungent and somewhat bitter.

The Greeks and Romans used pepper as both medicine and condiment, and Theophrastus wrote about it in 300BC. It is the oldest trade item from the Orient. The enthusiasm for pepper and spices declined with the fall of the Roman Empire, and the spice trade with it. With the changing fate of the spice trade and the increasing cultivation and distribution of the plants, pepper has become a universal seasoning.

In medicine it was used for gout, rheumatism, smallpox, scarlet fever, dysentery, typhus, cholera and bubonic plague. The ground seed was mixed with caraway seeds and honey, or a gruel made, well seasoned with pepper, for quinsies. It is most valuable for stopping profuse bleeding. A sprinkling of pepper over a cut is not as painful as it sounds, and is a sure and antiseptic method of healing. It is stimulant, carminative and digestive and good for dyspepsia, flatulence and nausea, as well as for diarrhoea.

The use of pepper in cooking is so much a matter of personal taste that it is probably best to use the milder white pepper in most dishes, and to produce black pepper for the table. A pepper mill in which the peppers, either black or white or a mixture of both, may be ground is the best and most aromatic way of individual seasoning.

Freshly ground black pepper figures in the following sauce which appeared in *The Cook's Oracle* of 1817. Rich men will find it equally enjoyable.

Poor man's sauce

Pick a handful of parsley leaves from the stalks, mince them very fine, strew over a little salt, shred fine half a dozen young onions; add these to the parsley, and put them in a sauce-boat, with three tablespoonsful of oil, and five of vinegar; add some ground black pepper; stir all together, and send it up.

Observation. — This sauce is in much esteem in France, where the people of taste, weary of so many rich dishes, to obtain the charm of variety, occasionally order the fare of the peasant.

PIMPERNEL

Anagallis arvensis
A. cerulea

A GALLANT SOLAR HERB

This miniature annual is widely distributed throughout the temperate regions of the world, and is common — and welcome — in Britain. It is naturalized in the USA.

The scarlet pimpernel frequents sunny banks, gravelly and sandy heaths, fields and gardens. It has creeping square stems carrying gentle green and egg-shaped paired leaves, which lie flattened face-upwards to the Sun, hiding the minute dots on their undersides. The neatly pointed flower-buds open to reveal petals not of a true scarlet, but ones lightly splashed with vermilion. During the long flowering period from May to September, fruits like little green bullets develop; these bend backwards when ripe and split and shake their seeds which are carried by the wind.

A deep blue variety, *A. cerulea*, rare in Britain, is more common in central and southern Europe, and there are intermediate varieties. The Greeks and Romans regarded the scarlet pimpernel as the male flower and the blue as the female, although they may have had doubts if presented with a white flower with a pink or purple eye.

In the company of other scarlet flowers, the pimpernel is said to have appeared in the soil of Calvary when Christ's blood fell to the ground. The plant was therefore taken as a talisman against witchcraft, and an application of its bruised leaves was advised to combat the embedding of splinters in human flesh by witches.

The Greeks used it for eye diseases, and Pliny and Dioscorides recommended a dose of twenty grains, four times a day, for epilepsy and melancholia. Gerard advocated its use for toothache. 'The juyce cures the toothach being snift up the nosthrils, especially into the contrary nosthril.' It was also used against the plague. Because of its colour it was accepted by the *Doctrine of Signatures* as a suitable plant to stop bleeding. It seems a very small flower to cure 'the bitings of serpents and madd dogges', but so it was claimed. A tincture of St John's Wort and pimpernel, or pimpernel alone, was used for brain diseases. In the Middle Ages it was used in salads and as a pot-herb.

Its early reputation as a cosmetic herb was endorsed by Culpeper, who said that 'the distilled water or juice is much esteemed by French dames to cleanse the skin from any roughness', but he also recommended its more serious use in expelling stones from kidneys and bladder, a purpose for which it is still prescribed, with caution.

Pimpernel has, in fact, been recommended for the treatment of almost every disease from hydrophobia to tuberculosis, but its reputation still stands in the treatment of mental and nervous diseases, epilepsy and jaundice, but modern authorities consider it a drug that should not be used without medical advice.

The generic name of *Anagallis* comes from the Greek word for pleasure, and it is no misnomer, for there is little doubt of the charm and cheerfulness embodied in this tiny plant. The specific name *arvensis* means growing in the fields. It belongs to the Primula family.

Its common names of poor man's weather glass and shepherd's barometer refer to the fact that the flowers will not open in rainy weather, nor even when rain is anticipated. It is also called poor man's clock due to its punctual time-keeping on sunny days for it opens at seven o'clock in the morning and closes at two in the afternoon. It is best gathered for drying in June and July.

PIPSISSEWA

Chimaphila umbellata

A perennial evergreen of northern temperate zones pipsissewa grows in large areas of the USA. It is a handsome plant, with leathery bright green leaves, strongly veined and sharply toothed. Sculptured waxy flowers of white or pink, marked with a deeper pink or purple ring, appear in spreading clusters from May until August. It belongs to the Wintergreen family and prefers the shelter of dry woods.

It is known as bitter wintergreen, ground holly and pine tulip. The name love-in-winter comes from its generic name of *Chimaphila*, derived from

Anagallis arvensis.

PIMPERNEL — in this case, scarlet pimpernel — illustrated in Curtis' *Flora Londinensis*.

The ovate leaves grow in flat rosettes directly from the root, each having several long ribs growing from the base of the leaf to the point. The flower stems are channelled, reaching 6–8in (15–20cm), and bearing spikes of greenish-white or purplish-green flowers from May to October. These flower-heads are marvellous miniatures of architectural beauty. It seems that the reputation of the plantain as a healing herb has diminished since the invention of the lawn-mower, for it was once regarded as the herbalist's answer to an impressive numbler of human ills. True appreciation was shown by Culpeper, who said of its time of blooming, 'It is in beauty about July'.

The plant proves its benevolent disposition by loving its enemy, travelling wherever the English emigrant has travelled, and settling wherever he has settled. The seeds probably accompanied stowaways carrying agricultural seed, which would account for its common name of Englishman's foot or white-man's foot. The name was used by Hiawatha when he described the coming of the white man to Indian territory.

PLANTAIN as shown in a plate from the second volume of W. Curtis' *Flora Londinensis*, 1817.

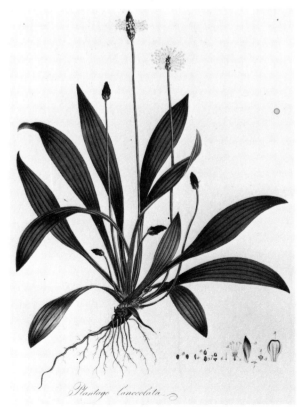

PIPSISSEWA, from the third volume of *Medicinal Plants*, 1880, by R. Bentley and H. Trimmen.

two Greek words for 'winter' and 'to love'. It is also called rheumatism weed, and for less obvious reasons, king's cure and prince's pine. The name pipsissewa is the white man's nearest equivalent to the American Indians' name for this useful medicinal plant.

It is used in the manufacture of tonics and is a valuable diuretic and astringent. A tea or poultice is made for the treatment of sores, tumours, blisters and other skin troubles. The dried leaves heal cuts and stop bleeding. It is also added to other medicines as a flavouring.

PLANTAIN

Plantago species

UNDER THE DOMINION OF VENUS

A perennial plant, common in waste places all over Europe and USA, plantain is of the *Plantago* genus, of which there are more than 200 species.

Wheresoe'er they tread, beneath them
Springs a flower unknown among us,
Springs the White-man's Foot in blossom.

The earliest name of plantain was waybroed or waybrode, which became corrupted into way-bread, giving the false impression that it was a herb always ready to nourish the weary traveller. In fact, no such nourishment may be expected, and its name simply indicates that it was bred at the wayside. Pliny records that 'Themison, a famous physician, sets forthe a whole booke of the hearbe waibred or plantaine, wherein he highly praiseth it; and challengeth it to himself the honour of first finding it out, notwithstanding it be a triviall and common hearbe trodden under everie man's foot'.

Plantago maintained its wayside reputation even in Burma, where travellers starting on a journey would hang a bunch on the pole of their buffalo cart to conciliate any evil spirit they might meet.

It is associated with St Patrick and is called St Patrick's leaf in Ireland, and Patrick's dock in the Isle of Man.

A piece of the root was once carried in the pocket to protect the bearer from snakebite, but anyone failing to take this wise precaution could still use plantain tea as a treatment when the inevitable happened. The name snakeweed in the USA is an echo from those days; it is also known there as rippleseed.

Plantain, apart from being good against jaundice, dropsy and falling sickness, was a trusted plant for healing wounds, no doubt because of its astringent properties. Shakespeare mentions it twice as a healer of broken shins. In *Love's Labours Lost,* Costard begs his companions for 'No salve, sir, but a plantain' to heal his wound; and in *Romeo and Juliet:*

Romeo: *Your plantain leaf is excellent for that.*

Benvolio: *For what, I pray thee?*

Romeo: *For your broken shin.*

The poet Shenstone wrote of the 'plantain ribb'd, That heals the reaper's wound.'

The ribbed leaves of the plantain gave it a place in the *Doctrine of Signatures* for the treament of the hands, fingers and nerves. Dooryard plantain, an affectionate US country name, was an old-fashioned cure for erysipelas, eczema, kidney and bladder diseases, stomach pains, back-ache, diarrhoea, burns and scalds, piles, sores and ulcers. The leaves pounded into paste stopped bleeding and gave relief to tumours, boils and carbuncles. A strong tea of 1oz (28g) of this pounded plantain to 1pt (550ml) boiling water, steeped for 20–30 minutes, was used with a syringe for haemorrhoids. A weak tea was given for bed-wetting.

Plantain juice, alone or mixed with lemon juice, is an excellent diuretic. The seeds, boiled in milk or broth, used to be taken as a laxative, and the warmed leaves were applied to draw out thorns or splinters from inflamed flesh.

Herbalists today prescribe plantain for asthma, bronchitis and for digestive weaknesses. They also advise plantain poultices for open sores and inflammation.

The leaves contain a soothing mucilage resembling linseed, and may be used for the same purposes. *P. lanceolata*, the ribwort plantain, is a British species whose mucilaginous coating was used by manufacturers for stiffening the finer kinds of linen. The leaves also yield a serviceable fibre from which paper may be made.

POKEWEED
Phytolacca americana

A strong-growing perennial of the Bloodberry family, pokeweed is native to the southern USA, as well as common in Mediterranean countries.

It is one of the best known North American plants, and most striking in appearance. It is smooth, strong smelling and succulent and has large fleshy poisonous roots with stout hollow stems whose pith is divided into discs. The large alternate leaves may grow to 8–12in (20–30cm) in length. The small white or greenish flowers are borne in long terminal racemes which eventually droop with the weight of their dark purple berries. The plant grows to a height of 4–12ft (1.2–3.6m), in waste places, along the damp edges of woods and in cultivated ground from Maine to Texas.

The young shoots, when boiled in two changes of water to remove their acridity, may be eaten as a vegetable. It is emetic and laxative, with narcotic properties. The dried root reduces inflammation and arthritic and rheumatic pains. It is sometimes used to adulterate belladonna, and as an ointment for skin diseases. Both berries and roots contain a dangerous drug.

It is also known as coakum, pokeroot, and pigeonberry, and was given the name of inkberry by the early settlers in the New World because the juice from the berries furnished them with ink.

The berries also produce a red dye if vinegar is added to the water, but the results are not permanent.

PRIMROSE
Primula vulgaris

UNDER THE DOMINION OF VENUS

A perennial, the primrose is native to Britain and Europe, and frequent among cold and temperate parts of the northern hemisphere.

Flourishing in meadows, copses, hedges and ditches, its short brown rootstock produces feathery yellow-green wrinkled leaves which appear aged in strange contrast to the flawless youth of the pale yellow, deceptively frail looking flowers, that grow on downy stems frequently stained with a rusty pink. There are two kinds of flower, 'pin-eyed' and 'thrum-eyed', and only one kind is found on each plant. Both have a delicate pale green tubed calyx, with a corolla of five petals. The 'pin-eyed' flower has within it only the green knob of the stigma. The 'thrum-eyed' shelters a ring of five anthers. Both root and flower contain a fragrant oil.

The occasional six-petalled primrose was believed to be lucky for love and marriage. It was considered unlucky to bring a single primrose into the house, and less than a bunch would bring disaster to a Worcestershire farmhouse, for the chicks and ducklings would die. If less than thirteen primroses were brought into a Norfolk farmhouse, it was believed that only that same number of eggs would be hatched by each goose. In Germany, however, it was believed that primroses could reveal the places where buried treasure lay hidden and that they also had the power to open locks, for which they were called *schusselblume*, the key-flower.

Shakespeare noticed not only the virginal look of this pale serene flower, but the fact that it often bloomed before the bees awoke in spring:

> *Pale primroses,*
> *That die unmarried, ere they can behold*
> *Bright Phoebus in his strength —*

The name comes from the Latin *primus*, first — the first rose of spring. It was also known as butter-rose and Easter-rose.

Primroses were once frequently used to decorate salads and sweets, crystallized for puddings and made into heady and delightful country wines. Izaak Walton frequently used primroses in fish dishes. Here is his recipe for a dish of minnows.

Izaak Walton's dish of minnows

— in the spring they make of them excellent minnow-tansies; for being washed well in salt, and their heads and tails cut off, and their guts taken out, and not washed after, they prove excellent for that use; that is, being fried with yolks of eggs, the flowers of cowslips, and of primroses, and a little tansy; thus used they make a dainty dish of meat.

Every spring women and children came into towns carrying baskets full of primroses, calling, 'Two bundles a penny, primroses, two bundles a penny!' It was not only for the sweet smell of the spring countryside that primroses were bought, for they were once of great importance in medicine. In Wales it was well known that primrose juice was a cure for madness. The roots pounded and the juice 'snuffed into the nostrils cured headaches and purged the brain'. Sodden in vinegar the flowers were a cure for scrofula. Bramble tops and primroses were made into an ointment used for spots and sores on the face.

Culpeper is unusually brief on the subject, merely telling his readers that he will instruct them how to make salves at the end of the book: 'make this as you are taught there, and do not (you that have ingenuity in you) see your poor neighbours go with wounded limbs, when a half-penny cost will heal them'.

Another learned herbalist wrote that 'a practitioner of London who was famous for curing the phrensie, after he had performed his cure by the due observation of physic, accustomed every yeare in the moneth of May to dyet his Patients after this manner; Take the leaves and the floures of Primrose, boile them a little in fountaine water, and in some rose and Betony waters, adding thereto sugar, pepper, salt and butter, which being strained he gave them to drinke thereof first and last'.

Today's herbalists say primrose tea, freshly made from the leaves and flowers, 2 teaspoonsfuls steeped in ½ cup of water, is good for rheumatism, gout, arthritis, and migraine, and as a general blood cleanser. A decoction of the rootstock, 2 teaspoonsfuls in a cup of water, may be taken for catarrh, coughs and bronchitis.

It is regarded as a safe, non-addictive cure for insomnia if an infusion is taken at bedtime.

POKEWEED: an 18th-century engraving by John Miller.

PRIMROSES being sold in the London streets: an engraving by L. Schiavonetti
after a painting by F. Wheatley, dated 1793.

ROSE, the plant of lovers, described in this charming illustration from *Tacuinum Sanitatum*, c. 1385.

ROSE
Rosa species

RED ROSES ARE UNDER JUPITER, DAMASK ROSES ARE UNDER VENUS, AND WHITE ROSES ARE UNDER THE MOON

'The Rose doth deserve the chief and prime place among all floures whatsoever, beeing not onely esteemed for his beauty, vertues, and his fragrant and odoriferous smell; but also because it is the honor and ornament of our English Sceptre, as by the conjunction appeareth in the uniting of those two most Royall Houses of Lancaster and York,' wrote Gerard. Similar sentiments must have been expressed by countless others.

Fossilized traces of the rose, 35 million years old, have been found in Montana, Colorado and Oregon. It has been established that all the many rose species are natives of the northern hemisphere, and all varieties south of the equator have been cultivated. The first recorded relationship of man with rose was discovered by Sir Leonard Woolley when he excavated the royal grave of Ur in Chaldaea and found evidence that the Sumerian King Sargon brought vines, figs and roses back to his country after a successful campaign 5,000 years ago.

It was not the beauty of the rose, however, that was the first concern of man. In the struggle for life the vital search for food and medicine must come first; in this the rose played its part. Flowers were brought in from the wild, tasted, tested and cultivated. Pliny listed thirty-two medicines that could be prepared from roses. Physic gardens and herbal cures evolved together. With the cultivation and the testing came the early manuscripts and the printed herbals, and after them the still-room books, with their receipts for 'melroset', 'sugar roset', syrope of roses', 'oyle of roses' and 'rose water'. These may be full of old-world charm to us today, but they are of greater importance as records of the earnest search for health through the knowledge of medicine. Even rose water, little more than a delightful perfume and flavouring today, was regarded by Gerard (and earlier herbalists) as vital in medicine and only of secondary importance in the kitchen:

'The distilled water of Roses is good for the strengthening of the heart, and refreshing of the spirits, and likewise for all things that require a gentle cooling. The same being put in junketting dishes, cakes, sauces, and many other pleasant things, giveth a fine and delectable taste. It mitigateth the paine of the eies proceeding of a hot cause, bringeth sleep, which also the fresh roses themselves provoke through their sweet and pleasant smell.

'Of like vertue also are the leaves of these preserved in Sugar, especially if they be onely bruised with the hands, and diligently tempered with Sugar, and so heat at the fire rather then boyled.

'The conserve of Roses, as well as that which is made by ebullition or boiling, taken in the morning fasting, and last at night, strengthneth the heart, and taketh away the shaking and trembling thereof . . .

'Take Roses at your pleasure, put them to boyle in faire water, having regard to the quantity; for if you have many Roses you may take more water; if fewer, the lesse water will serve; the which you shall boyle at the least three or foure houres, even as you would boile a piece of meate, until in the eating they be very tender, at which time the Roses will lose their colour, that you would thinke your labour lost, and the thing spoiled. But proceed, for though the Roses have lost their colour, the water hath gotten the tincture thereof; then you shall adde unto one pound of Roses, foure pound of fine Sugar in pure pouder, and so according to the rest of the Roses. Thus shall you let them boyle gently after the Sugar is put therto, continually stirring it with a woodden Spatula untill it be cold, whereof one pound weight is worth six pound of the crude or raw conserve, as well for the vertues and goodnesse in taste, as also for the beautifull colour.

'The making of the crude or raw conserve is very well knowne, as also Sugar roset, and divers other pretty things made of Roses and Sugar, which are impertinent unto our history, because I intend nether to make thereof an Apothecaries shop, nor a Sugar-Bakers storehouse, leaving the rest for our cunning confectioners.'

By this time other uses were being discovered, and Gerard noted: 'The white leaves (of white roses) stamped in a wooden dish with a piece of Allum and the juyce strained forth into some glased vessell, dried in the shadow, and kept, is the most fine and pleasant yellow colour that may be divised, not onely to limne or wash pictures and Imagerie in books, but also to colour meats and sauces, which notwithstanding the Allum is very wholesome.'

Culpeper said: 'Of the red Roses are usually made many compositions, all serving to sundry good uses, viz. Electuary of Roses, conserve both moist and dry, which is more usually called Sugar of Roses, Syrup of dry Roses, and Honey of Roses . . . The distilled water of Roses, vinegar of Roses, ointment, and oil of Roses, and the Rose leaves dried, are of very great use and effect. To write at large of every one of these would make my book swell too big . . . Honey of Roses is much used in gargles and lotions to wash sores, either in the mouth, throat, or other parts, both to cleanse and heal them . . . Rose leaves and mint, heated and applied outwardly to the stomach, stay castings, and very much strengthen a weak stomach.'

The medicinal rose, *R. gallica officinalis*, a variety cultivated by the Romans, was by the 13th century largely grown in the town of Provins, near Paris. Provins was by now the centre of the rose-growing industry, and by 1597, when Gerard published his herbal, the main street of the town was entirely occupied by apothecaries' shops. The Provins or Apothecary's rose was cultivated also in England, and it is generally accepted that it is the rose adopted as the emblem of the House of Lancaster.

North America's early settlers found their own uses for the native roses. The meadow rose, *R. blanda*, furnished hips that when boiled made an excellent soothing syrup for itches and sores. The dried flowers were powdered and made into a tea for heartburn, and physic for settling the stomach was found in the hips of the Carolina rose. Today, herbalists prescribe an infusion of the fresh or dried petals of *R. canina*, Rupert Brooke's 'English unofficial rose', to strengthen the heart and the brain.

Rose hips, with their high content of vitamin C, are of the greatest value. Rose-hip syrup is a popular preventative of the common cold, and is taken for kidney ailments, diarrhoea and dysentery, and to lighten menstrual pains. The leaves of the dog rose may be dried and infused as a substitute for tea.

The Greeks, Romans and Egyptians had long ago discovered how to extract the perfume from roses by steeping the petals in water, oil or alcohol, and from the Middle Ages the use of distilled rose water in perfumes and cosmetics, as well as in medicine, became part of everyday housekeeping. Housewives concocted sweet bags, pomanders, scented candles, perfumed gloves, toilet waters, pastilles and pot-pourri. Notes were made of weights and measures; pecks of rose petals and pints of spring water; of steeping and seething and straining and similar fruitful activities. Receipts were exchanged by friends and kin.

(left, above) ROSES in profusion form the frontispiece to Mary Lawrence's *Les Roses*, 1799.

(left, below) THE ROSE *Rosa lutea*, a 19th-century watercolour from the Reeves Collection of the Royal Horticultural Society.

That the conducting of these still-room experiments and the keeping of still-room books was not exclusively women's work is proved by the number of men who kept, and sometimes published for the benefit of others, these invaluable prescriptions. One of the earliest was Sir Hugh Platt, courtier and noted gardener. The following recipe is taken from his *Delights for Ladies*, 1594.

To make a speciall sweet water to perfume clothes in the folding being washed

Take a quart of Damask rose water and put it into a glasse, put unto it a handfull of Lavender flowers, two ounces of Orris, a dram of Muske, the weight of four pence of Amber-greece, as much Civet, foure drops of Oyle of Cloves, stop this close, and set it in the Sunne a fortnight; put one spoonfull of this water into a bason of common water and put it into a glasse and so sprinkle your clothes therewith in your folding: the dregs left in the bottome (when the water is spent) will make as much more, if you keepe them, and put fresh Rose-water to it.

Gervase Markham, poet, dramatist, soldier and prolific garden writer, describes how to perfume gloves in his book *The English Housewife*, 1675.

To perfume gloves

Take Rose-water and Angelica-water, and put to them the powder of Cloves, Ambergreece, Musk and Lignum Aloes, Benjamin and Calamus aromaticus: boyl then hang them in the Sun to dry and turn them often: and thus three times wet them and dry them again: or otherwise take Rose-water and wet your Gloves therein, then hang them up till they be almost dry; then take half an ounce of Benjamin, and grind it with the oyl of Almonds, and rub it on the Gloves till it be almost dryed in: then take twenty grains of Musk, and grind them together with oyl of Almonds and so rub it on the Gloves and then hang them up to dry, or let them dry in your bosome, and so after use them at your pleasure.

(right) THE ROSE *Rosa aimee vibert*, a plate by Alfred Parsons from Wilmot's *Genus Rosa*, 1910–14.

[143]

Sir Kenelm Digby, banished from England in 1643 for Royalist sympathies and subsequently made chancellor to Queen Henrietta Maria at the Restoration, found both the time and interest to describe how to make rose cakes or pastilles not only to sweeten the room but as an antiseptic inhalant. The instructions appeared in *Choice and Experimented Receipts*, 1668.

Rose pastills to burn

Take Benjamin three ounces, storax two ounces, Damask Rose-buds one ounce; grind the Roses by themselves, and the rest also: Then take Lignum Aloes, Amber, fine Sugar, Civet, powder of Cypress, half a quarter of a pound; grind these well together. Then mix it with gum Tragacanth dissolved in Orange-flowers or Rose-water and make them up.

Pomanders were also in general use against the plague, and although these most popularly took the form of an orange or apple stuck with cloves, they were also made of a mixture of aromatic and sweet herbs and spices in a solid form that might be carried or worn. *Mary Doggett. Her Book of Receipts*, 1682, contains a most practical and economical receipt for a 'sweet bagg' which, after pounding and working again at the end of a year, will apparently smell as fresh as ever. She also gives her original method of making a pomander.

A pomander

Take a quarter of an ounce of Civit, a quarter and a half quarter of an ounce of Ambergreese, not half a quarter of an ounce of ye spiritt of Roses, 7 ounces of Benjamin, allmost a pound of Damask Rose-buds cutt. Lay Gumdragon on rose water and with it make up your Pomander, with beads as big as nutmegs; when you make them up wash your hands with oyle of Jasmin to smooth them, then make them have a gloss; this quantitie will make seaven braceletes.

How to make 'Odoriferous Candles Against Venome and the Plague', 'Rose scented Beads for a Rosary', 'Rose scented Snuff' and 'A Bag to Smell unto to Cause One to Sleep', fill the pages of these little books; many such recipes have been gathered together by the late Eleanour Sinclair Rohde.

If it were not considered an *embarrass des roses*, a complete rose tea might be offered to garden-party guests. The idea is not so unusual as might be supposed, for rose petal delicacies were a feature of the Victorian tea-table.

Menu for a rose tea-party

Thinly cut wholemeal bread and butter with individual pots of rose-hip jelly. Rose-petal sandwiches, and small pink-iced cakes decorated with crystallized rose petals. Rose tea.

Rose-hip jelly

4lb (1.8kg) windfall apples
2lb (900g) firm ripe rose-hips
preserving sugar

Cut up apples, removing bruised parts and put into a preserving pan with enough water to cover, and 1pt (550ml) for the rose hips. Cook to a pulp, meanwhile putting rose hips through the coarsest cutter of the mincer. Add minced rose hips to cooked apple, and gently simmer for 10 minutes. Remove and leave for a further 10 minutes before straining through a jelly-bag. Leave to drip overnight.

Next day measure juice and allow 14oz (400g) sugar to each pint (550ml) juice. Weigh sugar and put it in oven to heat thoroughly. Boil juice for 3 minutes and add hot sugar. Test for setting, pour into warm jars and tie down.

Rose-petal sandwiches

Cut the white points from freshly gathered crimson or other sweet-scented petals. Cut bread and butter very thinly (it can be brown or white, or one of each together). Remove crusts before arranging rose petals, so that they may be seen at the edges of the sandwich. Rose-petal sandwiches were a feature at Balmoral tea-parties.

Crystallized rose petals

Any small iced cakes may be decorated with crystallized rose-petals. Beat the white of an egg gently to avoid making it frothy. Dip each petal into the egg-white. Spread them out on a large flat dish and sprinkle with castor sugar. Turn each petal carefully and sprinkle the reverse. Leave to dry in a warm room. An old recipe suggests dipping the petals in rose water instead of egg-white, and drying in the hot sun after sugaring.

Rose tea

A handful of crimson rose petals infused in a cupful of boiling water, sweetened if required with half a teaspoonful of honey. As soon as the

ROSE, on the right, and pea, from a 16th-century *Herbal and Bestiary ABC*. The garden pea, *Pisum sativum*, is now cultivated throughout almost the entire Northern Hemisphere, although originally a native of central Asia.

boiling water covers the petals, the colour drains out, and after infusing for a few minutes the petals are removed and a clear bluish-red perfumed liquid remains. It is soft, like scented rain water. If a larger quantity is required, do not use a metal teapot.

Rose water may be made by filling a saucepan with crimson petals, adding water and bringing them to the boil. Cover and simmer for a few minutes and then strain. A small jug of freshly made rose water would be welcomed by any newly arrived guest.

In that delightful classic *Cranford*, Mrs Gaskell says, 'I had often occasion to notice the use made of fragments and small opportunities in Cranford; the rose-leaves that were gathered even as they fell to make into a pot-pourri for some one who had no garden, the little bundles of lavender flowers sent to strew the drawers of some town-dweller, or to burn in the chamber of some invalid'.

Recipes for pot-pourri are to be found from ages past, but we learn from Mrs Earle, the author of *Pot-Pourri from a Surrey Garden*, that the original word meant a mixed stew or hotch-potch, an *olla podrida*, or favourite Spanish dish of various kinds of meat chopped finely and stewed with vegetables. The recipe she quotes is not her own, but 'a rich and opulent receipt' from *The Garden's Story*, 1895, by Mr Ellwanger. Such richness and opulence is hardly suitable for the present race of pot-pourri makers, enthusiastic as they may be, so a simpler version has been chosen, to be adapted or expanded to suit individual taste.

Pot-pourri

Gather the petals while young, at noon on a dry day. It is important that they should be thoroughly dried as quickly as possible. Wire trays ensure a good circulation of air, and a well ventilated room provides the ideal conditions. The mixture should not be made until every petal is completely dry, to avoid subsequent mildew. Rose petals should form the chief ingredient, with a combination of rosemary, thyme, lavender, the dried and powdered skin of an orange, a few bay leaves, half an ounce of powdered clove, and a teaspoonful of mixed spice. Most sweetly scented flowers from the garden are suitable, and any other aromatic herbs available. A few tiny rosebuds and half opened borage flowers, and one or two marigold petals may be laid on top to brighten the bowl.

Special packets of prepared spices can be bought from most chemists for the purpose of mixing with the flowers from one's own garden.

Rose wine

1½lb (680g) rose petals, all of one variety if possible
3lb (1.3kg) white sugar
1lb (454g) barley
1tsp dried yeast
1gal (4.5l) water

Boil the rose petals in ½gal (2.2l) water for 15 minutes. Boil barley in the other ½gal (2.2l) for 5 minutes. Leave to cool, and when both are at blood temperature strain them into the sugar and stir until the sugar is dissolved. Cream yeast in ½ cup warm water and add. Stir again and pour into wine jars which should be sealed with an air lock or a wad of cotton wool. Leave to ferment in a warm place for about a month, and when bubbling has ceased, pour the liquid into wine bottles through filter papers, and cork. Leave for at least a year.

ROSEMARY
Rosmarinus officinalis

A HERB OF THE SUN, UNDER THE CELESTIAL RAM

A perennial, rosemary is native to the Mediterranean area and to many parts of Europe, especially near the sea, from which it gets its name, *rosmarinus,* dew of the sea. The branches have a scaly bark and bear narrow evergreen leathery leaves, dark green above and downy white beneath. The flowers are pale lavender-blue or sometimes white and appear in April and May. The shrub can reach about 6–8ft (1.8–2.4m). The whole plant is aromatic.

An ancient plant, it is mentioned in an Anglo-Saxon herbal of the 11th century. Charlemagne was aware of its many virtues and ordered it to be grown on the imperial farm. It was early cultivated in the physic gardens for medicine, cookery and as a bee-plant. There is a tradition that the Countess of Hainault sent the first plants to her daughter in England, after Philippa had become Edward III's queen in 1328. From that time onwards it was one of the favourite herbs in stillroom, kitchen, bedroom and garden. In a linen cloth tied around the right arm it made the wearer 'light and merrie'. In the clothes-chest it rendered moths and insects noticeably less 'merrie', and if hidden under the bed the sleeper was delivered 'from all evil dreams'. The ashes were made into a dentifrice, and as a poultice gave sufferers whose legs were 'blowen with gout' much relief.

The essential oil was distilled by Raymond Tully in about 1330, and was generally believed to have preservative properties. Gerard advised that a garland of rosemary should be worn around the neck as a remedy against the 'stuffing of the head, and a cold braine'.

Culpeper said that 'the leaves shred small, and taken in a pipe, as tobacco is taken, helpeth those that have any cough, phthisick, or consumption'. He added that 'the leaves are much used in bathings; and made into ointments or oil, are good to help cold benumbed joints'. He believed that it was good for the eyesight, 'the flowers thereof being taken all the while it is flowering, every morning fasting, with bread and salt'.

John Evelyn found that rubbing his closed eyelids with spirits of wine in which a few rosemary flowers had been distilled, strengthened not only his sight but the rest of his senses, especially his hearing, a drop or two being distilled into the nose or ears.

What was the magic of this shrub that preserved health, beautified women, busied the cook and intoxicated the bees? It was used in the ale-house for dipping in tankards, and for stirring the cups at christenings. It was sold in the apothecaries' shops as a cure for hang-overs, or 'the affections of the head caused by wine', and its wood was made into 'lutes or such like instruments, for lovers' madrigals'. Queens have worn it at their bridals, and it has sweetened the graves of common men.

The whole character of the plant was expressed by William Langham in *The Garden of Health*, 1579: 'Seethe much Rosemary, and bathe therein to make thee lusty, lively, joyfull, likeing and youngly.' It is difficult to think what the medieval housewife would have done without it. Still-room books are full of its virtues. Particularly was it in favour for the treatment of the hair. This recipe is to be recommended, except for blonde hair.

Rosemary shampoo

A teaspoonful of chopped rosemary leaves to a cup of boiling water. Strain and massage the liquid into your scalp. Comb through and then shampoo in the ordinary way.

A recipe for rosemary perfume appeared in *The Accomplish'd Lady's Delight*, 1719, by Mrs Mary Eales (confectioner to Queen Anne).

A royal perfume to make your house smell like rosemary

Take 3 Spoonfuls of Perfect Rosemary and as much Sugar as half a Walnut beaten into small powder; all these boyle together in a Perfuming-pan upon hot Embers, with a few Coals.

Today's short-cut, which applies also to other aromatic herbs and shrubs, is to burn your prunings of rosemary on an open fire. The incense rising from rosemary cuttings, faded marigolds, chopped-down tansy, or best of all, chrysanthemums cut down in autumn, makes the thought of the coming winter a little easier to bear. The Elizabethans used rosemary clippings mixed with woodruff, and other aromatic plants, for strewing the floors of their houses.

One of the earliest known perfumed waters is Hungary water, made from a recipe given to

Queen Elizabeth of Hungary by a hermit in 1370. The original recipe remained in Vienna, but it is said to have been made by distilling the tips and flowers of rosemary with *aqua vitae* — the first mention of the employment of alcohol for extracting the essential oil from a plant. Rosemary is also one of the ingredients of eau de cologne.

An old recipe for rosemary wine is simple and can be used today. It makes a refreshing and unusual drink, especially for those suffering from a weak heart.

Rosemary wine

Infuse a bunch of rosemary tips (about 6in (15cm) long) in sound white wine for a few days. The wine will then be fit for use.

The following recipe is taken from the *Ladies Cabinet Enlarged and Opened, etc.*, 1654, by Lord Ruthven.

Honey of rosemary flowers

Take of Rosemary flowers a pound, clarified hony three pound, mix them in a glasse with a narrow mouth, set them in the sun and keep them for use.

Chicken joints with rosemary sauce

Fry young chicken joints in a little butter and oil. After browning, reduce heat, cover and cook for 25 minutes, turning once. Meanwhile prepare a sauce of the juice of one lemon, a tablespoonful of honey, and a little chopped rosemary. Heat and pour into a sauce boat. Serve the chicken joints with a slice of lemon and a sprig of parsley, watercress and small new potatoes.

Chopped rosemary leaves mixed with white breadcrumbs dredged over a joint of lamb an hour before serving greatly improves the flavour. A small quantity of the chopped leaves may be used to flavour puddings and cakes, and the flowers crystallized in the same way as rose petals (see p. 144), used for decoration.

In medicine, rosemary is tonic, astringent and stimulant. In the Middle Ages a posset was made of hot curdled milk and ale, honey and rosemary as a nerve tonic and for the heart. An infusion of a teaspoonful of the leaves and flowers in a cup of warm water is good for the digestion, but should be taken not more than once a day. A preparation of dried rosemary and coltsfoot leaves may be smoked for asthma. Oil of rosemary is good for rheumatism. Rosemary combined with equal quantities of skullcap, vervain and betony as an infusion for migraine is beneficial. For a headache,

a few drops of spirits of rosemary should be rubbed on forehead and neck, and the fumes inhaled. The Chinese take rosemary tea with a pinch of ginger as a digestive.

RUE
Ruta graveolens

A HERB OF THE SUN UNDER THE DOMINION OF LEO

An evergreen shrub with attractive blue-green much divided leaves and small yellow flowers, rue is very popular with flower arrangers.

It is also called the herb of Grace, because it was used in bunches for sprinkling holy water at the ceremony preceding High Mass on Sundays. It was known familiarly as herbygrass, and respectfully as the herb of repentance. It is mentioned only once in the Bible, in Luke *xi*:42, 43: 'But woe unto you, Pharisees! for ye tithe mint and rue and all manner of herbs, and pass over judgement and the love of God.'

The monk Walahfrid Strabo grew it in his garden at Reichenau in the 9th century, and in his *Hortulus* he claimed for it 'many a healing power . . . to combat hidden toxin and expel from the bowels the invading forces of noxious poison'. It was understood to be medicinally safe if gathered in the morning, but poisonous if picked later. Rue was supposed to improve the eyesight; Pliny stated that it was eaten in great quantities by the artists of his time for this reason. They also ate the leaves as a protection against the 'evil eye'. Happily, it seems to have outgrown its ancient and dubious quality of promoting love in man and diminishing it in woman.

As a medicinal herb it was considered good for toadstool-poisoning, the stings of hornets, bees and wasps, and the bites of serpents. The following recipe 'Against the Sweating Sickness' was prescribed in 1517: 'Take a handful of rue, called Herb-grace, an handful marygold, half a handful feverfew, a handful sorrel, a handful burnet, and half a handful dragons, the top in summer, the root in winter; wash them in running water and let them seethe soberly till night the half be consumed, then draw back the pot till it be almost cold, strain it and keep it close and use thereof morn and even, and when need is, oftener; and if it be bitter, allay it with sugar candy; and if it be taken afore the pimples break forth there is no doubt but with the Grace of Jesu it shall ament man, woman or child.'

RUE, here appearing in two strikingly different illustrations, one from an English manuscript from about 1100 in the possession of the Bodleian Library, Oxford (*left*), the other from *Tacuinum Sanitatum, c.* 1385.

The once-noted vinegar of the four thieves was an anti-pestilential vinegar containing rue, which was used during the plague of Marseilles. Invented by four anonymous villains, it was used for protection against infection when they broke into houses.

Rue has strong magical connections, and was used by and against witches. The circles and other signs of magic drawn by witches were no doubt of pagan origin, and rue was a necessary ingredient of their secret concoctions. 'Then sprinkles she the juice of Rue With nine drops of the morning dew,' wrote Drayton, in a description of a witch's incantation.

Aristotle had an ingenious explanation for the use of rue against witchcraft. He claimed that the Greeks were not in the habit of sitting down at table with strangers, and that this made them so nervous that they ate too quickly and suffered from flatulence and indigestion. They concluded, therefore, that they had been bewitched. As rue acted as an antidote to indigestion, they came to the conclusion that it must also disarm witches and dispel their charms. So a bundle of rue came to be used as a witch-finder, and fastened over the door it prevented witches from entering.

In modern medicine a substance called rutin, a product of rue, was used in World War II to treat high blood-pressure. Rutin tea is available in most health-food shops. It is a potent herb and should be taken sparingly, and not during pregnancy. It is thought to be a cure for cramp, and is used as a nerve tonic and in relieving the pains of rheumatism and sciatica. A teaspoonful of leaves may be infused in ¾pt (400ml) water, and a dessertspoonful of the liquid taken before going to bed. It should be said, however, that it does not suit everyone.

During the Great Plague rue was carried as an antiseptic, and it was strewn over the hustings on the occasion of the election of the Lord Mayor and Sheriffs at the Guildhall in London, and in the Law and Criminal Courts against the risk of gaol fever. Dickens referred to its use in Newgate in *A Tale of Two Cities*. Its ancient employment as a destroyer of fleas is no longer necessary, but there is an antiseptic virtue in the plant that we can still enjoy, for it is a repellant of flies. Grown in window boxes or around stables, barns and manure heaps, rue may be more than just a pleasure to the eye; it does not, however, like growing with mint.

Too bitter for popular culinary use in England, it was grown as a crop in Mitcham in the 19th century for the making of rue gin and cried in the London streets at a farthing a bunch. Its roots give a good red dye.

SAFFLOWER
Carthamus tinctorius

A hardy annual plant, safflower is possibly native to Egypt and the Mediterranean countries. It was introduced into England in the 16th century and is cultivated in a small way. It is largely cultivated in southern Europe, China, India and the USA.

A member of the Compositae family, safflower has stiff thistle-like leaves armed with small spiny teeth. The plant reaches a height of 1–3ft (30–90cm) and produces spiny heads of yellow-red flowers which develop into seeds resembling small white and shining shells. The flowers are known to have been worn in the wreaths and garlands of the ancient Egyptians.

The safflower florets are gathered just before withering, and are used for the dyeing of wool, silk and leather. The flowers give a yellow dye, and by means of alkalis the bright reds and purples of China silks were produced. It also produces a pink dye which was once used to dye red official tape in India.

Mixed with talc, a rouge was once made of it for actors. It was also the principal ingredient in macassar oil, a hair oil very popular with Victorian gentlemen.

The petals are added to certain dishes to give colour and flavour. In Poland they are used in certain types of bread. The flowers are sometimes introduced into pot-pourri. Its common names of American saffron, dyer's saffron, bastard saffron, and Mexican saffron are an indication of some of these uses. Safflower has been used as a substitute for saffron, although it is unrelated.

Safflower tea, made of 1 teaspoonful of the flowers in 1 cup of water, produces a strong perspiration when taken hot for colds. It is used for dropsy and measles, and it has a calming effect in cases of hysteria.

The following is a pleasant and health-giving

CARTHAMVS foliis ouatis integris ferrato-aculeatis. *Linn.* S. P. 830. *Ludw.* D. G. P. 325.
· · · · · tinctorius.
· · · · · officin.

SAFFLOWER, in J. Kniphof's *Botanica in Originali seu Herbarium Vivum.*

dish which is good as a starter, or with bacon rolls as a supper dish.

Courgettes in safflower oil, cider vinegar and honey

Trim either end from 1lb (450g) small courgettes and leave unpeeled. Slice thickly and add to a pan of boiling salted water. Reboil, simmer for 2

[150]

minutes, and drain. This removes any bitterness in the skins and preserves the colour. Heat 1tbsp safflower oil and 1oz (28g) butter, and add drained courgettes. Add 1tsp cider vinegar and ½tsp honey. Season with salt and freshly milled pepper. Cook for a few minutes until soft.

SAFFRON
Crocus sativus

A HERB OF THE SUN, UNDER THE DOMINION OF LEO

C. *sativus*, the true crocus, is cultivated in France, Spain, Sicily and Iran, and it is native to Greece and Asia Minor. In the past it was cultivated in England at Saffron Walden, to which it gave its name.

The lavender-tinted, lily-like flowers appear without the leaves in September. They rise straight from the corm, which is about the size of a nutmeg. The flowers contain a three-cleft deep orange stigma which hangs from the flower and is aromatic and bitter. When dried, these stigmas constituted one of the most valued and expensive spices in the world; the Arabs, Greeks and Romans used it in perfume, medicine and dyeing. The leaves, which succeed the flowers, are slender, dark green and have a white central line.

In biblical times saffron was of the highest importance, not only as a spice and perfume, but for its food-colouring properties. The aromatic, brilliantly coloured stigmas were packed together and sold as cake-saffron, and in this form conveyed from Persia to India for the colouring of curry.

Saffron was mentioned by Homer and Theophrastus; Pliny said that the benches of public theatres were strewn with the flowers, and the petals placed in small fountains to scent the banqueting halls. Saffron-scented essences were made to descend upon the people like dew, from the *velarium* forming the roof of the amphitheatre. Lucan, a Roman writer, described in *Pharsalia* how the blood runs out of a man bitten by a serpent, that it spouts out 'in the same manner as the sweet-smelling essence of saffron issues from the limbs of a statue'.

In 16th- and 17th-century England, saffron was considered a remedy for innumerable complaints. Because of its colour it was believed to be a remedy for jaundice. Lord Bacon advocated the syrups of dried roses, saffron, and apples to procure quiet sleep, and recommended that 'some pills, or a small draught of these things, should be used familiarly'. He claimed that what made the English people sprightly was 'the liberal use of saffron in their broths and sweetmeats'.

Gerard said that 'the eyes being anointed with the same [saffron] dissolved in milke or fennel or rose water, are preserved from being hurt by the small pox or measels'. He also claimed that steeped in water it could be used 'to limne pictures and imagerie'.

There is a tradition that saffron was smuggled into England by a pilgrim in the hollow of his palmer's staff, for 'if he had been taken, by the law of the country from whence he came, he had died for the fact'.

Saffron has always been costly, since usually the stigmas only are used, and these have to be gathered by hand. No less than 60,000 stigmas are needed to make 1lb (450g) of saffron, and only 4lb (1.8kg) can be obtained from an acre of ground. C. *sativus* should not be confused with the large and handsome C. *autumnalis* of our gardens, a poisonous plant which is used in medicine — but only under medical advice. It is in no way suitable for cooking.

Saffron was once used for dyeing, for colouring butter, for saffron-cakes and saffron-bread, and tansies. It used to be made into balls with honey, and when dried the balls were powdered.

It was so highly valued, even by the Puritans, that Samuel Hartlib, the friend of Milton, maintained that saffron was allowed to be picked on the Lord's day 'because it is concieved that God who hath made it so to flower, would not a thing so usefull for men's health should be lost of gathering'. In the 19th-century it was used, combined with sandalwood, cochineal and talc powder, in the making of rouge.

The famous French *bouillabaisse*, traditionally made of a specimen of every variety of fish caught off the coast of Marseilles, is best cooked in white wine and saffron, but an English *bouillabaisse* must be adapted to circumstance.

Bouillabaisse
several different kinds of fish
1 onion
1 clove garlic
sprig of parsley
piece of Seville orange peel
pepper
salt
spice
pinch of saffron
a little oil

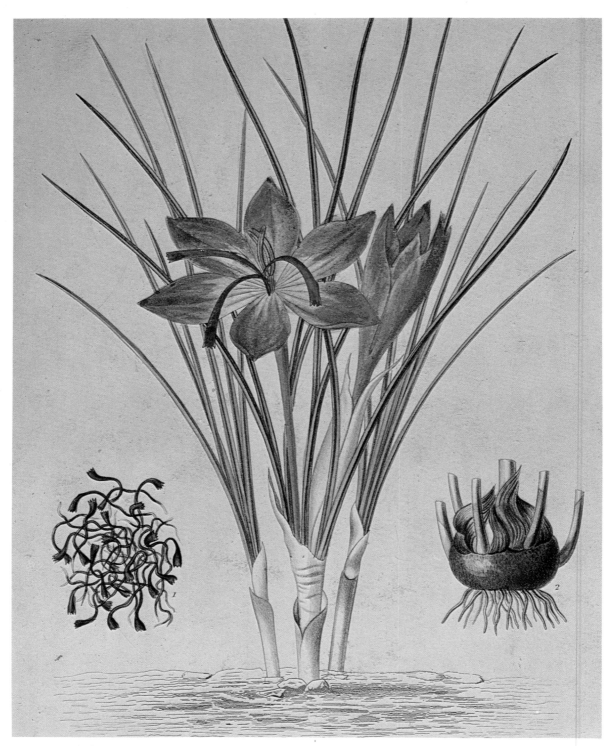

SAFFRON, the most expensive of all spices, comes from the crocus of the saffron flower, illustrated here in a 19th-century French engraving in the possession of the Bibliothèque Nationale des Arts Décoratifs, Paris.

(*right*) SAGE, from *Tacuinum Sanitatum, c.* 1385.

This dish should be made of several kinds of fish, the more the better, except for mackerel, pilchards and herrings. Place in large saucepan the onion, cut in 4 or 5 pieces, garlic, minced parsley, orange peel and flavourings; add sufficient water just to cover fish, but do not add fish and oil. Cook mixture well, then cut fish into pieces, and put it into pan over a fierce heat. The name bouillabaisse indicates that the cooking should be very fast — it should boil for about ¼ hour, according to the quantity and type of fish. Fennel, sage, or bay leaf may be added.

SAGE

Salvia officinalis

A PLANT OF JUPITER

A perennial, native to the northern shores of the Mediterranean, sage is cultivated in England, France and Germany. There are forty different wild sages in the USA. Sage is a member of the Mint family, and one of the most important medicinal herbs of antiquity. The Greeks dedicated it to Zeus and the Romans to Jupiter. It is the symbol of domestic virtue.

Gerard described its leaves as 'long, wrinkled, rough and whitish, like in roughness to woollen cloth threadbare'. It is a quiet, unexciting plant, and its name seems infinitely suitable, although the reference comes from the Latin, *salvere*, to be saved, due to its many uses in healing. The stems, on which grow purple or white two-lipped flowers in whorls, are square and hairy. The flowers appear in June, July and August. There are, however, many varieties of brighter and more attractive colouring; red-leaved, red and white, white, green and white, crisped and variegated in many forms.

'Sawge' as it was called in the Middle Ages, was grown for many purposes: the curing of 'falling sickness' (epilepsy), lethargy, palsy, stitch, cramp and plague. It was recommended for baths, gargles, hair-dye, and, of course, the 'bitings of serpents'. It was said that 'If women who cannot conceive ... will take a quantitie of the juice of sage, with a little salt, for four days before they company with their husbands, it will help them not only to conceive, but to retain the birth without miscarrying'.

In time of plague, sage juice was drunk with vinegar, and gargles were made with sage, rosemary, honeysuckle and plantain, boiled in wine or

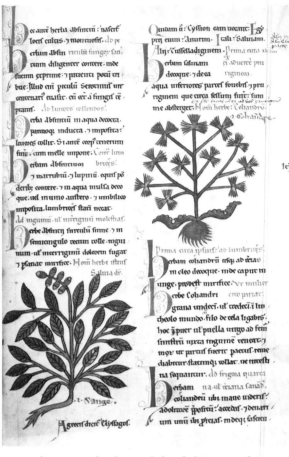

SAGE, shown at the lower left of this page from an English 13th-century manuscript. The plant depicted on the right is coriander.

water, with honey. In *The Knight of the Burning Pestle*, by Beaumont and Fletcher, 'wholesome broth, with sage and comfrey' is recommended as a cure for beaten bones.

Sage tea was as commonly drunk as China and Ceylon tea is today, and in the 18th century sage butter was one of the Church's great fasting dishes. An early 19th-century recipe for the curing of a relaxed throat gives the following: 'A handful of sage-leaves, a handful of fresh or dried rose-leaves, pour over them a pint of boiling water; in half an hour strain it off, and stir in two spoonfuls of honey and half a pint of vinegar.'

In 1845, Mrs Loudon described the making of sage cheese. 'In many parts of Gloucestershire, what is called Sage Cheese is made. For this a couple of handfuls of sage leaves and a handful of parsley are generally put into a portion of the evening's milk, and suffered to remain all night. In the morning the milk is warmed, and, after being strained from the leaves, it is turned to curd with the rennet in the usual way. In the mean time a portion of the morning's milk into which no colouring matter is put, is turned to curd by rennet; and the curds of both kinds are kept separate through the processes of draining and scalding, till they are ready to be put into the vat, when they are mixed accord to the fancy of the dairymaid. Sometimes the green curd is pressed into a tin or wooden mould, so as to form a dolphin or some other fanciful figure; in which case it is taken carefully out of the mould, and put into the vat without breaking it, and the white curd is crumbled between the fingers and pressed carefully and firmly round it. In other cases the sage and parsley leaves are only bruised, and the juice which is pressed from them is mingled with a portion of the morning's milk; or one portion of the milk is coloured red with the juice of beetroot, another green with the juice of spinach leaves flavoured with sage, and another yellow with the bruised petals of the marigold ... In other cases the whole of the milk is coloured and flavoured with sage.'

Sage is used to treat coughs, colds, headaches and fevers. An infusion of the leaves is used for sore throats as a gargle or a mouthwash. The gargle is made from 1pt (550ml) boiling water poured over a handful of leaves, with the addition when cool of a little vinegar and honey, or perhaps a clove and a small piece of alum about the size of a pea. Red sage is given for asthma, coughs, colds, bronchitis and tonsillitis. The whole herb is used.

Sage has tonic qualities and is good for the liver, and indeed for the whole digestive system. It is used as an invigorating bath additive, and the leaves rubbed on the teeth are said to keep them white. Like rosemary, it is included in hair tonics to restore grey hair to its original colour, and to remove dandruff. It is also used as a powerful herbal tobacco.

S. officinalis, garden sage, grows in profusion over the rocks in Crete where, in the sunshine, its fragrance is very powerful. One of the species produces galls which are formed by insects and are sold in the markets as sage apples for the making of a delicious conserve. It also grows in great abundance on the barren Adriatic coast of Yugoslavia, where the essential oils are sold for the making of perfumes.

It is a valuable bee-plant, and is used in the making of herb beer, to flavour wine, and in the perfuming of soaps.

In cookery, it is best known for its use in sage and onion stuffing for white meat. The same recipe can be used to stuff tomatoes or green peppers as a supper dish. It is excellent in sausages, pâtés and terrines. Chopped finely and beaten into cream cheese it makes a good sandwich filling.

When preparing sage and onion stuffing for a joint, make double quantities for further requirements. It can be frozen and used for many different purposes, such as the following quick and easy recipe:

Sage and onion soup
1 chicken-stock cube
1 heaped tbsp sage and onion stuffing
1tsp brown sauce
1pt (550ml) water

Boil the water with the chicken-stock cube, and gradually stir in sage and onion and sauce. Serve with a sprinkle of parmesan cheese.

Sage is essential in any herb garden, and can be used fresh or dried. It is at its most beneficial in the spring, and this is the best time for drying. It should be propagated by layering.

It is sad that John Evelyn was not more assiduous in his use of sage, for it was he who said, ''Tis a plant, indeed, with so many and wonderful properties as that the assiduous use of it is said to render men immortal.'

ST JOHN'S WORT
Hypericum perforatum

UNDER THE CELESTIAL SIGN OF LEO AND THE DOMINION OF THE SUN

A perennial native to Britain, Europe and Asia, St John's wort has spread throughout the eastern USA and Canada.

The *Hypericum* genus is large, consisting of both herbs and shrubs, most of which have opposite leaves and yellow flowers, varying considerably in size. *H. perforatum*, the commonest, has strongly ribbed leaves of a delicate green which may redden with age; the leaves are full of clear dots which may be easily seen if the leaf is held up to the light. The branched stem carries a wealth of golden flowers which are profusely dotted with black, during July and August. They have a lemony resinous scent and will leave a yellow, or sometimes red dye on the fingers if handled. At the end of August the seed appears, turning black when ripe.

ventured nowhere near. John Aubrey described how the haunted house of a friend was cleansed by a doctor who put St John's wort under the sufferer's pillow. The Scots used to wear a sprig of the plant against the 'evil eye', and the custom handed down from Welsh mothers to their daughters of pressing the leaves between the pages of their Bibles was still observed at the end of the 19th century. It was called the 'touch-leaf' or the 'touching-leaf'.

The house that had St John's wort hung above the door was safe from thunder, lightning and fire; and neither witches nor the devil himself could cross the threshold. With St John's wort tied to the cradle, no child could be taken for a changeling.

On 23 June, the feast of the vigil of St John, garlands of St John's wort and other flowers were hung at doors and windows. On St John's day a sermon was preached from a permanent stone pulpit in the corner of the first quadrangle of Magdalen College, Oxford; the quadrangle was decorated with St John's wort and other plants so that the meeting might more nearly resemble that of St John the Baptist and his followers in the wilderness. The herbs had to be picked early in the morning while they were still wet with dew, for it was thought to be dangerous to gather them after the Sun had risen.

Because of its red juice and the perforations of its leaves, St John's wort was accepted by the *Doctrine of Signatures* as a herb for healing wounds. The herbalists thought highly of it, and wrote of its medicinal qualities. Gerard gave directions for making 'an oile of the colour of bloud; which is a most pretious remedie for deep wounds and those that are thorow the body, for the sinues that are prickt, or any wound made with a venomed weapon. I am accustomed to make a compound oile hereof, the making of which you shall receive at my hands, because I know that in the world there is not a better.'

Culpeper described it as 'a most noble anti-venereal', and said 'It may be, if you meet a Papist, he will tell you, especially if he be a lawyer, that St John made it over to him by letter of attorney.'

George Herbert advised that 'Hyssop, valerian, mercury, adder's tongue, melilot and St John's Wort made into a salve, and elder, comfrey and smallage made into a poultice, have done great things'.

A salve made from the flowers was much used

ST JOHN'S WORT, from William Woodville's *Medical Botany*, 1832.

St John's wort was believed to have infinite healing powers derived from the saint himself, the red juice of its leaves representing his blood. It was therefore dedicated by the monks to St John the Baptist, and regarded as a protection against the devil. It was once known as *Fuga daemonium*, devil's flight. It was believed that the devil's hatred of the plant was so great that he tried to destroy it with a needle, thus causing the dots or pricks around the edges of the leaves. The name *Hypericum* is derived from the Greek, meaning 'over a phantom or apparition', and signifies that the scent of it was so obnoxious to Satan that he

SAMPHIRE illustrated at the top left of this page from an English 19th-century printed herbal.

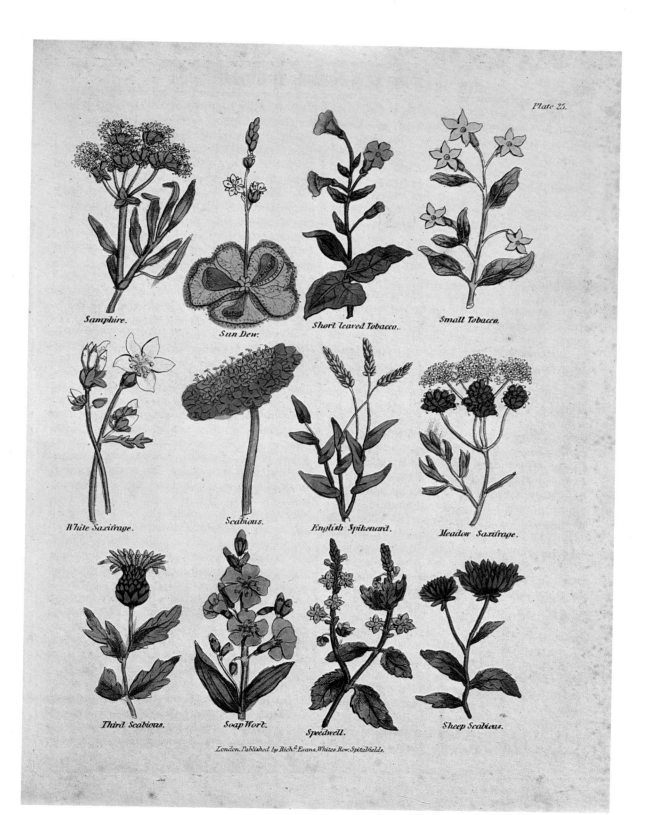

Plate 25.

Samphire.

Sun Dew.

Short leaved Tobacco.

Small Tobacco.

White Saxifrage.

Scabious.

English Spikenard.

Meadow Saxifrage.

Third Scabious.

Soap Wort.

Speedwell.

Sheep Scabious.

London. Published by Rich.ᵈ Evans, Whites Row, Spitalfields.

and valued in English villages for scratches and small wounds. The flowers were picked daily as soon as they blossomed, and made into gargles and lotions. An oil reddened with the juice was kept in apothecaries' shops for burns.

St John's wort has tonic and astringent properties, and in modern medicine is used as a cure for neuritis and for the prevention of haemorrhages. It is used as a dressing for minor wounds, scalds and blisters, and as a general pain-killer. A standard infusion is made of the chopped leaves, flowers and stems for stomach disorders, or it may be mixed with olive oil for external application for abrasions.

When making a tisane, a spray of any remaining St John's wort left in the tea-pot, if used as soon as it is cold, will be beneficial to most garden plants.

H. perforatum has become an abundant weed on the east coast of North America, and there are many other wild species. John Josselyn listed it as common to both England and New England. He said that cheeses wrapped in it would keep when they were carried on long sea-voyages.

The juice of the young tops and flowers is soluble in water, alcohol or vinegar. In water or alcohol a blood-red colour is obtained; in vinegar a fine bright crimson. When alum is used as a mordant, St John's wort picked in July gives grey; in August, greenish-yellow. By increasing the quantity of the mordant, and by the addition of various other solutions, rose, cherry or crimson can be obtained. Even the late summer flowers, when dried, will give a brownish-red colour.

SAMPHIRE

Crithmum maritimum

A HERB OF JUPITER

A perennial plant native to the rocky coasts of Europe, samphire is famous for perching in perilous places and leading intrepid samphire-gatherers to their destruction. This reputation is entirely due to Shakespeare's dramatic lines in *King Lear*:

Half way down
Hangs one who gathers samphire, dreadful trade!

William Turner, the first Englishman to study plants scientifically, mentioned samphire growing on the cliffs of Dover in 1568 — before Shakespeare's reference to it.

Samphire is not uncommon around the eastern and southern coasts of England, and as far west as Cornwall, but is rare further north. It grows in rocky crevices at any height, but not in the masses it once achieved. It may be found also on the low sandy shores of East Anglia, where it used to be sold in shops for pickling. Mrs Earle in her entertaining *Pot-Pourri* mentioned that in Norfolk, in 1899, 'they still make an industry of gathering it and pickling it'.

Samphire was dedicated to St Peter (whose name in Greek signifies a rock), the patron saint of all fishermen. Since the plant chose to grow only on the rocks of the seashore, it was called St Peter's herb, the herb of Saint-Pierre, or samphire. It was cried in London streets as crest marina.

It is an umbelliferous plant, with glaucous foliage full of an aromatic juice which has a hot spicy flavour; the young shoots are gathered in May for eating while fresh or for pickling. The white or greenish-yellow flowers bloom late in summer. The whole plant is strongly aromatic, 'beeing of smell delightful and pleasant', according to Gerard.

John Evelyn wrote in *Acetaria*, 1699, 'You cannot provide too much of this excellent ingredient in all crude salads'. It was eaten chopped and cooked in butter, or as a cold cooked vegetable. Anne Pratt wrote that samphire had been cultivated with success in sheltered situations, where the soil had been sprinkled with barilla (an alkali made from kelp), although why a sheltered situation was thought necessary for a plant that had once flourished on the windy coast is not clear. Mrs Lyell, the well known herbalist, nurtured a plant which she said cautiously 'has settled down with us and so far is thriving', but it seems that samphire is too wild a character to be cultivated.

Culpeper said of samphire that 'this is used more by the cook than by the apothecary', but he believed it to be digestive, and 'in some sort opening obstructions of the liver and the spleen'. 'If people will have sauce to their meat, they may take some for profit, as well as for pleasure', he advised.

Here are two receipts from the past, the first from an anonymous cook and the second from the famous Mrs Elizabeth Raffald.

Pickled samphire

Gather when green, and soak for 2 days in a brine of salt and water. Put in a stone jar with peppercorns and a little allspice. Cover with vinegar, and put the jar in a slow oven. It must boil only when it is green and crisp; if it is allowed to become soft it is spoiled. When cold, cork and cover the jar for storage.

To pickle samphire

Wash your samphire very well in sour small beer, then put it into a large brass pan, dissolve a little bay salt, and twice the quantity of common salt in sour beer; then fill up your pan with it, cover it close, and set it over a slow fire till it is a fine green, then drain it through a sieve, and put it into jars, boil as much sugar vinegar or white wine vinegar, with a race or two of ginger, and a few peper corns, as will cover it; then pour it hot upon your samphire, and tie it well down.

Although the plant is no longer common, it is not impossible to find, and it may be useful to learn that samphire may be kept all the year in a strong salt brine and water and soaked in vinegar before use.

SANICLE

Sanicula europaea
S. marylandica

A HERB OF VENUS

An umbelliferous plant, abundant in the middle and north of Europe, and on the mountains of tropical Africa, wood sanicle is found all over the British Isles, and *Sanicula* species are wild in many parts of the Americas. Our forefathers said, 'He that hath Sanicle, needeth no surgeon'. Over the centuries the reputation of some of our healing herbs dwindles and dies. This has been so with sanicle. It is a dull-looking plant, neither tall nor short, with dark green leaves and tufts of dull whitish flowers which may be pinkish or chocolate coloured when young. The flowers appear in May and June. The leaves are finely indented around the edges. The roundish seeds, covered with prickles, adhere to everything they touch. Anne Pratt assures us that it is extremely elegant.

In France, sanicle was known as *herbe de St Laurent* after St Laurence, who was put to death on a grid-iron; it was therefore invoked for burns and scalds, but this does not appear to be so elsewhere.

In England it was valued as a herb for treating wounds. Culpeper said: 'This is one of Venus's herbs, to cure wounds or mischiefs Mars inflicteth upon the body of man,' and he compared it with comfrey, bugle and self-heal. It may have found

more uses in the USA, where *S. marylandica*, black sanicle, or snakeroot, as it is called, was given for sore throats and fevers. It was taken in the form of root tea for skin troubles and even St Vitus' dance.

Today, we are inclined to ignore sanicle, but it is recommended for external use for skin diseases, mouth washes and gargles. Internally, it may be taken for chest complaints, coughs and catarrh, and a strong decoction of the leaves is good for piles.

SASSAFRAS

Sassafras officinalis

This tree of the Laurel family is a native of North America, where it grows abundantly; in parts of the southern USA the air becomes impregnated

SASSAFRAS is an evergreen of the laurel family. This picture shows the tree, from Nicholas Monardes' *Joyfull Newes out of the New World*, 1580.

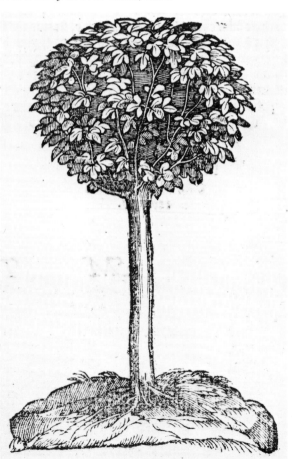

Flora Danica Tab. CCLXXXIII.

SANICLE, as illustrated in G. C. Oeder's *Flora Danica*. Members of the
genus *Sanicula*, all of which are commonly called sanicle, include
the black snakeroot, *S. marylandica*.

Cornus mas Odorata.
Sassafras.

Muscicapa Corona rubra.
The Tyrant.

SASSAFRAS: a detail of the leaves, blossom and berries from M. Catesby's *Natural History of Carolina*, 1731.

with its aroma. It is an ornamental deciduous tree, with mucilaginous twigs and foliage. It grows between 10 and 40ft (3 and 12m) high, according to situation, and has small yellowish-green flowers on pendant spikes and panicles, which bloom in May and June before the leaves appear. Male and female flowers are found on different trees. The leaves are pale green and downy on the underside. Sassafras fruit somewhat resembles that of the cinnamon, which gives the tree the common name of cinnamon wood. The trunk of the tree produces a useful hard wood.

The tree was first discovered by the Spaniards who were taught its medicinal value by the Red Indians. Nicholas Monardes, a Spanish herbalist, author of the first book on the use of herbs in the New World, wrote in 1569, 'The Spaniards did begin to cure themselves with the water of this tree and it did in them greate effectes, that it is almost incredible, for with the naughtie meates and drinkyng of the *rawe* waters, and slepying in the dewes, the moste parte of them came to fall into continuall agues.' Living as he did in Seville, he wrote of the use of sassafras as a pomander during a period of plague there: 'Many did use to carrie a peece of the Roote of the wood with them to smell to it continually as to a Pomander. For with his smell so acceptable it did rectifie the infected ayre.' The name sassafras evolved from Spanish efforts to pronounce the word saxifrage, which they believed to have similar virtues. It is also known as ague tree, from the belief that it was a cure for that unpleasant disease.

Sassafras was introduced to Europe by way of France, but it was Drake who brought the roots from North America to England. Here sassafras tea was immediately accepted as a cure for all ills, including drunkenness. The tea, called saloop, became the fashionable beverage among English gentlemen, who gathered at street stalls to partake publicly of the new brew while exchanging the scandals of the day. When it became known that sassafras tea was not the true saloop — which was the product of the tubers of a kind of orchid — and, even worse, that it was the North American Indians' cure for the French pox, it was considered discreet to cease the taking of such a remedy, at least in public. Saloop then became the poor man's beverage; it was sold in the streets at daybreak, and became one of the cries of London. Served with sugar and milk, it became the favourite drink of porters, coal-heavers and other hard-working men. At times it was combined with true saloop.

Sassafras tea became a dependable North American country spring medicine, and was often combined with other blood-cleansing herbs. It was mixed with broth for invalids and children, and given to babies after weaning. Powdered saloop could be obtained, and a dessertspoonful was then added to boiling water: after stirring, the preparation became a jelly, and it was customary to add white wine and sugar, or sometimes milk. Saloop and flour was made into bread. It is still taken for bladder, kidney, chest and throat troubles, but today is rarely given alone.

The root, wood, and bark of the tree possess the same medicinal qualities, and are used for rheumatism, gout and arthritis. The bark of the root contains a volatile oil which has antiseptic properties. A warm infusion of the bark is considered a good blood purifier and tonic for the bowels. Lotions are given as an eye-wash, and for skin diseases and eruptions.

SAVORY shown left in an entrancing decoration in Jean Bourdichon's 16th-century *Hours of Anne of Burgundy*.

NAMES.

SUMMER
SAVORY.

PARTS USED.

A.

G. Οΰμβρα.

PREPARATIONS.

L. Satureia hortensis,
sive Cunila Æstiva.

I. Savoreggia Pareudla.

G. Satury.

F. Sariette.

S. Axedrea, Axedrea,
Sageridu.

D. Keulen.

PLACE.
South of France.

TIME.
Flowers. July. October.

DESCRIPTION.

Square, stiff Stalks, long narrow Leaves, dusky green pointed seem perforated, growing by pairs. Empalement is 3 or 4 on footstalks at the Joints, with fine points, edged with pale purple hairs, flowers, Ovary in the bottom of the cup, light green in four parts, a light purple forked Style, Chives almost white dark purple Summits, white Transparent oval Farina, the Seed vessel in 4 parts, with a purple top & 4 naked Seeds in it. Aromatic Smell & Taste.

VIRTUES.
Good for Head & Nerves. Top in Flowers are best.

T. Sheldrake delin.

C. Hemerich sculp.

SUMMER SAVORY, shown right in a delicate illustration by Sheldrake from *Botanicum Medicinale*, 1759.

[163]

Oil of sassafras from both wood and bark is used for toothache, and is also made into a dentifrice. It is a useful essence in the making of the cheaper types of soaps and perfumes, and is a pleasant antiseptic wash. The roots produce a peach-coloured dye, and the bark, with an alum mordant, makes a good yellow.

The mucilaginous leaves have been used in the thickening of soup, and the young shoots were brewed into a kind of beer in Virginia. They are now employed in the flavouring of soft drinks. A rose-coloured tea is made from the dried bark, which is known as arthritis tea, and a few chips may be added to China tea.

The following is a 19th-century recipe.

Sassafras cordial

½lb. sassafras chips. 2ozs. sarsparilla, 1oz. gum arabic dissolved in white wine, 1oz. bruised juniper berries, 2ozs. ground pistachio nuts, 1oz. syrup of lemons, 2ozs. rosemary leaves and 1oz. marjoram, both finely shredded, 1oz. each of candied lemon and citron, 9ozs. sugar, 12 stoned and cut muscatel raisins, 3qts. sherry and 2qts. of proof spirits of wine.

These ingredients were put in a jar, corked and sealed, and the jar set in a bath of hot water. It was infused for a week; kept for 2 months, then strained and filtered, when it was ready for use. Sassafras cordial improved with age.

SAVORY, SUMMER

Satureia hortensis

A PLANT OF MERCURY

Both summer and winter savories are native to France and Italy, and were first cultivated in England in 1562. They were grown in the USA by the first English settlers and Josselyn included both in his list of *Garden Herbs as do thrive*. Of the fourteen species known, only *S. hortensis* and *S. montana* are commonly grown in Britain. Both were regarded by the ancients as herbs belonging to the satyrs, hence the name *Satureia*. Pregnant women were warned to avoid them.

Summer savory is still a neglected herb which might be put to more and better uses. It is highly aromatic and flourishes in light soil, but needs sunshine. It is beneficial to grow summer savory near to beans. It can also be grown indoors as a pot-plant. It should be picked just before flowering and hung up to dry for winter use.

Summer savory is a hardy annual, with erect stems about 1ft (30cm) high. The pale lilac to purple labiate flowers, which appear from July to September, are attractive to bees. A description in the *Cyclopaedia of Botany, c.*1800, has a domestic quality: 'The leaves are oblong and narrow; they stand two at each joint, with a quantity of young ones in their bosoms.'

It is a member of the Mint family, with a peppery flavour slightly resembling thyme. An infusion may be taken for indigestion, and a decoction applied to an aching tooth gives relief. A sprig of either of the savories is soothing if applied to wasp- or bee-stings, and both are good insect repellents. The whole plant may be used in medicine, but generally speaking it is more distinguished as a culinary herb.

Useful in salads, sausages and many meat and egg dishes, its most valuable use is as a stuffing for chicken or fish.

For fish stuffing and forcemeat balls

3oz (85g) soft breadcrumbs
1dssp chopped savory, green or dried
1tbsp chopped onion
grated rind and juice of 1 lemon
2oz (56g) butter
1 egg
salt and pepper

Gently fry onion without browning. Add to other ingredients and bind with egg. Use for stuffing fish, chicken or veal, or to roll into balls or small sausages for frying.

SAVORY, WINTER

Satureia montana

A PLANT OF MERCURY

A shrubby perennial, winter savory is not widely grown in Britain. It is better known, however, in Europe, where it is called the bean herb and served with all sorts of bean dishes. It is a bushy evergreen shrub, peppery and aromatic, and was used for knot gardens and shrub mazes. The stems are woody and much branched, with pale purple labiate flowers. It grows best in poor soil and makes an attractive rockery plant.

Culpeper wrote of both savories: 'Keep it dry by you all the year, if you love yourself and your ease, and it is a hundred pounds to a penny if you do not: keep it dry, make conserves and syrups of it for your use; and withal, take notice that the summer kind is best.'

Winter savory, however, is listed by Frances Bardswell as one of the nine most useful perennial kitchen herbs. It resembles marjoram in flavour and much improves a steak pudding. Izaak Walton used it frequently. Here is a modified version of his recipe.

Izaak Walton's recipe for roasted pike

'First, open your pike at the gills, and if need be, cut also a little slit towards the belly; out of these take his guts and keep his liver, which you are to shred very small with thyme, sweet marjoram, and a little winter savory.' Walton's following items, pickled oysters and anchovies, you may perhaps decide to dispense with. The next, 1lb (450g) butter, may be reduced to 4–6oz (113–170g), according to the size of the fish. The herbs are mixed with butter, a blade of mace added, and the pike, or whichever whole white fish you are using, stuffed. A spit is thrust through the fish's mouth and out at the tail. The stuffed fish is then roasted.

Walton has a complicated way of binding up the fish with tape and split sticks, so that it does not fall to pieces before it is done, but today's cook needs only to reach for her roll of foil, wrap the fish and let the aromatic filling ooze into the fish at its will. When done, combine this sauce with the juice of two oranges, a little claret, pour over the fish and serve garnished with slices of orange.

SCURVY GRASS
Cochlearia officinalis

UNDER THE DOMINION OF JUPITER

An annual or biennial, scurvy grass is native to northern Europe, North America and Asia. It is found wild in the marshy districts of Britain, and was probably introduced from Holland, where it grows plentifully.

This low-growing plant has thick flat leaves, longer than broad, of a dull bluish-green. Small white flowers bloom all the summer, giving out an unpleasant smell. The globose fruits that follow contain small reddish-brown seeds. It prefers growing in salt mud, but however far from the sea it may be found, it will always taste salty. In the past it was believed that 'there are, by the wise dispensation of Providence, such species of plants produced in every country, as are made proper and convenient for the meat and medicine of the men and animals that are bred and inhabit therein. So in Denmark, Friesland, Holland, where scurvy usually reigns, the proper remedy, Scurvy-grass, doth plentifully grow.'

It is believed to be the famous *Herba Britannica* of the old herbalists, who advised its use by sailors hundreds of years before it was discovered that scurvy arose from the lack of vitamin C which that plant supplies. The dried herb or a bottled distillation was carried on board ship.

It was not only at sea that this affliction occurred. The diet of the poor in big cities also was insufficient and unsuited to their needs, and scurvy was known on land as well as on sea. So much was scurvy grass in demand that it was grown in the physic gardens and in corners of cottage gardens as well. Women would collect it from river marshes for the apothecaries. In the 17th century it was cried in the city streets: 'Here's watercresses and scurvy-grass, Come buy my sage of virtue, ho!' It was also called spoonwort — a translation of *Cochlearia*, its botanical name — from the shape of its leaves.

The following recipe used to be made for a health-giving drink in the early 19th century.

To make scurvy grass whey

Boil a pint of blue milk, take it off to cool, then put in two spoonfuls of good old verjuice, set it over the fire, and it will turn to a fine whey; it is very good to drink in the spring for the scurvy.

Another health drink of the same period was made from 2 pints of scurvy grass juice, 1 pint brooklime juice, 1 pint watercress juice, and the juice of several Seville oranges, mixed and strained. It was to be taken two or three times a day. Scurvy grass was also made into beer, syrups and conserve. Today, the juice mixed with orange juice is still often regarded as a useful spring tonic, and a gargle is made for ulcers and sores in the mouth. It has also been used to cure venereal disease, and in the treatment of dropsy and rheumatism. It is stimulating, aperient and diuretic.

The following recipe is from the receipt book of Elizabeth Cleland, 1759, and was quoted by Eleanour Sinclair Rohdes in her *Garden of Herbs*.

Sallet of scurvy grass

Being finely picked short, well soaked in clean water and swung dry, dish it round in a fine clean

a.

b.

c.

[166]

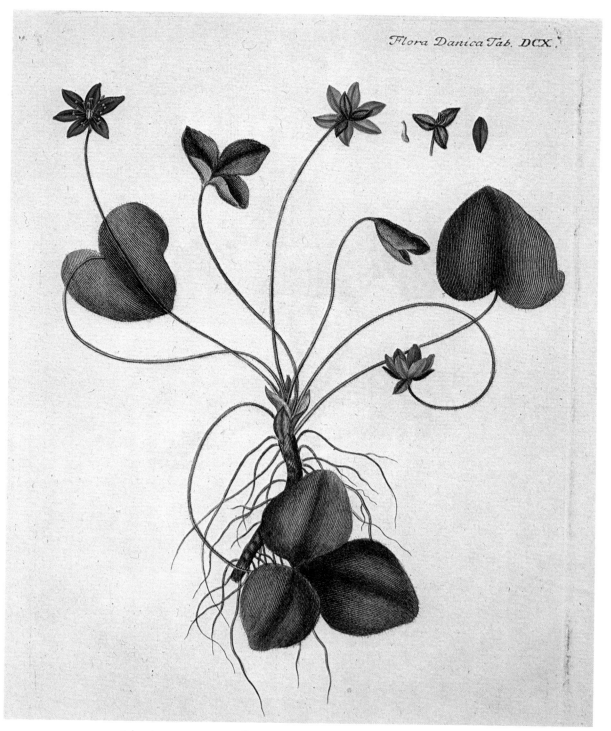

(*above*) SKULLCAP, or scullcap, as shown in G. C. Oeder's *Flora Danica*.

(*left*) SCURVY GRASS, or spoonwort, which has both medicinal and culinary uses, is today a surprisingly neglected herb. This illustration of it is from *Flora Medica*, 1829.

dish with capers and currans about it, carved lemon and orange round that and eggs upon the centre not boiled too hard, and parted in halfs, then oyle and vinegar; over all scraping sugar and trim the brim of the dish.

SELF-HEAL

Prunella vulgaris

UNDER THE DOMINION OF VENUS

A perennial native to many countries, self-heal grows along the waysides in New England as a plant introduced from Europe, and it is very common in Britain. It is a low-growing herb, with square stems which are a little hairy, and a root full of fibres. The creeping stems throw out new plants in all directions. The dark green leaves are paired, and the labiate flowers, each set in a purple calyx, may be deep purple, lilac or sometimes white. They grow in dense, short spikes, about 6in (15cm) high, and appear in July and August. They are fertilized by bees. The corolla in profile resembles a little bill-hook, which gained it a reputation as a healer of wounds made by sickles, scythes and other sharp instruments, and a place in the *Doctrine of Signatures*. Carpenters certainly made use of the herb as a vulnerary, and gave it the names of carpenter's herb, sicklewort, hookweed and hook-heal.

Gerard had complete faith in this herb. 'There is no better wounde-herbe in the world than Self-Heale is, the very name importing it to be very admirable upon this account and indeed the Virtues doe make it good, for this very herbe without the mixture of any other ingredient, being onely bruised and wrought with the point of a knife upon a trencher or the like, will be brought into the form of a salve, which will heal any green wounde even in the first intention, after a very wonderful manner.'

It was once called brunella, a word derived from the German *bräune,* meaning quinsy, since it was used to heal that condition. Linnaeus, however, softened the word to the prettier *Prunella,* which remains its generic name. Neither Greeks nor Romans seem to have known this herb.

Culpeper said that 'if it be accompanied with Bugle, Sanicle, and other the like wound-herbs, it will be more effectual to wash or inject into ulcers in the parts outwardly', and that 'the juice hereof, used with oil of roses to anoint the temples and forehead, is very effectual to remove the headach; and the same mixed with honey of roses cleanseth and healeth all ulcers in the mouth and throat, and those also in the secret parts. And the proverb of the Germans, French and others, is verified in this, *that he needeth neither physician nor surgeon, that hath Self-heal and Sanicle to help himself.'*

The New England settlers found it a handy cure for all those mysterious 'female troubles' and as a tonic. A root tea was made for liver and stomach disorders, and was taken for epilepsy. It was commonly prescribed as a vermifuge. The dried herb was made into an infusion, sweetened with honey, for a sore throat and for ulcerated mouths.

It is still used in herbal treatment as a general tonic, and as an infusion made of 1oz (28g) of the dried herb to 1pt (550ml) of boiling water. Externally, it is used in poultice form as a cleansing herb for wounds and to stop bleeding.

SKULLCAP

Scutellaria galericulata

An herbaceous plant, skullcap is scattered throughout the world and particularly abundant in the Americas. There are about 90 known species, 30 of which are found in North America, and only 2 in England — the common skullcap and the lesser skullcap.

Scutellaria galericulata, the common skullcap, is a handsome plant, with dark wrinkled leaves, green above and pale beneath. The flowers, which are labiate and bright blue, grow in pairs from the axils of the leaves, each pair facing the same way. They bloom from June to September. It frequents the borders of rivers and ponds, and is by no means common. *S. minor* is a low bushy perennial with downy lanceolate leaves and pinkish-purple flowers each with a spotted lower lip. The flowers grow in pairs and bloom from July to October. The plant is not common, except in the West of England.

'Skull' is an abbreviation and corruption of *Scutellaria,* meaning a little dish, from the shape of the calyx. As soon as the flowers fall off, the upper lip of the calyx closes on the lower one, giving the seed vessel the appearance of a cup with a lid. The small seeds resemble little nuts and appear in each calyx, and when the parchment-like box is dried, the seeds fall to the ground.

It is not surprising that the name has changed over the years — it was originally scullcap — since, when inverted, the calyx resembles a helmet with the visor raised; this formation has given it the common name helmet-flower. When righted, the calyx returns to its dish-shape or its *Scutellaria* design. Without these complications it can be likened to a small blue snapdragon. The plant was first recorded in 1576 by l'Obel, who was botanist to James I.

Traditionally, the plant is held to cure infertility, and in the past it was used to treat the tertian ague, that strange fever which manifested itself every third (or every other) day.

It is used today for the relief of epilepsy, convulsions and fits and St Vitus' Dance. It is also given to help withdrawal from drug and alcohol addiction. Both British and American varieties are known to be sedative, and *S. laterifolia*, Virginia skullcap, has been claimed to be the finest nervine ever discovered. All kinds of nervous complaints respond to this herb, even insanity, and for this reason it has become known as madweed. It also has the reputation of curing hydrophobia, and in districts where this has happened it is called mad-dog skullcap.

SKUNK CABBAGE
Symplocarpus foetidus

A perennial swamp plant, skunk cabbage is native to northern and middle USA. The flowers appear first, often pushing their way through snow and ice in February. They arrive completely covered in a purple and yellow-green hood-like spathe, the flowers themselves being inconspicuously small and purple, which may be variegated with red and yellow. The leaves appear in about April; at first they are rolled up and they then expand to become wavy-edged and spade-shaped, up to 3ft (90cm) long. The fruit that follows remains green.

This member of the Arum family gives out a smell like a skunk or a pole-cat and is pollinated by carrion flies. Regardless of these disadvantages, it proved a useful plant to the early settlers. The rootstock and seeds were used for tuberculosis, pleurisy, whooping-cough, asthma and hay fever. As a poultice the root was dried and powdered, and sprayed over open wounds. The leaf bases were applied to reduce swellings. It is still used as a tea made of 1 teaspoonful of rootstock and roots steeped in a cupful of water, for coughs and catarrh.

Most of its common names, such as stinking pole, skunkweed and swamp cabbage, are unflattering, but it is regarded as a handsome plant for the water-garden.

SLIPPERY ELM
Ulmus fulva

One of the most important herbal medicines comes from this small tree, which is abundant in the USA and Canada. It has rough branches and long toothed leaves with hairs on both sides. The leaf buds are covered with yellow wool. The flowers are inconspicuous and stalkless. Its popular names are American elm, moose elm, Indian elm and red elm, and its leaves are known as British tea. It is both an old-fashioned remedy and one of the most valuable herbal medicines today. It is an official drug of the United States Pharmacopoeia.

Slippery elm has wonderful healing properties in its inner bark, which is used in a coarsely powdered form for poultices, and finely powdered for the making of mucilaginous drinks. Bowel and bladder troubles, lung ailments, diarrhoea, stomach and kidney illnesses, boils and ulcers, and infected sores can all be treated with slippery elm in one form or another. It is used in the making of cough-drops. Its mucilaginous properties are valuable in easing childbirth. It is made also into pessaries and suppositories.

Slippery elm tea is made of 1 tablespoonful of the powdered bark to a pint (550ml) of boiling water, soaked for an hour and then simmered for a few minutes.

SORREL
Rumex acetosa

UNDER THE DOMINION OF VENUS

A perennial, sorrel is native to Europe, Asia and parts of North America. *R. acetosa* is the common indigenous English sorrel, a member of the Dock family, and an old pot-herb. John Josselyn listed it among the plants thriving in New England in 1672. The leaves are large and arrow-headed, and change from green to rusty-red and almost crimson, according to the soil in which they grow and the time of year. The flowers grow in whorled spikes of reddish-green which turn to purple in late summer. Stamens and pistils grow on different plants. The plants are deeply rooted and grow to a height of 2–3ft (60–90cm).

Although a useful culinary herb, it is seldom grown in the herb garden since it is easily obtainable in the fields and seeds too freely to be desirable as a garden plant. Alice Morse Earle, the

3224.

W. J. H. del.

Pub: by S. Curtis, Glazenwood Essex. Mar. 1 1833.

(*left*) SKUNK CABBAGE, an illustration by Curtis for the *Botanical Magazine*.

SORREL, *Rumex acetosa*, as depicted in *Flora Medica*, 1829. It should not be confused with the sorrel tree, or sourwood, *Oxydendrum arboreum*, a deciduous tree found in southern parts of the USA.

American author of *Old Time Gardens*, wrote with a marked lack of appreciation that 'none reign more absolutely in every inch of the fields than that poverty stricken creature, the Sorrel'.

In Ireland, on Tara Hill, where from June until August the meadows are red with sorrel, it is said that the leaves are stained with the blood of the Irish rebels who fell in the ''Ninety-eight'.

Both common sorrel and wood sorrel, *Oxalis acetosella*, were once used in the making of verjuice, a popular condiment in the cookery of former days. In Izaak Walton's *Compleat Angler*, an obliging milkmaid tells him, 'If you come this way two month's hence, I'll give you a syllabub of new verjuice'. A mixture of sorrel and other acid plants, such as vine leaves, unripe grapes and crab apples, was taken to sharpen the appetite. For this reason sorrel was often called sourgrass, or green sauce, after a green sauce made by blending the leaves with sugar and vinegar, to eat with cold meat. It was called also cuckoo's meat by the old herbalists, because it was believed that cuckoos ate it to clear their throats — a lubricant that few cuckoos of our time seem to require.

Both sorrel and scurvy grass grow in the Arctic regions, a fact noted in *A Journal of a Voyage to Baffin's Bay* (1850–1), when antiscorbutic plants were of the greatest value. John Evelyn said that as an antiscorbutic sorrel takes the place of oranges and lemons, and the juice was considered a good cooling drink for fevers.

The French sorrel, *R. scutatus*, introduced to England in 1596, is now grown in preference to the common sorrel for use in salads, soups and as a cooked vegetable. When chopped up in a salad, no vinegar is required. The leaves were once used in the making of ale, and for removing the rust marks from linen and stains from the hands. It gives a good greenish-yellow dye, and for this purpose the leaves can be used all summer, although they are best during the spring.

Herbalists today use it as an infusion for jaundice, liver complaints and internal ulcers. As a lotion it heals boils, abscesses and sores. A poultice relieves inflammation. It is used also as a gargle for sore throats.

For making sorrel vinegar, the leaves can be collected in a jar from the fields, washed and replaced in the jar and filled to the top with wine vinegar. Seal with cork or waxed paper — but never with a screw-top, for vinegar eats into and destroys the metal.

In cookery sorrel can be made into a purée to use with pork or duck, or the chopped leaves sprinkled into omelettes and other egg dishes. The leaves can also be dipped into batter, then lightly fried and garnished with parsley. Without doubt, its most popular use today is in sorrel soup.

Iced sorrel soup

equal quantities of sorrel and beetroot tops
½pt (275ml) iced water
1 large cucumber
½pt (275ml) vinegar
1tsp cayenne pepper
3 eggs
2 small onions
1pt (550ml) single cream

Mix sorrel and beetroot tops and boil until soft. Press out as much water as possible and blend. Slowly add iced water until mixture is a little thicker than cream.

Slice half cucumber and steep in vinegar and cayenne pepper. Hard boil eggs and cut small. Chop the green ends of onions small and add them to paste. Put paste in individual soup bowls and divide cream between them. Add other half cucumber sliced, and some hard-boiled egg to each dish. Refrigerate until required, and serve decorated with ice shavings.

SOUTHERNWOOD

Artemisia abrotanum

A HERB OF MERCURY

The common southernwood of the English garden is native to the south of Europe. Although a small shrub which seldom flowers in England, it grows to a large size in the Holy Land, where it bears nodding yellow blooms in profusion. The name southernwood is a contraction of southern wormwood, meaning that it is the European plant indigenous to Spain and Italy. Field southernwood is native but rare in Britain, growing only in Norfolk and Suffolk. Both varieties are related to mugwort and wormwood. Taken by the settlers to the New World, this useful herb survived the long journey only to succumb to the rigours of the New England winters. However, it is now successfully naturalized in the USA.

Garden southernwood, more strongly aromatic than the field variety, has finely divided sage-green leaves arranged in clusters of uneven length. The plant reaches a height of 3–5ft (90–150cm) and uneven length, can be a vigorous spreader. Once thought of only as a cottage-garden plant it

SOUTHERNWOOD, from William Woodville's *Medical Botany*, 1832.

mattress. Conveniently, it was later discovered also to be a cure for the 'French disease'.

It was known as the old man of southern Europe or, affectionately, old man, and, true to the contradictions of rural nomenclature, lad's love. The latter name comes from country lads making an ointment from its ashes to encourage their beards to grow. Parkinson claimed that the ashes of southernwood mixed with old salad oil would cause the growth of a beard, or hair on a bald head. Although 'In cases of baldness southernwood has in fact no particular magic, but given a reasonable amount of hair to work upon it is, like rosemary, an excellent tonic, and has been made and sold as hair pomade'. It is also recommended as an invigorating bath infusion.

More certain are its virtues as a moth and flea deterrent, and if planted near fruit trees it will repel fruit-tree moths; planted near cabbages, it keeps away the cabbage white butterflies whose progeny wreak such havoc among the leaves.

Although not possessing any outstanding cosmetic virtues, it did have a small part to play in a charming Mayday custom of dew-collecting, described in 1824 by George Calvert of Kirkby Moorside. 'To collect may dew to beautify the skin, they go forth carrying on a pole a flower board, which one of them doth go first bearing it as it were a banner. Each damsel has a silver spoon and doth carry a pretty broom fashioned of fine Lad's Love and Lavender sprigs so that it be like unto a small broom for to sweep and to lick up the dew into a silver bowl or china cup; all do hold firmly to its virtues for to clear and beautify the skin.'

With other such strongly aromatic herbs, it was regarded as a preventive against the plague and placed with rue by the side of a prisoner in the dock to guard that unfortunate against gaol fever. It was a special favourite with the London poor, and the street cry of 'Here's southernwood That's very good!' was a welcome sound.

Sir John Hill advocated its use for insomnia in *The British Herbalist* in 1772.

Sir John Hill's receipt for southernwood tea

Chop four ounces of the leaves fine and beat them in a mortar with six ounces of loaf sugar till the whole is like a paste. Three times a day take the bignesse of a nutmeg of this. It is pleasant and one thing in it is particular, it is a composer and always disposes persons to sleep.

Early in the 19th century Richard Brook prescribed the following decoction for fomentations:

has been promoted, not only to the herb garden but to the outer edges of white and silver-leaved borders, where grey moves imperceptibly into grey-green.

It belongs to the Compositae family, but since it sets seeds so rarely it needs to be increased by cuttings. It was brought to Elizabethan England and, it is said, has been maintained by cuttings ever since. Pliny seems to have been aware of the difficulties of propagating this plant, for he said, 'For of seede, much adoe there is to make it come up. And when it is above ground, the young plants are removed and set, as it were in Adonis gardens, within pots of earth; and that in summer time, after the manner of the hearbe and flower Adonis.'

To the Greeks and Romans it was a magic plant, and according to Pliny it was thought to have aphrodisiac qualities when placed under the

Richard Brook's decoction

One ounce each of dried southernwood, tops of sea wormwood and camomile flowers, with half an ounce of dried bay-leaves, in six pints of distilled water. Boiled and strained.

To English palates southernwood has too astringent a quality to be a popular culinary herb, although in Italy it is eaten raw and cooked as a vegetable. It was used in Europe for flavouring beer. It produces a good yellow dye for wool.

SOYBEAN

Soja hispida

A small hairy plant of the Bean family, soybean is native to India and China. It is cultivated in India for its seeds and made into the sauce called soy. Soybean has been cultivated in China for over 4,000 years and is considered one of the five sacred grains, the others being rice, barley, wheat and

SOYBEANS, from a 19th-century Indian work, *Flora of India.*

millet. It produces so much protein that it has been used in many parts of the world as a substitute for milk and called China cow. The residue, or cake, is used for manure.

It was brought to the USA in 1804 by a Yankee clipper-ship returning from China. Not until World War II was the potential of the soybean realized, and extensive cultivation begun.

From its beginnings in China, Japan and India, when the salted beans were used as condiments, or a sauce was made to be eaten with fish, the uses have increased in the most varied directions. The oil is employed in the making of margarine, in paints, plastics and other industrial products, and in fish-canning.

Soybeans roasted and coarsely ground are used as a substitute for coffee, and the flour is mixed with wholemeal flour to make bread. It contains a protein comparable to all forms of animal meats. Soybean sprouts constitute one of the most nutritious foods available, and after sprouting the vitamin levels increase. They contain calcium and zinc and are the highest source of protein in vegetables. They may be sprouted at home and are increasingly popular.

Soybeans may be fried, served with mayonnaise in salads, or offered in bowls as an accompaniment to drinks. Two tablespoonfuls of soya flour mixed with water and boiled until thick, strained and blended with vegetable oil, as for mayonnaise, makes soy butter.

Soybean soufflé

3 cups sieved soybeans
4 eggs, separated
1tbsp grated onion
2tbsp chopped chervil
½tsp thyme
¼tsp marjoram
salt

Preheat oven to 400°F (200°C). Beat soybeans with egg yolks, and stir over low heat until mixture thickens. Stir in onions, herbs and salt to taste. Pour mixture into well buttered 1½pt (825ml) soufflé dish and bake for 45 minutes or until set.

STRAWBERRY

Fragaria species

UNDER THE DOMINION OF VENUS

A perennial, strawberry is native to the whole of the northern hemisphere except the tropics.

A 19TH-CENTURY Colombian poster advertising the pharmacy of Lambardi and Fernandez, now in the possession of the Bibliothèque Nationale, Paris, Étampes.

Although common in both France and Britain, the berries are more abundant in cold countries, such as Sweden. Its small fruits bear some of the most widely dispersed seeds in the world, owing to their popularity with birds, which carry them great distances.

The wild strawberry, *F. vesca*, is a member of the Rose family. The plant is erect, growing to about 6in (15cm) high, with leaves divided into three or sometimes four leaflets, which are deeply veined, dark green and toothed. These leaflets sometimes turn to scarlet in the autumn, echoing the fruit, which are carried like little red pincushions among the green. The white flowers, resembling small single roses, appear in April and May, and throughout the summer; flowers and fruit appear together. In England it is one of the joys of sunny chalk downs. It is dedicated to the Virgin Mary.

Its name has been the subject of much argument. There are those who believe that it derives from the fact that the runners on which the new plants are rooted resemble straws; that plants and fruit are strewn or strawn about the ground; or that it comes from the practice of protecting the fruit with straw (although the name came centuries before the practice). Perhaps the most convincing theory is that they are, in fact, strayberries, from the trailing or straying of their new growth.

The strawberry leaf has been adopted as the emblem of the English nobility; a duke's coronet has eight leaves, an earl's eight, and that of a marquis four. The leaves are worn in the coronets of the younger members of the royal family.

There are at least nine varieties of wild strawberry in North America, of which *F. virginiana*, also indigenous to Canada, is probably the most abundant. The Indians made good use of such abundance by bruising the fruit in a mortar and mixing it with meal to make strawberry bread; and the early settlers, delighted to find so pleasant and useful a herb, made wines as well as tonics for stomach-ache in babies or bowel trouble in

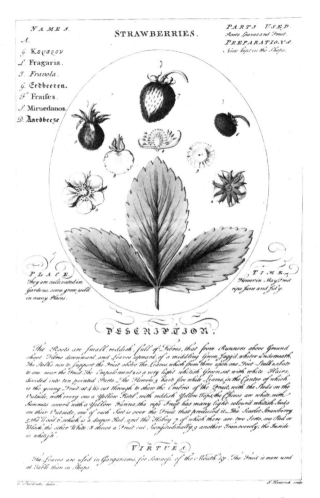

STRAWBERRIES of various kinds appear in this plate from Sheldrake's *Botanicum Medicinale*, 1759. At top left the name of the plant is given in seven languages.

children. *F. virginiana* was introduced to English gardens in 1629, and was also cultivated in France.

The earliest mention of the 'stroeberie' is in a Saxon plant list of the 10th century. By 1300, wild strawberries were beginning to be taken into gardens and cultivated, so that by 1580 Thomas Tusser could mention it with confidence as one of his *Five Hundred Pointes of Good Husbandrie*:

Wife unto thy garden and set me a plot
With Strawberry rootes of the best to be got.
Such growing abroade, among thornes in the wood
Well chosen and picked prove excellent good.

In 1629 Parkinson grew in his garden a different variety, taken from the wild, which he said was 'pleasant to behold, and fit for a Gentlewoman to weare upon her arm, etc. as a raritie instead of a flower'.

At this time the cry of 'Strabery rype' was heard around London streets. During the 18th and 19th centuries strawberries were brought to the markets in baskets carried by women on their heads. These carriers were principally from Twickenham and Isleworth, and their fragrant but heavy loads were carried backwards and forwards twice a day, a distance of 40 miles or more. Soon the strawberry women were coming from farther afield — Irish, Welsh and Shropshire girls, all known alike as 'the Shropshire girls' — starting about midnight in parties of almost a hundred, making night-travelling safe from footpads, to find employment in the neighbourhood of London during the summer. The strawberry season ran from the third week of June until the first week of August, and except on Sundays everyone worked an eighteen-hour day from 3 in the morning until 9 at night. The strawberries were measured out in 'pottles', long, pointed baskets which may be seen in some of the old engravings of 'The Cries of London'.

In the 18th century the modern large red strawberry was evolved, following the introduction of *F. virginiana* from North America, *F. chilensis* from South America and *F. grandiflora* from Surinam, by crossing them with the native species. From 1870 onwards strawberries became increasingly popular crops with Scottish growers.

The shape and the colour of the fruit caused it to be classified according to the *Doctrine of Signatures* as a cure for heart disease. Lotions and gargles were prescribed for mouth, throat and eyes, and 'to fasten loose teeth'. Richard Brook wrote: 'To ladies, and those who wish for good and clean teeth, there is nothing better than cleaning them with strawberries'.

An excellent tea was made from wild strawberry leaves, or from an infusion of strawberry leaves and woodruff. The leaves were used as a lotion for the complexion and as a bath additive for those who suffered with 'grievous aches and paynes of the hyppes'. A recipe for a face wash, from *The Good Housewife's Handmaid*, 1585, combines strawberries and wild tansy distilled in 3pt (1.7l) new milk. The leaves and roots boiled in wine and water was taken as a cooling drink for internal inflammations. Linnaeus claimed that wild strawberries had cured his gout.

Both wild and garden varieties possess considerable medicinal value, except for those who are allergic to them. The leaves can be used instead of tea or coffee for a pleasant drink that tones up the system and acts as an appetizer. Two large hand-fuls of the leaves infused in 1qt (1l) boiling water may be made and taken internally for diarrhoea and dysentery, or for jaundice, heart conditions and fevers. It is astringent and restrains haemor-rhage, excessive menstruation and threatened abortion. Externally, a lotion is good for eczema and styes, or for anti-wrinkle cosmetic purposes. A concoction of root and herb is good for ulcers and liver disorders.

In the 17th century there was a tremendous interest in the making of strawberry cordials and wines.

A cordial water of Sir Walter Raleigh

Take a gallon of Strawberries, and put them in a pinte of *aqua vitae*, let them stand four or five dayes, strain them gently out, and sweeten the water as you please, with fine Sugar, or else with Perfume.

A receipt for strawberry wine remains from 1669. It comes from *The Closet of Sir Kenelm Digby Opened*, published by his man-servant after Sir Kenelm's death.

The strawberry wine of Sir Kenelm Digby

Bruise the strawberries and put them into a Lin-nen-bag which hath been little used so that the Liquor may run through more easily. You hang in the bag at the bung into the vessel before you put in your Strawberries. The quantity of the fruit is left to your discretion for you will judge there to be enough of them when the colour of the wine is high enough. During the working, you leave the bung open. The working being over, you stop your vessel.

SWEET CICELY

Myrrhis odorata
Ozmorrhiza longistylis

UNDER THE DOMINION OF JUPITER

A perennial, sweet cicely is native to Britain and many parts of the world. The American sweet cicely, *Ozmorrhiza longistylis*, grows in low-lying moist country and flowers in May and June. Sweet cicely has a thick root with large feathery and aromatic foliage, which is dark green above and pale beneath. The white flowers are carried in compound umbels, giving way to large brown

seeds. The plant reaches 2–5ft (60–150cm). It is strongly flavoured with anise and has the scent of lovage. The old herbalists described the plant as 'so harmless you cannot use it amiss', wherein lies its danger, for its close relatives, hemlock, water hemlock and fool's parsley, have a very similar appearance and are all extremely poisonous.

It is the plant of St Cecilia and was known affectionately as sweet cis. Its name, *Myrrhis odor-ata*, comes from the Greek word for perfume. It was also called shepherd's needle, from its long, sharply pointed fruits. In Scotland and northern England, where it grows abundantly, the seeds, ground finely and mixed with bees-wax, were used in the 17th century to polish furniture and floors. It was regarded as a preservative against the plague.

It was valued in the 16th century as a pot-plant, and Gerard claimed that the roots were 'most excellent in a sallade, if they be boiled, and after dressed as the cunning Cooke knoweth how

SWEET CICELY from G. C. Oeder's *Flora Danica*, 1813–18.

better than myself'. He added that, for old people, 'dull and without courage, it rejoiceth and comforteth the hart, and increaseth their lust and strength'. It was widely cultivated in England, and the herbalist William Turner wrote, 'I never saw greter plenty of it than I have seen in the hortyard [kitchen garden] or Pebroke Hall in Cambridge, where I was sometime a pore fellow'. It was much used in cooking by the French and the Dutch, and Germans made use of its seeds instead of cloves or caraway seeds.

Sweet cicely found growing in the woods of Canada, Alaska and parts of North America was used for many medicinal purposes. The root and herb were given as a pleasant tonic to invalids and new mothers. A root drink was mixed with honey locust, *Gleditzia triacanthos*, as a restorative and beverage. It was also a poultice plant for wounds and sores. It was taken for coughs, flatulence and digestive complaints, and for much the same illnesses as in England.

In France, the macerated seeds were taken in brandy, for most purposes an acceptable drink. In many parts of Europe the roots were boiled and eaten with oil and vinegar. Sweet cicely combined with tarragon and chopped finely gives a pleasant flavour to omelettes, and the shredded leaves of cicely alone give a suggestion of anise to a salad. The roots can be candied and used for the same purposes as angelica.

To candy sweet cicely roots

Cut the roots into short pieces and boil them until tender. Drain and soak for an hour in a syrup made of 1lb (450g) sugar to 1½pt (825ml) water, and a little lemon juice. Drain off the syrup, which can be used for flavouring puddings and stewed fruit. Dry the roots in a cool oven.

Sweet cicely turnovers

Roll out thinly enough pastry for your company and cut into squares. Chop a handful of sweet cicely and a few sorrel leaves, with any thick ribs removed, and a little brown sugar. Place a spoonful on each square of pastry and fold corner to corner, as for apple turnovers. Brush with a little top of the milk, sprinkle with brown sugar, and bake. Serve hot.

TANSY
Tanacetum vulgare

UNDER THE DOMINION OF VENUS

A hardy perennial, tansy is widely spread over Europe. It was one of the earliest plants brought to North America by the settlers. It was cherished in New England herb gardens, from whence it spread to the dooryard and thence to the farm lanes. By 1746 tansy was growing wild along the hedgerows of Pennsylvania and became part of the American country scene: it was used not only for preserving life in the form of proprietary medicines, but also at times of death: corpses were sometimes preserved in a coffin full of tansy. The generic name *Tanacetum* comes from the Greek *athanasia,* meaning immortality, for the flowers when dried do not wilt. It is dedicated to St Athanasius.

Tansy is a bold-looking, upstanding plant, growing 2–3ft (60–90cm) high. The stems are

TANSY, from Crispin de Pas's *Hortus Floridus*, 1614.

grooved and angular, with dark green feathery leaves. The hard bright rayless flowers, earning it the name of bachelor's buttons, or sometimes bitter buttons, bloom in June and July. It is a good, showy plant for the herb garden and flourishes in sun or shade.

Tansy was a popular disinfecting herb for strewing in public places, especially during the Great Plague. It was used to rub over meat to make it distasteful to flies, but too generous an application could make the meat distasteful to the family as well. A bunch of dried tansy 'buttons', stripped of the leaves, hung in the modern kitchen is a good fly repellent. Planted in the orchard, tansy is a valuable companion plant, as it helps discourage fruit-tree moths. Rubbed on a dog's coat, it helps to discourage fleas. Tanacetum oil is a well known fly- and insect-repellent. Rich in potassium it is also useful on the compost heap.

Its use as a cosmetic was known as early as 1527. 'I have heard that if maids will take wild Tansy and lay it to soak in Buttermilk for a space of nine days and wash their faces therewith, it will make them look very fair,' wrote an old herbalist, and the advice was taken by American maids as well.

Culpeper wrote of the wild tansy, or silver-weed as he called it, although the two herbs are unrelated, 'Now Dame Venus hath fitted two herbs of one name, one to help conception, the other to maintain beauty, and what more can be expected of her?' What, indeed? On the garden tansy, Culpeper said, 'Dame Venus was minded to pleasure women with child by this herb, for there grows not an herb fitter for their use than this is; it is just as though it were ordained for the purpose. This herb, bruised and applied to the navel stays miscarriages . . . Let women that desire children love this herb, for it is their best companion (their husbands excepted).'

The herb is carminative, vermifuge, and a good fever medicine, causing the patient to perspire. It is good for sciatica and improves the circulation. A teaspoonful of tansy infused in a cup of water drunk twice daily, or a hot fomentation of tansy tea applied externally to varicose veins, bruises, styes or minor swellings, is recommended treatment, but the dosage must be carefully regulated, as the plant contains certain poisons. A lotion can be made for the treatment of freckles, sunburn and pimples.

Tansy bitters, made of tansy leaves placed in a bottle of New England rum, was a favourite spring tonic in North America a century ago. A cold infusion was an American country tonic for convalescence after illness, and for dyspepsia, hysteria, and jaundice, although it has been said that overdoses could make the patient considerably worse. It was used in an old mining area of South Dakota in the making of whiskey.

The juice, or the shredded leaves, beaten with eggs and fried, were eaten as a digestive. The root was preserved with honey or sugar for gout.

For culinary use, although the strongly flavoured leaves might be eaten in salad, Evelyn considered that they were fitter 'tho' in a very small quantity, for the Pan, being qualified with the Juices of other fresh Herbs, Spinach, Green Corn, Violet, Primrose-leaves, etc., at entrance of the Spring and then fried brownish and eaten hot with the Juice of Orange and Sugar'.

An 18th-century cook book gives a similar type of recipe.

To make tansey pancakes

Beat four eggs, and put to them half a pint of cream, four spoonfuls of flour, and two of fine sugar, beat them a quarter of an hour, then put in one spoonful of the juice of tansey, and two of the juice of spinage, with a little grated nutmeg, heat all well together, and fry them in fresh butter — garnish them with quarters of Seville oranges, grate double-refined sugar over them, and send them up hot.

Since the whole plant is bitter, the eating of tansy at Easter was regarded as representing the bitter herbs of the Passover. Tansy teas as well as tansy puddings were highly esteemed during Lent, and a tansy cake was the reward to victors in the Easter games. It was traditionally eaten at Trinity College, Cambridge, on Easter Monday and Tuesday.

Many tansy recipes are still available in old cookery books, but are either too extravagant and complicated or are likely to be too bitter for today's cooking. Mrs Raffald gives recipes for 'A Boiled Tansey Pudding', 'A Baked Tansey Pudding', 'A Tansey Pudding With Almonds', and 'A Tansey Pudding of Ground Rice'.

Tansey pudding

Blanch and pound a quarter of a pound of Jordan Almonds; put them in a stew-pan, add a gill of syrup of roses, the crumb of a French roll, some grated nutmeg, half a glass of brandy, two tablespoonfuls of Tansey juice, three ounces of fresh butter, and some slices of citron. Pour over it a pint and a half of boiling cream or milk, sweeten, and when cold mix it; add the juice of a lemon, and eight eggs beaten. It may be either boiled or baked.

Today's uses of tansy are more limited, although gipsies still value it for medicinal and culinary purposes. It can be shredded finely for cakes, puddings, omelettes and salads, especially to celebrate Easter.

Oil of tansy is occasionally used in the making of perfumes, toilet water and bath essence. A good yellow-green dye can be extracted from the leaves before the plant blooms.

TARRAGON
Artemisia dracunculus

UNDER THE DOMINION OF MARS

A perennial herb native to southern Europe and parts of Asia and Siberia, tarragon is cultivated in the sunny and dry areas of the USA. There are two culinary types, the French and the Russian, and both are cultivated in England. It was first grown in the royal gardens in Tudor days.

Tarragon has long, narrow and smooth leaves, the French variety dark green, and the Russian a lighter green. The flowers are small, yellow and black, and appear in July, August and September — but they rarely open. The plant reaches about 2ft (60cm). It grows best in poor soil, but requires warmth and sunshine, and plenty of space. It does not set seed in the USA and Britain, and must therefore be propagated by cuttings and root division. It is safer to cover it in winter. It may be grown in a pot on a sunny kitchen window-sill.

The name tarragon is derived from *dracunculus*, meaning a little dragon. It is a member of the Wormwood family, and like most of them it possesses a strong and individual flavour more popular in France than in Britain. The dried herb is more aromatic than the fresh, and French tarragon has a sharper flavour than Russian. Its oil is used in perfumery.

In medicine it is employed as a diuretic, and for digestive purposes and catarrh. It is cooling and carminative and helps purify the blood. Tarragon tea, made of an infusion of ½ teaspoonful of the dried plant in ½ cup of water, helps to overcome insomnia. John Evelyn regarded it as 'highly cordial and friend to the head, heart and liver'.

For drying, hang it in loose bunches for a week. For freezing, cut young tops and tie in bunches. Wash thoroughly and dry on absorbent paper. Immerse in boiling water for 1 minute. Plunge into ice-cold water for 2 minutes. Drain and place in freezer bag. Keep in freezer until required.

In cookery it is used chiefly in sauces and vinegars. Florence Bardswell described it as the one and only correct flavouring for sauce tartare. It is also used in ravigote sauce and béarnaise sauce.

Sauce tartare

6 fluid oz mayonnaise
1 chopped hard-boiled egg yolk
1 medium grated onion
1tbsp chopped chives
1tsp chopped chervil
1tbsp chopped capers
2tsp wine vinegar

Mix the ingredients well and allow to stand an hour before using.

Ravigote sauce

6 fluid oz mayonnaise
1tsp mustard powder
1tsp chopped tarragon
1 chopped onion
1tbsp chopped capers
1tbsp cider vinegar

Mix the ingredients together and serve cold with fish or hot with veal.

Sauce béarnaise

2tbsp cider vinegar
2tsp tarragon
1tsp parsley
peppercorns
1 small chopped onion
bay leaf
¼ cup stock
1½oz (32g) butter
2 egg yolks

Boil chopped onion, bay leaf, peppercorns and half the parsley and tarragon in the vinegar until reduced to half. Strain into a basin and reserve the liquid. Heat a double saucepan, or a basin in a saucepan. Mix the egg yolks with a little of the stock and put into the double boiler, stirring constantly. Add butter, a little at a time, stirring. When the mixture has thickened, add the rest of the stock and the reserved liquor. Add the rest of the parsley and tarragon and serve hot with grills.

A LABEL of the pharmaceutical company of I. Louys, who could supply not only such delights as chocolates but also chloroform and leeches.

(*left*) TARRAGON, as depicted in J. Zorn's *Abbildüngen von Arzneygewachsen*, 1780–87.

THYME

Thymus species

A PLANT OF VENUS, UNDER THE SIGN OF ARIES

Common thyme, *T. vulgaris*, is a cultivated form of *T. serpyllum*, the wild thyme or mother of thyme, which is native to the greater part of Europe. Common thyme was cultivated in England by the middle of the 16th century and sold in London markets. It is perennial, with a tough woody root and hard stems which grow to a height of 12–18in (30–45cm). The dark green leaves are tiny and aromatic, and it bears whorls of little two-lipped lilac-coloured flowers from May

[181]

THYME, from an illustration which appears in the first volume of W. Curtis' *Flora Londinensis*, 1817.

to September. There are a number of other useful and decorative varieties: *T. aureous*, a bright gold; *T. citriodorus*, a lemon-scented thyme which has a silver-leaved form; *T. serpyllum coccineus*, which has red flowers; and basil and orange thymes.

Thyme is an excellent bee-plant and was always planted near hives; its leaves were rubbed on the hives. Pliny said: 'Honey-mistresses and such as keep bees hope to have a good yeare, when they see the Thyme to bloome abundantly.' It grows wild on the hillsides of Greece and gives Greek honey its distinctive flavour. Butterflies love it, too.

The name thyme comes from a Greek word meaning 'to fumigate', and a type of incense was made from the plant to drive away insects. It was a favourite strewing plant, and part of every well equipped still-room. The good housewife kept it always handy beside the kitchen fireplace, for thyme keeps its aromatic quality for years.

In the pioneer gardens of New England thyme was grown for both cooking and medicine. The plant was collected while in flower, dried and saved for use as a tea for excessive menstruation, or for general aches and pains. As a medicine, oil of thymol is used by herbalists for throat, chest and digestive illnesses, and for laryngitis, bronchitis and whooping-cough. In fact, as Culpeper said so long ago, 'It is a noble strengthener of the lungs, as notable a one as grows'. It is antiseptic and forms an ingredient of some disinfectants. Oil of thyme, 'thymol', is added as an antiseptic to mouthwashes and toothpastes.

Thyme tea is made from 1oz (28g) dried leaves to 1pt (550ml) water, strained. One or two tablespoonfuls may be taken two or three times a day for all chest complaints, and for indigestion. Externally, thymol oil with olive oil is an excellent liniment for rheumatism.

Thyme is a good ground-cover plant, and in crazy-paving it repays careless steps with a generous perfume. In company with a bay leaf and a sprig of parsley, it softens and scents our bath water. With alum as a mordant, thyme gives an attractive grey-gold, and mixed with a tin mordant, it makes a good yellow.

The varieties used in cooking are usually the common, the lemon and the orange. Green leaves may be mixed in stuffings, but the dried leaves have a stronger taste. Courgettes, cut into 1in (2.5cm) thick slices, dropped into boiling salted water for 3 minutes, and then strained and gently cooked in butter, with a little black pepper and a teaspoonful of thyme, is a delicately flavoured summer vegetable, and the following sauce is delicious on entrées, fish, or veal cutlets.

Italian herb sauce

Put 2tbsp finely chopped onion into a pan with 1tbsp oil, stir over gentle heat until soft but not brown. Add 4tbsp stock, or ½ stock cube in ½pt (275ml) of water, boil and reduce a little. Add a chopped mushroom, a dash of cayenne, the juice of a ¼ of a lemon, a squeeze of garlic, a little chopped thyme, and a glass of dry sherry.

TURMERIC
Curcuma longa

A perennial plant, turmeric is native to eastern India, the East Indies, Madagascar, and most of the Pacific Islands. It is cultivated in Tobago, Sumatra, Java, Bengal and — the best — China. The pale yellow wrinkled roots spread far, having many circular knots from which arise four or five spear-shaped leaves. The yellowish-red flowers grow in loose scaly spikes. The hard roots, not unlike ginger, may be powdered and applied to ulcers. The roots were also used for liver and bowel complaints, and for the treatment of jaundice. Turmeric belongs to the Ginger family.

The plant is a gentle stimulant, but is seldom

TURMERIC, the oriental herb from whose rhizome can be extracted a yellow spice used for flavouring and colouring foods, often as a cheaper substitute for saffron. This picture is from Chaumeton's *Flore Medicale*.

safflower. Unsized paper, tinged with a solution of turmeric, and known as turmeric paper, is used as a test for alkalis.

As a food colouring and flavouring it is used in pickles and chutney, mustard powder blends, and curry. It gives a yellow tinge to rice and is sometimes used as a substitute for saffron. It may be used for colouring cakes, or for making kedgeree.

Curry powder

3oz (85g) turmeric
4oz (113g) coriander
1oz (28g) black pepper
1oz (28g) ginger
¼oz (7g) cayenne pepper
¼oz (7g) cinnamon

Mix the ingredients together and keep sealed in a wide-mouthed bottle.

Indonesian rice

1lb (450g) Patna rice
1pt (550ml) milk
½pt (275ml) water
1tsp turmeric powder
2 eggs
watercress
salt

Bring milk and water to the boil, add rice and seasonings, and cook until liquid is absorbed, stirring to prevent burning. Leave on a low heat for 5 minutes. Finish by steaming rice until it is cooked. Make an omelette with the eggs, and cut into strips. Put rice into a dish, and decorate with omelette strips and watercress. Serve with roast chicken.

used in medicine now except for colouring. It yields a small quantity of gold-coloured essential oil, and has a strong smell and a pungent taste. In the 19th century it was used as a hair bleach.

Its principal use is as a dye. The natives of the Pacific Islands use it for painting their bodies, and members of the Vishnu sect in India make a distinguishing perpendicular mark on their foreheads with turmeric. It is also used to colour yellow varnish and to dye cottons. The chopped roots are powdered and dissolved in water. After the cloth is dipped into this solution it can be mordanted with ash extract or with citric acid to obtain yellow; with iron water followed by calcium hydroxide for gold brown; and for scarlet, the cloth is first dyed with turmeric and then with

VALERIAN

Valeriana officinalis

A HERB OF MERCURY

A handsome perennial, native to a large part of Europe and the USA, valerian is also found throughout Britain.

The root of *V. officinalis* sends out numerous fibres, and has valuable medicinal properties. The stem is hollow, round and grooved, and more or less hairy. It terminates in two or more pairs of flowering stems which reach 3–4ft (90–120cm) high. The leaves are paired, dark green, and the under-surface is covered with short soft hairs. The flowers, which appear in June, July and August, are small, pink or flesh-coloured, with a scent disagreeable to most people, giving it the old country name of phu. However, the scent was better appreciated in the East, where baths were scented with it. It also possesses a fascination for cats and rats.

Valerian was supposed to inspire love, and was therefore employed as a love philtre, for it was believed that if a girl wore valerian she would never lack lovers. It also preserved folk from thunder and lightning, and was used both for and against witchcraft. It was dedicated to St Bernard.

As well as having importance as a simpler's plant, it was cultivated by the 'valerie-growers' in Derbyshire and sold to the druggists. The plant owes its generic name to its medicinal value: *Valeriana* from the Latin, meaning 'powerful', and *officinalis* indicating its official value. Valerian has achieved the fame of a book to itself — Sir John Hill's *The Virtue of Wild Valerian in Nervous Disorders* — which reached its fourth edition in 1772.

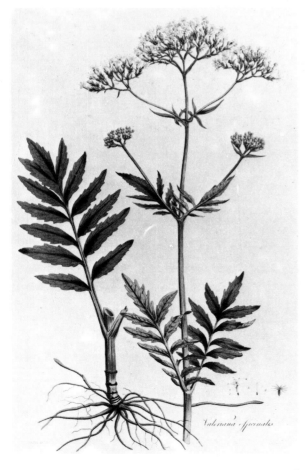

Valeriana officinalis

It has been discovered that the bacillus of typhoid fever is killed in 45 minutes in air impregnated with the vapour of oil of valerian.

The red-spur valerian, classified by Linnaeus as *V. rubra* but now known to botanists as *Centranthus rubra*, was a garden plant in England in the 17th century, but was already widely naturalized, particularly on the cliffs of the Isle of Wight. It flourishes in chalky places and in old walls, ruined castles, churches and railway cuttings.

The spurred flowers, which are bright pink, near-crimson and white, bloom from June to September. The smooth light green leaves, sometimes covered with a sea-green bloom, are in complete contrast to *V. officinalis*. It has little medicinal value, but in some parts of Europe its leaves were eaten as salad. The seeds of some species were formerly used in embalming the dead. It was a much-loved flower in old gardens under the names of pretty Betsy and bouncing Bess.

VERVAIN
Verbena officinalis

A PLANT OF VENUS

A weedy plant of the Verbena family, vervain is native to Europe, China, Japan and many parts of the world. It is native to and common in England, less common in Scotland, and rare in Ireland. It escaped from cultivation in the USA, where it has established itself along the roadsides. In England vervain grows abundantly on waste ground. Philip Miller in 1754 noticed that it never grew farther than ¼ mile away from human habitation. An inconspicuous plant, with little beauty and less scent, it has square wiry stalks which are very strong and a little hairy; the stalks are sometimes purplish and rise to 2ft (60cm). The narrow, notched leaves are dusky green above and pale green beneath. The small lilac or purple flowers open only two or three at a time, from June to October.

Why should this undistinguished herb have been venerated in so many ways and by so many races? It was used by the ancient Druids in their lustral water, and for divination and incantations. They extracted the juice by steeping the plant in cold water, by boiling, and by infusing in wine. They used it in salves, ointments and fumigations, and in magic medicine. They ordered the plant 'to

VALERIAN shown in a plate from the third volume of W. Curtis' *Flora Londinensis*, 1817.

[184]

A PAIR of 18th-century French apothecaries' jars, labelled to contain gentian and safflower.

be gathered about the rising of the dog-star, but so as neither sun nor moon be at that time above the earth to see it'. Also, 'that before they take up the hearbe, they bestow upon the ground where it groweth, honey with the combs, in token of satisfaction and amends for the wrong and violence done in depriving her of so holy a hearbe'.

It is believed that vervain was introduced by the Druids into Rome, where it was called *Britannica* and became a ritual cleansing plant. According to Livy, it was made into little bundles with which they swept the altars dedicated to their gods and dusted the table of Jupiter. To the Romans the name *Verbena* meant altar plant. In honour of this *herba sacra,* as it was called, a festival called *verbenalia* was held annually. Vervain was dedicated to

Venus, and as a love-plant it had to be picked by a Roman bride to wear at her wedding. When Roman heralds-at-arms were despatched with a message of war they wore a chaplet of vervain. The herald was called a *verbenarius*, and claimed immunity, the vervain serving as a flag of truce or a red cross. Hippocrates, the first doctor to separate medicine from magic, used vervain as one of his list of 400 simples; he applied it to wounds and prescribed its use in fevers and nervous disorders.

With the coming of Christianity, other superstitions arose around this mysterious plant. It was believed to have grown at the foot of the Cross, and there was a special ritual for uprooting the plant. In Brittany it was known as the herb of the Cross, and it was ritually crossed and blessed.

Vervain was used for and against witchcraft, being one of the chief ingredients in enchanters' spells and potions, and yet having the reputation of 'hindering witches of their will'.

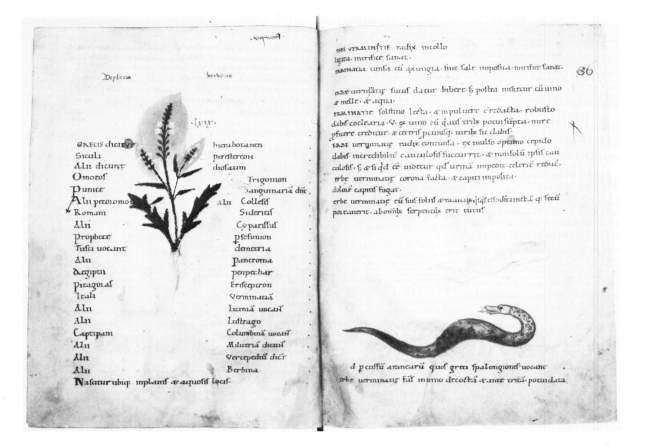

For making the true love powder

Take elecampane, the seeds and flowers, vervain, and the berries of mistletoe. Beat them, after being well dried in an oven, into a powder, and give it to the party you design upon in a glass of wine and it will work wonderful effect to your advantage.

Vervain also had the power over dreams.

To prevent dreaming

Take the vervain and hang it about a man's neck, or let him drink some of the juice in going to bed; certainly he will not dream if he does so.

Over the centuries the battle for and against vervain as a medicinal herb has continued. Gerard distrusted it, and said, 'Many odde old wives fables are written of Vervaine tending to witch-craft and sorcery, which you may read else-where, for I am not willing to trouble your eares with reporting such trifles, as honest eares abhorre to hear ... Most of the late Physitions do give the juice or decoction hereof to them that hath the plague: but these men are deceived, not only in the way they looke for some truth from the father of falsehood and leasings, but also because instead of a good and sure remedy they minister no remedy at all; for it is reported, that the Divell did reveale it as a secret and divine medicine.' Culpeper, on the other hand, advised it for all manner of ills, including ulcers and haemorrhoids, and said: 'Applied with some oil of roses and vinegar to the forehead and temples, it easeth inveterate pains and aching of the head, and is good for those that are frantick.' He believed it to be useful for either inward or outward application.

In the New World, men and women sought for healing herbs in the countryside to heal their sick; *V. stricta*, the wild blue verbena they discovered, was good for an upset stomach; the dried leaves of *V. hastata* made a herb tea for a cough cure, and white verbena, *V. urticaefolia*, was used in a root tea to treat profuse menstruation and mental illnesses. The lemon-scented verbena was grown in European gardens during the late 18th century, and because of its delicious perfume it became valuable in the making of soaps, toilet waters and perfumes. By now the magic of the plant was fading, but beliefs die hard, and in the first year of Victoria's reign, in the supplement to the British *Pharmacopoeia* 'necklaces of vervain roots, tied with a yard of white satin ribbon' were recommended for the cure of scrofula. It was too late. The miraculous cures, the cult-mysteries, the love-philtres and the incantations had ended with a yard of white satin ribbon.

But vervain was not forgotten with the end of the belief in vervain magic, and its real uses in natural medicine were discovered, or perhaps many of them rediscovered, when the mists of superstition were eventually diffused.

Homoeopathic medicine has cleared the name of vervain, and it is now used in the treatment of nervous disorders, epilepsy, asthma, whooping-cough and pneumonia. A decoction made from the whole plant is given for eczema and other skin complaints; a standard infusion of flowers, leaves and stalks taken as a nerve tonic; or 1oz (28g) each of vervain, skullcap and valerian as a tisane for migraine. The plant may, after all, be recognized by its old-fashioned name of simpler's joy.

VERVAIN, shown here from two English manuscript sources, one dating from about 1100 (*left*) and the other from the 13th century (*below*). Both associate the herb with the serpent: among vervain's numerous virtues was its efficacy in ameliorating the effects of snake-bite.

WATERCRESS
Nasturtium officinale

UNDER THE DOMINION OF MARS

A hardy perennial, watercress is native to Europe, India, Brazil and Australia, and is naturalized in the USA. The root is long and creeping, the thick stems have numerous rootlets springing from beneath, and the alternate leaves are dark green, bronze or purplish. The cruciform flowers, which grow on terminal spikes, are small and white, and bloom from June to August.

Nicholas Mesner was apparently the first man to cultivate watercress in Germany, in the 16th century. Cultivation followed in Holland, and after more than 100 years it was introduced into England.

The simplers supplied the herb shops in Covent Garden and the Fleet and Newgate Markets. They collected from hedges and streams not only watercress but dandelions, scurvy grass, nettles, bitter-sweet, valerian, feverfew, hedge-mustard, and a variety of other simples. Although the strong flavoured wild cress was preferred, watercress growing was profitable as a branch of market-gardening, and in the small gardens in the immediate vicinity of London watercress, radishes, parsley, and other herbs and flowers were not sent to market but sold in small quantities on the spot.

At the Farringdon market, however, the green-stuff sellers had to be on their rounds in time for the mechanics' breakfasts. At the principal entrance to the market was an open space running the entire length of the railings in front, and here the cresses were sold from the hampers in which they had been brought from the country. A candle fixed in the middle of the bright green cresses cast curious patterns on the ground in the surrounding gloom, where a group of skinny,

[187]

WATERCRESS being sold on the streets of London — one of the pen-and-ink illustrations from E. Hull's series of 'London Cries'.

pinched-faced little girls would gather the cold wet leaves into bunches to fill the 'shallows' that they would carry round the streets crying: 'Creases, young water-creases.'

Richard Brook wrote in about 1800: 'The Water-cress has long been cultivated as a salad in this country, and the quantity raised in the neighbourhood of London is truly astonishing. Every morning throughout the year, although there are something like two millions of inhabitants they have all Water-cresses within call, and can have them to breakfast if they choose.'

A watercress bed must be cleaned with wooden rakes of all debris before planting. The cuttings or rooted plants are set out by hand, and the beds given a shallow flooding as soon as they begin to take hold. The beds last indefinitely, but need to be replanted from time to time, to maintain cleanliness and freedom from weeds. Cress still grows wild where streams are unpolluted.

Watercress has been eaten for centuries by men and women who no doubt benefited by its generous supply of vitamin C. It is used medicinally for anaemia and eczema; for cysts, swellings and tumours. A teaspoonful of the juice in milk or water is beneficial as a spring tea. It should not, however, be taken during pregnancy. Herbalists advise it for stiffness, cramps and rheumatism; for nerves and heart conditions.

Apart from its use in salads and sandwiches, it makes an excellent soup.

Watercress soup

1 bunch watercress
1½oz (32g) butter
1oz (28g) flour
1¼pt (690ml) milk
pinch nutmeg
salt and black pepper
1 chicken stock cube
a little cream
paprika

Wash and pick over watercress, removing any yellow leaves and coarser parts of stalks. Make a roux with butter melted in ¼pt (135ml) milk. Blend cress with 1pt (550ml) milk in liquidizer and gradually add this to roux. Crumble stock cube and add to mixture. Add nutmeg, salt and black pepper to taste. Bring to boil very slowly, stirring all the time. Do not allow to boil. Serve in soup bowls with a swirl of cream, a light shake of paprika, and croutons.

WELD

Reseda luteola
R. lutea

The oldest yellow dye-plant in the world, weld is native to the sandy soils of the Moroccan coast and the shores of the Mediterranean. It is also native to Britain. It was cultivated around Paris and in other regions of France. It is a well known plant throughout Europe. The wild weld, *R. lutea*, is biennial, and does not give so much colouring as the cultivated variety, which was treated as an annual. It is bushier, shorter, and a deeper yellow, and frequents chalky cliffs, the corners of fields and roadsides, and is at home in abandoned stone quarries and lime-kiln rubbish, and often springs up on the rubbish tips around coal mines. It is abundant in Scotland, and blooms in June, July and August.

R. luteola, the cultivated weld, was known as dyer's weld, dyer's weed, dyer's rocket, greenweed (in Kent and Sussex), and yellow weed. All parts of this classic dye-plant, mentioned by Dioscorides, went into the making of a pure lemon yellow, rendered permanent with alum. It gave the artist's paint-box the colour known as Dutch pink, and was used to make blue cloth green. It

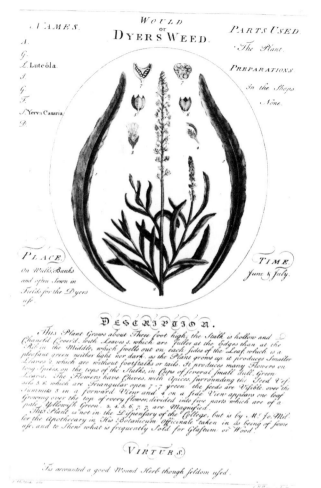

was added to madder to make an orange dye. Cotton, silk, linen and woollen materials respond equally well, and it was employed by calico-printers, colour-makers, and paper-hanging manufacturers.

The plant is erect, with narrow wavy-edged leaves and a long black root. The greenish-yellow flowers, which appear in midsummer, resemble those of the garden mignonette to which it is related, although it lacks the characteristic perfume and attractive burnt-orange stamens. The seed-pods are globular and gathered like small purses. The flowers, seeds and stalks turn yellow when the plants are ripe for harvest — a little earlier or later would be detrimental to the dye. It can, however, be hung by the roots and dried for later use.

Weld was considered to be useful against those two threats to medieval life, 'the bitings of venomous creatures' and the plague.

Weld flowers follow the course of the Sun, even on a cloudy day.

WILLOW, BLACK
Salix nigra

Black willow, the pussy willow, is native to North America. It grows on river banks, and can reach heights of 15–25ft (4.5–7.6m). It has a rough, blackish bark and dull green glaucous leaves, which become black when dry. It has similar properties to white willow and is also quick-growing.

According to Gerard, Dioscorides said that the bark 'being burnt to ashes, and steeped in vinegar, takes away cornes and other like risings in the feet and toes'. The bark and catkins were used as an anti-aphrodisiac and sexual sedative, for which an infusion was advised. Culpeper agreed that 'the leaves bruised and boiled in wine stay the heat of lust in man or woman, and quite extinguish it, if it be long used'. He also prescribed it to lessen other fevers.

Willows were once used in the process of tanning, and their leaves give a good cinnamon dye. In March and April the catkins are a great attraction to bees.

WILLOW, WHITE
Salix alba

A TREE OF SATURN, GOVERNED BY THE MOON

The white willow is a deciduous tree found in moist places in North Africa, central Asia and Europe. It was introduced into the north-eastern states of the USA. There are 250 known species of willow, and 17 or 18 are native to Britain, where the white willow, or the Huntingdon willow, grows along the riversides to a height of 60, 70, or even 80ft (18, 21 or 24m). Thomas Fuller, in the middle of the 17th century, said that it grew with such incredible speed in Buckinghamshire that 'the profit by willows will buy their owner a horse, before that any other tree will pay for his saddle'. The generic name *Salix* is derived from *salire*, to leap, and it was said that 'it groweth with that speed that it seemeth to leap'. It flowers in April and May.

The wonderful story of willow begins in the

WHITE WILLOW, as illustrated in *Pharmaceutisch Medicinisch botanik*, 1828, by Daniel Wagner.

WINTERGREEN
Gaultheria procumbens

Native to North America, wintergreen is a shrub found in pine forests, woodlands and clearings. The creeping stems, which cover a considerable amount of ground, send up erect branches, from 3–6ft (90–180cm) high, which have dark leathery leaves. From the top of the stems hang pinkish-white bell-shaped flowers, which bloom from May to September. These turn into scarlet berry-like capsules, which were once made into bread. The leaves are spicy and aromatic, and have been used as a substitute for or combined with tea, from which it received the name of mountain teaberry, or Canada teaberry. These leaves, which should be collected in the autumn, may be boiled like spinach. The berries afford food for game, which has earned the plant the names of grouseberry, partridge-berry and deer-berry.

Wintergreen oil, used both internally and externally, was an old-fashioned remedy for rheumatism and rheumatic fever, sciatica, dropsy, diabetes, bladder disorders and skin diseases. It

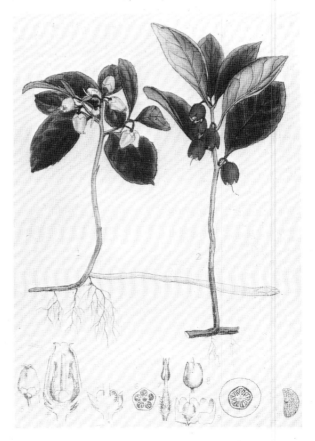

first century, when Dioscorides wrote about his use of willows for medicinal purposes, a use that has continued unbroken until this day. Believers in the *Doctrine of Signatures* held that because the willow flourished in damp places it must be good for rheumatism. It so happened that they were proved to be right, because the inner bark contains salicin, from which salicylic acid was derived in 1838. This is closely related to aspirin, which has now displaced willow bark from popular use. The tree once served as a symbol for deserted lovers.

White willow tea is an infusion of the shredded bark in a cup of cold water, brought to the boil, simmered for 2 minutes, and then left to stand for 15 minutes, which is the standard dose for arthritic and rheumatic pains. A decoction from the bark is used for a bath for weak babies. The bark of all the species is astringent, tonic and stomachic. White willow bark may be had from most herb shops.

WINTERGREEN: a plate from R. Bentley and H. Trimmen's *Medicinal Plants*, 1880.

was good for eye lotions, gargles, poultices, and antiseptic washes. The oil, which contains methyl salicitate, a close relative of aspirin, is obtained by distillation. It is still sometimes used by sportsmen in massaging muscles.

Today, combined with menthol and eucalyptus, it is much in use for flavouring toothpowders, liquid dentifrices, pastes, etc. In perfumes, the essence requires to be used with extreme caution, since it is exceedingly powerful. Well blended with other essences, it imparts a rich floral fragrance in soap.

WITCH HAZEL
Hamamelis virginiana

A deciduous shrub native to the eastern states of North America and Canada, witch hazel, *H. virginiana* or *virginica*, is grown in gardens for its much treasured yellow tassels which appear in September and October, when other flowers are few. The varieties grown in England bloom between December and February. It grows in damp woods and produces several branching stems, covered with smooth grey bark, from one root. The yellow flowers appear after the leaves have fallen. They are followed by black nuts which expel their round hard seeds like bullets from a shotgun, earning it the name of snappy-hazel. It is known also as winter-bloom and tobacco weed.

Its medicinal qualities were known to the American Indians. Both leaves and bark are astringent, tonic and sedative. Its astringent action is due to its relatively high tannin content, and it is of great value to sufferers from varicose veins. Preparations can be used for vaginal douches, excessive menstruation, diarrhoea and minor burns. It can be used as a poultice for inflammation, a wash for bed sores, and a lotion for stings. In dried form as snuff it stops nose-bleeds if sniffed up the nostrils.

Hamamelis water, or witch hazel water, is derived from the witch hazel brush, that is, the twigs bearing the flowers, collected in the autumn after the leaves have fallen. (Its oil is better in quality in the autumn and winter.) Witch hazel water can be bought at chemists and is good for bruises, small wounds, swellings and sprains.

Witch hazel is a valuable treatment for piles, when it may be used either as a suppository or an ointment. A gargle for sore throats is made from a heaped teaspoonful steeped in boiling water for 30 minutes.

It is employed in some toilet preparations as a skin tonic, to tighten up tissue and remove red veins. Mixed with rose water it is refreshing as an eye-bath, or as eye-pads for tired eyes.

WOAD
Isatis tinctoria

A PLANT OF SATURN

A biennial widely distributed in Europe, Asia and North Africa, woad was also cultivated in Asia and many parts of the world before the introduction of indigo. Woad is common in Britain. It is a member of the Mustard family. Its tall, upright stems grow to a height of 2–3ft (60–90cm). Its bright yellow flowers grow in panicles, with small yellow spear-shaped bracts between. It blooms in June and July, giving out a faint perfume of honey. It was Caesar who reported that the Britons painted themselves blue with woad when they went into battle. According to Dioscorides, the leaves of woad are strongly astringent and help to stem the flow of blood.

Woad was probably the earliest blue dye

WOAD illustrated in the first volume of F. and C. Regnault's *La Botanique mise à la portée de tout le monde.*

Le Pastel ou la Guède
Isatis tinctoria. L. S. P.
Ital. Guado. Angl. Woad. Allem. Waid.

known to the western world, and it became an important commodity at medieval fairs. In Germany and France the story was much the same. In France cultivation was continuous from the 13th to the 18th centuries. By the end of the 16th century there were 220 master dyers in Paris alone. Natural dyes were used up to the 1880s, when aniline dyes began to appear.

For British subjects engaged in the cultivation of woad, however, not everything went smoothly. In 1597 the people around Southampton raised objections 'because the common sort of people find themselves greatly grieved withal, for that, after woad-sowing, there will grow no grass, nor anything else to feed on' — a fact already known to the cultivators, who had discovered that it was necessary to move the crop after two years, because 'if long continued it robs the soil'. Parkinson reported another disadvantage: woad growers 'hath found it to be the cause of the destruction of their Bees: for it hath been observed, that they have dyed as it were of a Flix, that have tasted thereof'. This must have been serious indeed, for honey was of the greatest importance at that time.

But in spite of these allegations woad was still cultivated, as it had been before the beginning of the Christian era. The leaves were cropped four, five or six times a year, and immediately carried to the mills and pulped between immense wooden rollers turned by horses, each led by a man. The woad was heaped, drained, kneaded and rolled into balls, two handfuls of the pulp to each ball. The balls were then dried, powdered, wetted again and fermented or 'couched', and left to ferment for nine weeks, during which time they had to be sprinkled and turned frequently. A dark clay-like substance resulted, which was the dye. Parkinson described how dyer's-weed (*Reseda luteola*) changed to green any cloth or silk first dyed blue with woad, 'and for these uses there is great store of this herbe spent in all countries and thereof many fields are sowen for the purpose'. Philip Miller reported that dyers used it 'for laying the Foundation of many Colours, especially all Sad-Colours', for it was true that woad's durable dark blue could be reduced to many different shades of blue, and could also be used in the fixing of other colours.

With the advent of indigo, however, which gave brighter, livelier shades of blue, if not so durable, the role of woad became a secondary one of fixing and reinforcing the newer, more attractive indigo colours. The last two woad-mills in Lincolnshire creaked to a halt in the 1930s, never to turn again. Cultivation of woad in France and Flanders continued, but only to improve the colour and quality of the indigo dyes, and the introduction of aniline dyes completely changed the scene.

The plant's use in medicine in the treatment of St Anthony's Fire and for plasters and ointments for ulcers and inflammation was always overshadowed by its commercial employment in dyeing. Now it is grown only for those enthusiasts who still have the desire to research and experiment on an ageless craft.

WOODRUFF

Asperula odorata

A HERB OF MARS

A perennial, woodruff is native to Europe, Asia and North Africa, and is cultivated in the USA. A member of the Bedstraw family, it frequents

WOODRUFF, condemned by Culpeper as 'provocative to venery'. This illustration is drawn from an English manuscript dated about 1100 in the possession of the Bodleian Library, Oxford.

woodlands and shady places in Britain. Many slender square stems rise from its fibrous and matted roots and creeping rootstock. The narrow leaves surround the stems in successive whorls, each whorl having six to eight leaves. They were likened by the old herbalists to the rowel of a spur, and it was called wood-rove, from the French *rovelle*, a spur. Its name woodruff is equally descriptive, since these neat green whorls are set around the stem like a lace ruff. The tiny four-petalled flowers, usually white, but sometimes faintly tinged with pink, bloom in May and June, followed by bristly fruit. Although unrelated, it seems like a smaller and prettier sister of goose-grass or cleavers. Gerard said that the woodruff 'being made up into garlandes and bundles, hanging up in houses in the heat of the summer, doth very well attemper the aire, coole and make freshe the place, to the delight and comfort of any of such as are therein'. The plants grow to a height of 6–12in (15–30cm).

The perfume, only faint in its green stage, grows stronger with time, and is retained for many years. Garlands of woodruff were used for church decoration, especially on St Barnabas' Day, and on St Paul's Day. The star-shaped whorls pressed in books keep the pages scented for as long as they lie hidden. Sprigs in drawers and cupboards release a scent of new-mown hay.

The Elizabethans valued woodruff as a strewing herb, and for scenting their linen and stuffing their mattresses. They kept it, with other sweet-scented herbs, in pierced boxes to perfume their rooms, and made it into sweet-bags, and 'fancy snuffs to make a man merrie'. Incredibly, Culpeper declared that this innocent and charming flower 'is said to be provocative to venery'.

In Germany woodruff was gathered on May Day to make a delicious cooling drink with strawberries, Rhine wine and sugar. They called it Mai-trank, May drink or May bowl. It was also employed in the flavouring of liqueurs.

It was once used in perfumery. Woodruff contains a crystalline chemical principle known as coumarin, and in 1868 Sir William Perkin produced artificially this same coumarin, with its perfume of hay and woodruff, which is used in the making of scents and toilet articles.

It was used in the Middle Ages as 'an excellent cordial drink' for jaundice and liver complaints, and the bruised leaves were laid on open wounds. Today, it is sometimes combined in mixed herbal teas as a cure for migraine and bladder complaints, and as a tonic for nervous conditions and depression, and in recovering from a fever. It must be used with caution, however, for taken in quantity it can produce sickness and symptoms of poisoning. Two teaspoonfuls of the powdered leaves and not more than one cupful a day is the recommended dose.

WORMWOOD
Artemisia absinthium

GOVERNED BY MARS

A hardy perennial herb, native to Europe and introduced into North America, wormwood has now spread to Asia and to most parts of the world. The woody rootstock produces many bushy stems which grow to a height of 2–4ft (60–120cm). The leaves are alternate, covered with fine silky hairs, deeply cut and grey-green. Tiny yellow-green flowers appear from July to October.

It derives its name from Artemis, goddess of chastity, known as Diana to the Greeks. In ancient

WORMWOOD, or absinthe, shown as illustrated in an English 13th-century manuscript.

WORMWOOD being ground, as depicted in *Tacuinum Sanitatum, c.* 1385.

times it was believed to counteract poison. Shakespeare caused Oberon to touch Titania's eyelids with it, to counteract the effects of love-in-idleness, the wild pansy:

> *Be as thou was wont to be;*
> *See as thou was wont to see:*
> *Dian's bud o'er Cupid's flower*
> *Hath such force and magic power.*

Wormwood is frequently referred to in the Bible, chiefly for its bitterness: King Solomon mentioned it in warning his son against the seducing arts of a strange woman: 'The lips of a strange woman drop as a honeycomb . . . but her end is as bitter as Wormwood'.

A. absinthium has always been used as a vermifuge, hence the common name wormwood. It was also strewn about chambers and in cupboards to keep away moths and insects, including fleas. Pieces of wormwood were hung up in cottages for this purpose. It has been discovered that wormwood should be kept away from all other medicinal herbs, as it inhibits the growth of many. Wormwood tea, sprayed on the ground in spring and autumn, is a great discourager of slugs and beetles.

It was cultivated in the environs of London for medicinal use and with its relative, mugwort, was cried about London streets. In July 1760 a rumour spread through the city, causing great consternation, that plague had broken out in St Thomas's Hospital. The following morning in Covent Garden the demand for rue and wormwood was so great that the price rose by 40% and gardeners were employed all that day in bringing supplies of these herbs to the market. The report proved to be false, but when later investigations were made on the essential oils of medicinal herbs, it was found certain bacteria were killed by the evaporation of some of these oils — including oil of wormwood.

Burton advised pillows stuffed with wormwood for insomnia. Culpeper recommended it for scurvy, and in 'the hypochondriacle disorders of sedentary men'. He recommended the following recipe: 'Take of the flowers of Wormwood, Rosemary and Black Thorn, each of a like quantity, and half this quantity of Saffron; boil them in Rhenish wine, but put not in the saffron till the rest are almost boiled: this is the way to keep a man's body in health.' He devoted many pages to Wormwood and became very passionate in the writing. Of sea wormwood he said: 'A Papist got the toy by the end, and he called it Holy Wormwood; and in truth, I am of opinion, their giving so much holiness to herbs is the reason there remains so little in themselves . . . Of all the wormwoods that grow here this is the weakest; but doctors commend it, and apothecaries sell it. The herb is good for something because God made nothing in vain . . .' On Roman wormwood he was even more outspoken: 'And why Roman, seeing it grows familiarly in England? It may be so called, because it is good for stinking breath, which the Romans cannot be very free from, maintaining so many bawdy-houses by authority from His Holiness.' He thought well of the common wormwood. 'A poor silly countryman hath got an ague, and cannot go about his business; he wishes he had it not, and so do I; but I will tell him a remedy, whereby he shall prevent it: Take the Herb of Mars, Wormwood, and if infortunes will do good, what will fortunes do?'

Today, herbalists advise wormwood for jaundice, indigestion, constipation and kidney disorders. Oil of Wormwood is used in liniments for sprains, bruises and lumbago, and in fomentations for rheumatism and inflammations. An infusion of the leaves and stems stimulates appetite and soothes stomach pains. Because of its bitterness it is more palatable sweetened with a little honey; two tablespoons should be taken night and morning. Excessive use is dangerous, and pure wormwood oil is a strong poison which should be used only as liniment. It is of value for gout and rheumatism when used as a bath additive.

Wormwood as a drink has an ancient history, probably starting with the Saracens. It used to be steeped in wine, a custom thought to be derived from the ancients, who drank it before and after wine to counteract its effect. The essential oil of wormwood, which is dark green, was in the past infused with ale and beer to make purl, a liquor which hard drinkers were in the habit of taking in the morning. The name purl was also given to a mixture of hot beer with ginger, or maybe gin, and sugar as a morning drink in more leisurely days. The seeds were also employed in Scotland by the distillers of whisky.

But it is in the making of absinthe that wormwood is best known. In the Lamentations of Jeremiah, iii, 15, there is the expression 'He hath made me drunken with wormwood', which makes it possible that absinthe, or a similar drink, was known in the time of Jeremiah. The basis of absinthe is the drug absinthol, extracted from wormwood, and used with anise in the making of this highly intoxicating liqueur. Whole fields of wormwood were cultivated in France for that purpose, and millions of gallons were imported from other parts of Europe. Habitual drinking of too much absinthe may cause absinthism, which can lead to complete paralysis. A pleasant and less dangerous practice in the 18th century was the drinking of small quantities of absinthe in tokay.

Wormwood is used also in the making of vermouth (*wermuth*: wormwood) to give the drink its characteristic bitter flavour.

The following receipt for a caudle, a beverage given to sick people and to their visitors, comes from a 19th-century cook-book.

To distil caudle water

Take worm-wood, hore-hound, feather-few, and lavender-cotton, of each three handfuls, rue, pepper-mint, and Seville orange peel, of each a handful, steep them in red wine, or the bottoms of strong beer all night, then distil them in a hot still pretty quick, and it will be a fine caudle to take as bitters.

Wormwood, groundsel and elderflower salve

1lb (450g) lard
1 good handful of each of the fresh herbs

Cut the herbs into pieces 1in (2.5cm) long. Put into an earthenware pot in the oven with the lard; and slowly heat until boiling-point is reached. Simmer for ½ hour with the lid on. Strain into pots and tie down when cool. Excellent and helpful for bruises, sores and inflammations.

YARROW
Achillea millefolium

UNDER THE DOMINION OF VENUS

Yarrow is a European immigrant which has made itself at home on the hillsides and roadsides of the USA. It has a native American counterpart in *A. occidentalis*, which is similar, and numerous others such as *A. multiflora*, which are also natives. The leaves are dark green, aromatic and lacy, finely divided and exceedingly numerous — hence its name of milfoil, a thousand leaves. The stem rises from the centre to a height of 8–10in (20–25cm). The flowers, which appear from June to September, are small, white or tinged with pink or purple, and strongly but not unpleasantly scented. The plant is commonly found in dry pastures.

It is well known for its styptic qualities, and its ancient names indicate its former uses; souldier's woundwort; knyghten milfoil; and sanguinary or nose-bleed, for which generations of country folk

YARROW: an exquisite decoration from Jean Bourdichon's 16th-century *Hours of Anne of Burgundy* shows a detail of the head of the plant.

Achillea Millefolium

YARROW: a plate from Curtis' *Flora Londinensis, c.* 1785.

ecaries' shops, and pounded and mixed by housewives in still-rooms in town and country. Country people used the bruised herb or an ointment made of it, for burns and small wounds. Its bitter leaves were once used as a flavouring for beer.

Throughout the Middle Ages yarrow was regarded as a witch-plant, strong in incantations and with power for and against withcraft. It was believed that carrying yarrow in a wedding bouquet ensured seven years of happiness.

In North America the early settlers used it for diarrhoea and feverish colds. They applied the fresh leaves for eczema and rashes, and treated childish sufferers from ear-ache with wads made of yarrow leaves moistened with an infusion of the herb which were plugged into their ears. They, too, followed the classical hero and used yarrow as a wound-plant, making an infusion of the leaves or using it in the form of ointment.

The whole plant may be dried and used in an infusion for debility, loss of appetite, and as a tonic in convalescence. It relieves headaches, fevers, excessive menstruation, indigestion and palpitations. It is given for diseased conditions of the gastro-intestinal tract. A standard infusion of the leaves and flowers may be made, and a wine-glassful taken night and morning. It is recommended for measles, chickenpox and smallpox, and is found to be excellent for haemorrhages, and in the treatment of Bright's disease and diabetes.

A receipt for the treatment of rheumatism was used at the beginning of the 19th century.

Tincture of yarrow

Take of flowers of Yarrow . . . . four ounces;
— Alcohol   . . . . one pint.

Let them stand for a few days, then strain: add to the liquid a handful of the flowers, let these stand another day, than strain again and filter.

Forty or sixty drops of this tincture will frequently give relief in severe rheumatic affections.

In about 1800, Richard Brook advised his readers: 'To those who wish to smoke *untaxed tobacco*, the dried leaves of yarrow will be found one of the best English substitutes.'

Another species, *A. ptarmica*, taller and with larger daisy-flowers, was dried and used by the Scots as snuff, from which it was given the name of sneezewort and old man's pepper. A double variety of sneezewort has been cultivated, and grows in gardens under the name of bachelor's buttons.

employed the herb. Achilles is said to have been the first to use yarrow as a herb for healing wounds, 'healing them who were his soldiers after the battle of Troy'. He first learnt the use of the herb from Chiron, and it is this legend that is the source of its generic name. It is known to the French as *herbe au charpentier,* the herb that heals the wounds made by the sharp tools of the carpenter. It was a very profitable herb in camps, where it was called militaris.

Yarrow was one of the favourite Saxon simples mentioned in the herbal *Materia Medica*, which still forms the basis of popular English herbals. Through the centuries yarrow has been grown in physic gardens; it has been used for healing the sick in convents; gathered by simplers to be dried, weighed and measured in apoth-

APPENDICES

CONVERSIONS

Imperial	US Customary	Metric
1 pint	1.2 pints	570 millilitres
0.833 pints	1 pint	470 millilitres
0.42 pints	1 cup	235 millilitres
1.76 pints	2.1 pints	1 litre
1 fluid ounce	0.96 fluid ounces	28.4 millilitres
1.04 fluid ounces	1 fluid ounce	29.6 millilitres
1.76 fluid ounces	1.7 fluid ounces	50 millilitres
1 quart	1.2 quarts	1.14 litres
1.66 pints	1 quart	0.95 litre
1 ounce	1 ounce	28.4 grams
1.76 ounces	1.76 ounces	50 grams
1 pound	1 pound	0.45 kilograms
2.2 pounds	2.2 pounds	1 kilogram

TITLE PAGE from a book dated 1530: *The qualities of waters and herbs. With the regimen to counter pestilence. Made and compiled by medical men of the city of Basle in Germany.*

OVEN TEMPERATURE CONVERSIONS

Celius or Centigrade °C	Fahrenheit °F	Gas Mark	
110	225	¼	very cool
130	250	½	very cool
140	275	1	cool
150	300	2	cool
170	325	3	moderate
180	350	4	moderate
190	375	5	moderately hot
200	400	6	moderately hot
220	425	7	hot
230	450	8	very hot
240	475	9	very hot

DYERS' PLANTS

Material	Mordant	Colour
Agrimony	—	Yellow
Bedstraw	—	Coral
Coltsfoot	Copperas	Green
Dandelion	Alum	Light yellow
Dandelion	No mordant	Purple, magenta, red
Elderberry	Alum	Soft blue, lilac
Elderberry	Chrome	Purple
Elder root	Alum	Dark yellow
Elecampane	With wortleberries	Blue
Golden rod	Alum	Yellowish-tan
Golden rod	Chrome	Old gold
Madder	Alum and tartar	Lacquer red
Madder	Chrome	Garnet red
Meadowsweet	Alum	Greenish-yellow
Meadowsweet	Copperas	Black
Nettle	Alum	Greenish-yellow
Nettle root	Alum	Yellow
Pokeweed	Vinegar	Red, not permanent
Rose hips	Alum	Grey/rose
Rue	—	Red
Safflower	Alum	Yellow
Saffron	Alum	Yellow
St John's wort	Alcohol	Blood red
St John's wort	Vinegar	Crimson
St John's wort	Alum	Greenish yellow
Sassafras bark	Alum	Yellow
Sassafras root	—	Peach colour
Sorrel	—	Greenish yellow
Southernwood	—	Yellow
Tansy	Alum	Yellow green
Thyme	Alum	Grey/gold
Thyme	Tin	Yellow
Turmeric	Ash extract	Yellow
Turmeric	Citric acid	Brown/yellow
Turmeric	Calcium hydroxide	Gold/brown
Turmeric	With safflower	Scarlet
Weld	Alum	Lemon yellow
Weld	Chrome	Golden yellow
Willow	Alum	Rose/tan/cinnamon
Woad	Ferrous sulphate	Green/olive
Woad	—	Blue

(*right, above*) A GROCER'S SHOP, from a 16th-century woodcut by Jost Amman.

(*right, below*) AN 18TH-CENTURY glove and perfume shop is depicted in this engraving after Retif de la Bretonne.

HERBS AND SPICES USED THROUGHOUT THE AGES IN PERFUMERY AND COSMETICS, INCLUDING THE CARE OF TEETH AND HAIR

Angelica
Anise
Balm
Basil
Bergamot
Cardamom
Caraway
Cinnamon
Coriander
Cowslip
Cuckoo-pint
Dill
Elder
Fennel
Figwort
Lavender
Lovage

Marjoram
Mint
Pimpernel
Primrose
Rose
Rosemary
Safflower
Saffron
Sage
Southernwood
Strawberry
Tansy
Valerian
Vervain (verbena)
Willow
Wintergreen
Witch hazel
Woodruff

A HERB CALENDAR

Basil	Fit for drying about the middle of August
Chervil	Fit for drying about May, June, July
Elder-flowers	Fit for drying about May, June, July
Fennel	Fit for drying about May, June, July
Marjoram	Fit for drying about July
Mint	Fit for drying about the end of June, July
Parsley	Fit for drying about May, June, July
Sage	Fit for drying about August, September
Savory (summer)	Fit for drying about the end of July, August
Savory (winter)	Fit for drying about the end of July, August
Tarragon	Fit for drying about June, July, August
Thyme	Fit for drying about the end of July, August
Thyme (lemon)	Fit for drying about July and August
Thyme (orange)	Fit for drying about June and July

Herbs should be gathered on a dry day, cleaned and dried immediately in a cool oven. The leaves should then be picked off and bottled at once, either separately or mixed.

HERBAL TEAS OR TISANES

Agrimony	A substitute for tea
Angelica	Feverish colds
Balm	A refreshing summer drink
Basil	Digestive. Coughs
Bergamot	Digestive. Tonic
Borage	Cool summer drink
Catmint	Colds. Sedative
Chamomile	Relaxing. Digestive
Clove	Nausea
Coltsfoot	Coughs
Costmary	Catarrh
Cowslip	Migraine. Insomnia
Dandelion	Tonic. Blood purifier
Elderflower	Additive to China tea
Elecampane	Coughs
Fennel	Digestive
Ginger	Colds
Ginseng	Tonic
Golden rod	Tonic. Morning sickness
Horehound	Sore throat. Bronchitis
Hyssop	Carminative
Marjoram	Prevents sea-sickness
Meadowsweet	Cool summer drink
Mint	Digestive
Nettle	Blood purifier. Haemorrhoids
Red Clover	Digestive
Rosemary	Headaches
Rue	Take sparingly for high blood pressure
Safflower	Colds
Sage	Tonic
Sassafras	Old-fashioned spring medicine
Slippery elm	Gastritis, colitis, enteritis. Coughs, etc.
Southernwood	Sedative
Strawberry leaves	Summer punch
Sweet Cicely	Tonic
Thyme	Fatigue
Woodruff	Migraine. Use sparingly
Yarrow	Tonic

Do not experiment with making your own herbal teas without medical advice.

Never brew herbal teas in metal saucepans and teapots — always use enamel or earthenware pots. Herbal teas may be taken with honey or lemon but seldom with milk. A number of these teas and tisanes are obtainable at health food stores.

HERBS AND SPICES USED IN MODERN COOKERY OR WINES

Allspice
Angelica
Anise
Balm
Basil
Bay
Bergamot
Borage
Caraway
Cardamom
Cayenne
Chervil
Chicory
Chives
Cinnamon
Clove
Coriander
Costmary
Dandelion
Elder
Fennel
Garlic
Ginger

Hyssop
Lovage
Marjoram
Mint
Mustard
Nettle
Nutmeg and mace
Paprika
Parsley
Pepper
Rose
Rosemary
Saffron
Sage
Savory
Sorrel
Soybean
Sweet Cicely
Tansy
Tarragon
Thyme
Turmeric
Watercress

THE FRONTISPIECE of a 17th-century pharmacopaeia, now in the possession of the Musée d'Histoire de la Médecine, Paris, showing the interior of a pharmacy.

CARICATURES from the 19th century of the various facial expressions of grocers.

BEE-PLANTS

Alfalfa
Angelica
Balm
Basil
Bergamot
Borage
Chamomile
Catmint
Chicory
Coriander
Dill
Fennel

Hyssop
Lavender
Marjoram
Meadowsweet
Mint
Parsley
Red clover
Savory (summer and winter)
Sweet Cicely
Thyme
Willow

BIBLIOGRAPHY

All mentions of Culpeper, Gerard, or Parkinson in the text refer to:

Culpeper, Nicholas, *Complete Herbal* (Manchester, 1826)

Gerard, John, (ed Marcus Woodward), *Leaves from Gerard's Herball* (New York, 1969)

Parkinson, John, *Paradisi in Sole Paradisus Terrestris* (London, 1629)

Anon, *Herb Growing at Mitcham* (Croydon Natural History and Scientific Society, Croydon, 1959)

Anon, *The Cook's Oracle* (London, 1817)

Acton, Elizabeth, *Modern Cookery* (London, 1845)

Bardswell, Frances A., *The Herb Garden* (London, 1930)

Bath, Marchioness of, *Cottage Domestic Economy* (Frome, 1829)

Brook, Richard, *Cyclopaedia of Botany*, vols 1 and 2 (London, *c*.1800)

Brooklyn Botanic Garden Record Handbooks:
    Dye Plants and Dyeing, vol 20, no 3 (New York, 1978)
    Natural Plant Dyeing vol 29, no 2 (New York, 1978)

Conway, David, *The Magic of Herbs and Spices* (London, 1973)

Dampney, Janet, and Pomeroy, Elizabeth, *All About Herbs* (London, 1977)

De Candolle, Alphonse, *Origin of Cultivated Plants* (London, 1886)

Earle, Alice Morse, *Old Time Gardens* (New York, 1902)

Earle, C.W., *Pot-Pourri from a Surrey Garden* (London, 1897)

Edlin, H.L., *British Plants and their Uses* (London, 1951)

Fielder, Mildred, *Plant Medicine and Folklore* (New York, 1975)

Folkard, Richard, *Plant Lore, Legends and Lyrics* (London, 1884)

Grieve, M., *A Modern Herbal* (London, 1976)

Grigson, Geoffrey, *The Englishman's Flora* (London, 1960)

Harvey, John, *Early Gardening Catalogues* (London, 1972)

Hemphill, Rosemary, *Herbs and Spices* (London, 1966)

Hill, Jason, *Wild Foods* (London, 1944)

Jenkins, M. and N., *Medicines and Spices* (Journal of the Garden History Society, Reading, 1976)

Joice, Jean, *Some Bygone Garden Herbs and Plants* (Ipswich, 1977)

Kloss, Jethro, *Back To Eden* (Santa Barbara, 1975)

Lee, Mrs R., *Trees, Plants and Flowers* (London, 1859)

Leighton, Ann, *Early English Gardens in New England* (London, 1970)

Leyell, Mrs C.F., *The Magic of Herbs* (London, 1932)

Leyell, Mrs C.F., *Herbal Delights* (London, 1937)

Loudon, Jane, *The Lady's Country Companion* (London, 1845)

Lucas, Richard, *Secrets of the Chinese Herbalists* (New York, 1977)

Lust, John, *The Herb Book* (California, 1974)

Mayhew, Henry, (ed Peter Quennell), *Mayhew's London* (London, 1949)

Miller, Philip, *The Gardeners Dictionary* (London, 1754)

Moldenka, Harold, *North American Wild Flowers* (New York, 1949)

Philbrick, H., and Gregg, Richard B., *Companion Plants* (London, 1976)

Phillips, Henry, *Sylva Florifera* (London, 1823)

Phillips, Henry, *Flora Historica* (London, 1824)

Pratt, Anne, *Flowering Plants of Great Britain* (London, *c*.1870)

Prime, Cecil, *Lords and Ladies* (London, n.d.)

Raffald, Elizabeth, *The Experienced English Housekeeper* (1782)

Ranson, Florence, *British Herbs* (London, 1949)

Rendall, Vernon, *Wild Flowers in Literature* (London, 1934)

Rhind, William, *A History of the Vegetable Kingdom* (London, n.d.)

Rohde, Eleanour Sinclair, *A Garden of Herbs* (New York, 1969)

Rohde, Eleanour Sinclair, *The Old English Herbals* (London, 1972)

Rohde, Eleanour Sinclair, *Rose Recipes* (New York, 1973)

Sanecki, Kay N., *Discovering Herbs* (London, 1973)

Sanecki, Kay N., *The Complete Book of Herbs* (London, 1974)

Savage, F.G., *The Flora and Folk Lore of*

Shakespeare (London, *c.*1923)

Smith, John, *Dictionary of Economic Plants* (London, 1882)

Thompson, C.J.S., *The Mystery and Lure of Perfume* (London, 1927)

Thompson, C.J.S., *The Mystic Mandrake* (London, 1934)

Tuer, Andrew W., *Old London Street Cries* (London, 1885)

Tusser Thomas, *Five Hundred Points of Good Husbandry* (London, 1931)

Tynan, Katharine and Maitland, Frances, *The Book of Flowers* (London, 1909)

Walker, Winifred, *All the Plants of the Bible* (London, 1959)

Walton, Izaak, *The Compleat Angler* (London, 1949)

Wilkinson, Lady, *Weeds and Wild Flowers* (London, 1858)

ACKNOWLEDGEMENTS

The publishers acknowledge the following:

Colour

Bibliothèque Nationale, Paris: 39 (left), 42, 81 (top; bottom), 102 (bottom), 111 (top), 130 (top), 153, 162

Bodleian Library, Oxford: 25 (top), 39 (right), 57, 60, 89, 145

J.–L. Charmet: 2, 7, 17, 43, 47, 52, 67, 75, 84, 85, 96, 110 (top; bottom), 117 (bottom), 120, 125, 131, 152, 175, 181, 185

Lesley Gordon: 35, 88 (top left)

Royal Botanic Gardens, Kew: 10, 11, 14 (top), 25 (bottom), 32 (left), 34, 49, 64, 71, 74, 79, 92, 98 (left), 103, 106, 107, 113, 134, 160, 163, 166, 167, 170, 171

Royal Horticultural Society: 142 (top; bottom), 143, 157

Victoria and Albert Museum, London: 20 (left), 24, 29, 53, 98 (right), 99, 130 (bottom), 138, 139

Black and white

Austrian National Library: 128

Bibliothèque Nationale, Paris: 9, 12, 15, 16, 20 (bottom right), 28, 61, 68, 76, 101, 108, 115 (top), 117 (top), 140, 149 (right), 194, 195, 199 (bottom)

Bodleian Library, Oxford: 8, 36, 37, 40, 41, 70, 91 (top), 93, 97, 102 (top), 111 (bottom), 123, 149 (left), 154, 186, 187, 192, 193

J.–L. Charmet: 197, 199 (top), 201 (top; bottom)

Lesley Gordon: 88 (bottom left)

Royal Botanic Gardens, Kew: 14 (bottom), 20 (top right), 23, 26, 27, 30, 32 (right), 34, 38, 45, 46, 48 (top; bottom), 51, 54, 55, 56, 59 (bottom left; top right), 63, 66, 74, 77, 78, 82, 83, 86, 88 (right), 91 (bottom), 94, 95, 105, 115 (bottom), 116, 118, 119, 121, 124, 129, 135 (top; bottom), 147, 150, 156, 159, 161, 173, 174, 176, 177, 178, 179, 181, 182, 183, 184, 189, 190 (top; bottom), 191, 196

Victoria and Albert Museum, London: 188

Eileen Tweedy took many of the photographs.
The publishers would like to thank the Royal Botanic Gardens, Kew for their considerable co-operation.

INDEX